LANGUAGES OF IRAQ, ANCIENT AND MODERN

Edited by J.N. Postgate

British School of Archaeology in Iraq
2007

Dedicated to the memory of

Rabi' al-Qaissi
Manhal Jabr
Riyadh al-Douri
Nabil al-Safi
Hayef Shinyar

and other colleagues
in the State Board for Antiquities and Heritage
whose lives have been lost since April 2003

Printed and bound at the University Press, Cambridge

ISBN 978-0-903472-21-0

© The British School of Archaeology in Iraq

CONTENTS

The minaret at Tauq (Daquq) in the Turkman speaking zone
Photo: J.N. Postgate

PREFACE

This book derives from a "study day" of the same title, held by the British School of Archaeology in Iraq on 15th November 2003, in the rooms of the British Academy. The School is grateful to all the speakers for their contributions on the day, and for their patience during the long process of converting these into the present volume. We are much indebted to the British Academy for providing the venue, and to the Trustees of the Charlotte Bonham-Carter Memorial Fund for very generous subventions both to the costs of the event, and towards the publication. A grant from the British Council Iraq has also helped to defray the costs of producing the volume.

The contributions are very varied. Our collection describes three dead languages, three which are very much alive, and one whose history stretches back from the present day to antiquity, but whose future seems precarious. The long and complex history of Aramaic is one reason why it occupies more space in our volume than Arabic. Arabic of course is quantitatively and culturally the principal modern language of Iraq, and it may seem perverse that it receives less space than some others: but the aim of our meeting and this collection was not to give a comprehensive account of one of the world's great languages, merely to describe the Iraqi dialects of spoken Arabic in recent times. Arabic has been described many times, whereas we believe it would be hard to find a substitute for our contributions on Kurdish and Turkman.

For their permission to use images, or help in supplying them, we are indebted to the Trustees of the British Museum, the Curators of the Babylonian Section of the University of Pennsylvania Museum, Béatrice André-Salvini, Konrad Volk, Giorgio Buccellati, Ulrich Seeger, Fabrizio Pennacchietti, Lamia al-Gailani-Werr, Aage Westenholz, Gernot Wilhelm, Joyce Blau, Zubeida Barwary, The Vatican Library, George Kiraz and Kristian Heal, and Jennifer Lee at The Rare Book and Manuscript Library, Columbia University. The Editor is very grateful to Eleanor Robson for her assistance in adapting Jeremy Black's contribution for publication. Thanks go also to

Sibby Postgate for creating the maps and designing the cover, to Joan Porter MacIver, Dominique Collon and Jon Taylor of the British School of Archaeology in Iraq, and to Tony Mansfield and Noel Robson at C.U.P. for their assistance in the final stages of production.

Jeremy Black was the joint organizer of the study day and his untimely death has been a cruel blow to his colleagues and is a great loss to anyone interested in Iraq's languages. He would have wished this volume to be dedicated to the memory of our Iraqi colleagues, known and unknown, but I would like to remember him here as well, very fondly.

Nicholas Postgate
March 2007

List of illustrations

Introduction

Nicholas Postgate

University of Cambridge

Today the people of Iraq speak at least four languages from three major language groups: Arabic, Aramaic, Kurdish and Turkman. Four thousand years ago, in 2000 BC, the same was true: Akkadian, Amorite, Hurrian and Sumerian. Like modern Iraq, ancient Mesopotamia was a composite and complex phenomenon, with all the tensions and creative synergy that implies, and languages are one of the principal identifying features of the different groups making up the population. Not for nothing was the Tower of Babel there! Our meeting concentrated on the languages themselves, but it was with the common awareness, whether expressed or not, that they are but one facet of the entire civilization.

Language diversity naturally entails language contact. In the courts of kings and the imperial capitals, nationalities and languages rubbed shoulders. The English word dragoman derives (rather tortuously) from Akkadian *targumannum*, which described the interpreters needed by the governments of four thousand years ago. Even before this there were probably Meluhhans from the Indus at the court of the Kings of Akkad, and there were certainly Egyptians living at Nineveh in the 7th century BC. A Babylonian correspondent of the Assyrian king comments that "there are many tongues living in the city of Nippur under the protection of the king my lord". The splendour of the Abbasid Caliphate drew to Baghdad scholars from all over the Muslim world from Cordoba to Bokhara.

One of the proud boasts of King Shulgi of Ur was that he knew not only Sumerian but also Amorite and Elamite:

"Also I know the Amorite language as well as I do Sumerian. ..... mountain people walking in the hills ....., they greet me and I reply to them in the Amorite language. Also I know the Elamite language as well as I do Sumerian. ..... in Elam ....., they greet me and I reply in Elamite" (translation from ETCSL).

He was not shy about his talents, and in another passage he claims to speak the language of the north, Subartu, and says: "When I provide justice in the legal cases of Sumer, I give answers in all five languages". One of Shulgi's most famous successors,

Hammurapi, was less inclusive in his attitudes, dismissing the people of Subartu, Gutium and Tukrish as people "whose mountains are distant and whose language is contorted".

Western scholarship has allowed the Hellenistic intrusion to drive a wedge between the study of ancient and modern Iraq, but we should not allow this to mask the real continuity. Arabic and Aramaic speakers have been around in the country since the days when the accumulated knowledge and literary traditions of more than 2000 years of Mesopotamian civilization were gathered by Assurbanipal into his palace at Nineveh. On the back of my office door in Cambridge I keep a palm-fibre belt used by date-harvesters, not in case I feel a sudden urge to climb a palm-tree, but as a reminder that its modern Iraqi name, *tebelye*, can be traced back to the time of Hammurapi. This is only one of many ancient words surviving in the modern vocabulary. When the reader of the Gilgamesh epic is exhorted to admire the masonry of the city-wall of Uruk, it is described as of baked brick, with the same word as is used today, *ājūr*. As Stephanie Dalley has shown, there are echoes of Gilgamesh himself in the Arabian Nights, and of the Babylonian flood hero Ut-napishtim in Persian literature. Kurdish tales about a mythical eagle called Simurgh, along with many similar folktales from the Middle East and even Europe, must have an ultimate ancestor in the epics of Lugalbanda and Etana written down millennia ago. The sayings of Ahiqar, attributed to the vizier of Assurbanipal's father, turn up not only in Aramaic but also in Armenian and Old Slavonic. The major 9th century Arabic treatise on agriculture attributed to Ibn Wahshiyyah is called the Nabataean Agriculture, implying that it came from an Aramaic source; and even if we cannot prove it was so, it doesn't seem a completely implausible idea.

Of course our list of languages is far from exhaustive. At different times within the frontiers of modern Iraq we know there were speakers of yet other languages, and there must have been some we will never know about. Urartian, closely related to Hurrian, was certainly present in the far north-east of the country. Gutians and Kassites raided from the eastern hills at different times. Amorites infiltrated from the western desert. Although the Kassites and the Amorites established major dynasties which ruled for centuries, their own languages were soon submerged beneath Akkadian, and we know of them almost solely through their names, like Hammurapi or Burnaburiash. Other ruling elites must have used their languages from time to time, such as Greek, and Iranian languages under the Seleucid, Parthian and Sasanian dynasties. Recently Farsi has been spoken in homes round the great Shiite shrines, and since the First World War families in Baghdad talk Armenian. In the wake of frequent deportations, policies pursued famously but by no means exclusively by the Neo-Assyrian and Neo-Babylonian monarchs, isolated pockets of all sorts of uprooted langages must have existed. Most lost their mother tongues quite quickly: even the communities of Jews, like their compatriots at home, soon switched to Aramaic. The Turkman communities sandwiched between Arabic and Kurdish have tenaciously preserved their language for several centuries: but they were not deportees in the normal sense, rather military colonists, and this may not be coincidental.

It is no surprise that the natural geographical zones of the country correlate strongly with the distribution of its languages. For most of recorded history the main languages of the central urban belt have been flanked on one side by a different Semitic language belonging to the desert dwellers to the west and south, and on the other by one or more different linguistic groups spoken by mountain folk to the north and east, most recently one from the Indo-European family. And even within the central language zone there are often northern and southern geographical regions. Just as, within Akkadian, Assyrian became the dialect of the north and Babylonian of the south, so with modern spoken Arabic, Muslawi has its own identity which distinguishes it from the dialects of the south. Time does not allow us to explore the rich veins of dialects fully, but with Aramaic, which can be tracked through 30 centuries, and is the ancestor of Syriac, Mandaean and Neo-Aramaic, we have allowed ourselves more space to describe its different manifestations.

The mention of Syriac reminds us that we are not talking only of colloquial vernaculars. Several of our languages had, and have, an existence in their written incarnations which stretches well beyond the chronological and geographical range within which they were spoken. Not only Aramaic, in the Syriac and Mandaean scriptures, but Arabic, of course, and much earlier Sumerian and Akkadian: sometimes as the vehicle of scholarship and science, sometimes of diplomacy and commerce, and sometimes of religion. The first chapter in the science of linguistics itself was written in Mesopotamia. Again, with written languages, there are some we have had to leave out, like Hebrew, Ancient North Arabian, and Ottoman Turkish. And before leaving the field to the specialists, let us spare a thought for the unwritten languages we shall never recover. Did Romany people pass through Iraq on their way to Europe from North India? Did the mysterious Slubba, who knew the desert better than any bedu, originally speak Arabic or some other tongue? Was there a language even older than Sumerian at the dawn of Mesopotamian civilization?

Fig. 2.1 Photograph and hand-copy by H. Behrens of a tablet of the "Axe of Nergal" (UM 55-21-327 = 3N-T 43).

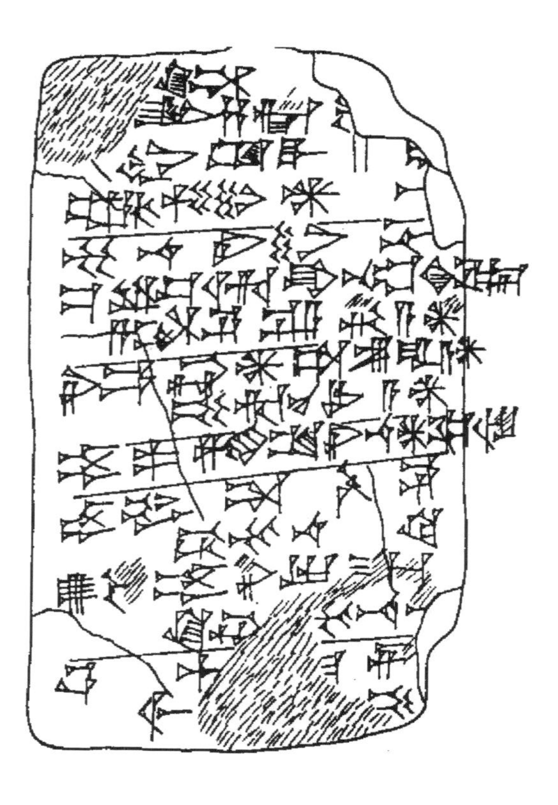

Reproduced with the permission of the Curators of the Babylonian Section, University of Pennsylvania Museum, and with the kind assistance of Kevin Danti.

Sumerian

Jeremy Black[1]

University of Oxford

In a Sumerian state letter of about 2000 BC an ambassador is complaining to his master about the (as he considers) inadequate reception he has met with on presenting his credentials. What he says in Sumerian is

ka egalaše ğenağune lu silima lugalğake en libintar
'When I arrived at the palace gate, no one asked after the health of my king'.

One might start with an analysis of that sentence just to give something of the flavour of Sumerian. The writing system to some extent obscures the morphemic and, probably, the phonetic structure, so:

ka e-gal-ak-še ğen-a-ğu-ne lu-e silima lugal-ğu-ak-e en nu-bi-n-tar-Ø

(Phonetically: ğ = 'ng'; š = 'sh'; Ø = zero.)

ka e-gal-ak-še is in the terminative case ('at')
(ka 'gate'; e-gal 'palace, great house'; -ak = genitive; -še = terminative)

ğen-a-ğu-ne is a verbal phrase
(ğen 'go' + -a nominaliser; -ğu 'my'; -ne = verbal phrase marker)

lu-e is in the ergative case
(lu 'someone; a person'; -e = ergative case marker)

silima lugal-ğu-ak-e is in the inanimate dative case
(silima from Old Akkadian *šulmum* 'health'; lugal 'king, great man')

en nu-bi-n-tar-Ø is a verbal expression
(en is in the absolutive case; nu-bi-n-tar-Ø is the verb;

---

[1] The text as presented here has been adapted and enlarged by Eleanor Robson from Jeremy Black's talk given at the Languages of Iraq day in November 2003, of which he was one of the organizers. The additional material has largely been quarried from his own teaching notes.

en ... tar 'to ask about' is a 'phrasal verb', i.e., noun+verb;
bi-, -n-, -Ø are respectively markers of the inanimate dative, ergative, and absolutive cases; nu- = negative. 'Someone ... did not' = 'no one ... did').

The word 'Sumerian' we use today goes back to the late 19th century AD, when it was rendered as 'Šumerian', derived from the Akkadian *šumeru (*šuwerum), māt šumeri* 'land of Šumer'; Sumerian eme-gir 'noble tongue, Sumerian', kiengir 'Sumer'. As far as we can tell its homeland as a spoken language was in southern Iraq.

The chronological range of written Sumerian as we know it runs from about 3100 to about 100 BC, although it declined as a live spoken language from just after 2000 BC. Only a handful of languages in the world can boast so long a continuous attested tradition. In its written form it was used throughout Mesopotamia, and is found in use also in Syria as a scribal language by 2400 BC, and later in ancient Turkey. The earliest known writing is in Sumerian, and we witness a gradual development in the writing system's ability to represent the language. In its first, pictographic, stages it largely consisted of rebus writing of nouns; by 2500 BC the scribes were placing the cuneiform signs in their 'correct' order, and the earliest texts which are written fully enough for us to be able to begin reading date from about this time. By 2100 BC, the grammatical affixes on nouns and verbs were being written in full. Most of the surviving Sumerian writing dates from the thousand years 2500 to 1500 BC, and during all that period Sumerian was living in a complex cultural relationship with an unrelated group of Semitic dialects: Old Akkadian, Eblaite, Old Babylonian, and Amorite. During the second half of that thousand-year period, Sumerian passed from being a vernacular language, essentially of a particular geographical area, to a situation where no one had it as a mother tongue. We know nothing of the relatives of Sumerian or the predecessors from which it developed, none of which was ever written down.

Modern scholars tend to divide the language as we see it in the written sources into a number of phases (all dates approximate):

Old Sumerian (2500-2300 BC)

Old Sumerian was already in contact with Old Akkadian, as shown by loan-words in both directions, and assumed Sumerian influence on Old Akkadian and Old Babylonian word order from Sumerian (West Semitic languages not being verb-final). However, written Eblaite is also rigidly verb-final and the spoken tongue can hardly have been influenced by Sumerian. But there is the possibility that *written* Eblaite, which is to a considerable extent written allographically in Sumerian, was pronounced in a different order from its writing. Actually the so-called 'natural' Verb-Subject-Object order of other Semitic languages is only attested from Ugaritic (1300 BC), Aramaic, and Hebrew onwards.

There is some Old Sumerian literature, which is very difficult to read; and many administrative and legal documents.

Agade (Akkadian) Period (2300-2100 BC)
From this period there are bilingual inscriptions, and some literature. Sumerian was used in Sumer; but this was the first period of Akkadian ascendancy.

Neo-Sumerian Period (2100-2000 BC)
This period saw the renaissance of Sumerian as an *official* written language; some linguistic developments from Old Sumerian; and the composition of much elegant and beautiful literature.

Old Babylonian Period (2000-1600 BC)
The Old Babylonian period witnessed the gradual decline of Sumerian, although it was still a crucial vehicle of Mesopotamian culture. Most surviving literary manuscripts date from this period; many were probably committed to clay only ephemerally, in order to memorise orally tradited literary compositions. This was also the beginning of the bilingual tradition, and of the explicit writing of grammatical affixes etc.

Post-Sumerian Period (1600-100 BC)
By this time there was very little composition, but still careful copying of literary texts. What composition there is shows a language almost artificially close in word order and syntax to Akkadian, and failure to understand phrasal verbs (see below), so that for instance ki ... ğar = *šakānu* gives munkiğar instead of ki munğar!

How we know Sumerian

The first clay tablets with Sumerian on turned up around 1850 in Layard's excavation of the library of the last major Assyrian king at Nineveh, near modern Mosul. These were written more than a millennium after the spoken language died out. The first large-scale excavation of a Sumerian site began in 1877 when the French consul at Basra, de Sarzec, started digging at Telloh, the capital of the state of Lagash in southern Iraq. The first attempts at decipherment started when the cuneiform script itself was deciphered, over the years 1846-1857. After much heated debate about whether Sumerian was a 'real' language or simply a cryptographic writing of Akkadian, the first serious grammar of the Sumerian language was published in 1911, and the first reliable grammar in 1923.

In addition to straightforward decipherment on a contextual basis, our understanding of the language is also assisted by:

(i) interlinear Akkadian translations for the whole of many literary compositions. These may sometimes be inaccurate when later in date, but remain invaluable;

(ii) extensive and highly complex native lexicographical traditions with Sumerian-Akkadian vocabularies (at least 50,000 entries), often with pronunciation indicated phonetically for Akkadian speakers:

si-iz-kur : AMARxŠE : *ka-ra-bu*

'the sign AMAR with the sign ŠE written inside it, together pronounced sizkur, corresponds to the Akkadian *karābu* "prayer"'.

(iii) texts written by Babylonian grammarians, with their analysis of Sumerian morphology.

In this chapter, which is intended simply as a first overview of the Sumerian language, I have used both a 'phonemic transcription' system and a normalised rendering of the syllabic Sumerian spelling, indifferently as either seemed to be appropriate, and have omitted the usual diacritics used to distinguish homophonous signs since the study of the writing system is a separate matter. (For an example of our transliteration system see the inscription presented in the Appendix.) I have also assumed a sort of unified Sumerian grammar, vaguely synchronic, since it is hardly possible in this space to take note of grammatical developments between Old Sumerian and 'Old Babylonian' Sumerian, although these certainly occurred, as might be expected over a period of six hundred years or more.

Syntax

A few remarks on the general structure of Sumerian. In general it would be described by linguists as an isolate, without known relatives; as agglutinative, conveying grammatical information by annexing particles to a (usually) unvarying base; partially ergative; with Subject-Object-Verb word order, and mostly right-branching noun phrase structure; and having two genders (animate and inanimate).

Typical are the chains or complexes, with at their core a nominal or verbal base (more or less unchanging), surrounded by *clitics* – unemphatic, often contracted words that are spoken or written as if they formed part of the preceding or following word (respectively called *proclitics* and *enclitics*) – and with dependent chains or complexes subordinate to them.

Central to the grammar is the opposition between animate and inanimate; in some cases a collective plural can be treated as an inanimate singular. The use of some cases is restricted to either animate or inanimate nouns, and this is linked to the basic axis of verbal rection between ergative on the one hand and absolutive on the other. Associated with a verb can be one participant (absolutive 'subject'); two participants (ergative 'subject' and absolutive 'object') or three (ergative, absolute and one of the other cases). There are rather few true adjectives: most can be regarded as non-finite ('participial') forms of verbs.

Word order is fairly rigid, with ergative standing first in the clause and verb last, although other words can be preposed or postposed for special effect. There are few true conjunctions, and subordinate clauses can be seen as enormous noun phrases placed under a particular nominal rection in relation to the main clause.

Phonology

With a dead language, there are no tape recordings, and the last person with even a traditional knowledge of the pronunciation of Sumerian died about 2000 years ago. Our reconstruction of Sumerian phonology is of course heavily dependent on our reconstruction of *Akkadian* phonology, and while there is good reason to think that Akkadian had a broadly similar phonetic inventory to other Semitic languages, including those living today, the crucial fact is that the writing system in which Akkadian is preserved for us was originally invented for recording Sumerian, and yet the numerous Sumerian loan-words into Akkadian always appear, in these twin orthographies (twin in the very literal sense of their common origin), to undergo certain phonetic alterations.

Consonants

Put briefly, we assume that (on the basis of the comparative *Semitic* evidence) that Akkadian had parallel sets of voiced and unvoiced consonants *b d g z* and *p t k s*. (It also had 'emphatic' [pharyngeal] *ṭ q* and *ṣ*.) To notate these it borrowed from Sumerian two parallel sets of signs for what we may symbolise as B D G Z and P T K S. However, in Sumerian loan-words in Akkadian, spelled according to Akkadian orthography, Sumerian B D G Z were apparently heard as *p t k s*. So were P T K S. So one hypothesises that Sumerian had two parallel sets of stops/sibilants distinguished from each other perhaps by being aspirated or non-aspirated, or ejective (with simultaneous glottal stop) or imploded, or non-ejective or non-imploded, and that the distinction was not perceptible to Akkadian speakers, who none the less borrowed the parallel sets of signs to notate their own opposition (which may have been) b/p d/t g/k z/s. Conventionally we write the Sumerian also as b d g z, p t k s, and we just have to put up with the fact that neither Sumerian bulug nor Akkadian *pulukku* are exact representations of phonetic reality. Sumerian P T and K occur only in virtual initial position (or medial in the case of T, possibly explaining why it was sometimes, intervocalically, notated as r, presumably flapped). This may increase the likelihood of them having been aspirates or ejectives. In addition there is š, a guttural of some sort ḫ, liquids l and r, nasals m and n. Because of variant and phonetic spellings it has been possible to establish the existence of ğ, generally regarded as representing 'ng' (velar nasal), though other possibilities are conceivable. Possibly a different sort of r occurs in some words as an intervocalic, flapped, allophone of -d/t- (see above; the 'd/r' [not 'dr'] phoneme), and there may be an allophone of g which sounded closer to b in a few words (abrig/agrig). However, it is not necessary to posit the existence of liminal phones to explain what may simply be phonetic alternation, allophony, within a particular phoneme. The sounds w and y probably also occurred.

With the exception of the continuants m s š z, all the consonants – i.e., b d g ḫ l r n ğ – are amissible in word-final position. That is, they can be dropped at the end of a word. However, they re-appear before a vocalic ending; for instance, barag 'dais' or (in phonetic spelling) ba-ra; but genitive baraga (for barag+ak).

Vowels
There are four vowels, a e i u. Possibly there is a short/long distinction sometimes. A certain amount of vocalic assimilation takes place.

Some verbal proclitics assimilate to the vowel of the following syllable in so-called *forward vocalic assimilation*:

ḫe- > ḫeme-	but ḫaba-, ḫumu-
ša- > šaba-	but šibi-, šumu-
nu- > numu-	but libi-, laba- (n>l)
u- > umu-	but ibi-, aba-

In *reverse vocalic assimilation* the verbal affix -ed- and the enclitics -en, -e, -enden, -enzen, -eš, and -ene assimilate after a verbal base ending in -u- followed by a labial, liquid or ḫ:

-šub-u, -šum-unzen, -šub-uš, -gul-ude, -kur-unden, -luḫ-ude;
but: -dug-eš, -tud-enzen, -ḫuğ-e.

Vowel crasis or elision occurs with some enclitics, as, for instance:

-ani+a > -ana 'of his'; -bi+a > -ba 'of its';
ğu+a > -ğa 'of my';
lu+e > lu 'a man' (+ ergative case marker);
-bi+e > -bi 'its' (+ inanimate dative case marker).

The question of whether Sumerian was a tonal language (or had pitch variation) has been raised because of the existence of a considerable number of apparent homophones. There *are* many homophones or homophonous elements, but few really impossible to distinguish on syntactic or functional grounds: so there are probably no more true 'homophones' than, say, English. We know very little about stress or other, suprasegmental, considerations, of course.

Lexical categories

The two major lexical classes are (1) nouns (nominals), and (2) verbs. Minor (small, closed) classes are (3) pronouns, (4) adjectives, (5) conjunctions, (6) interjections, (7) adverbs, (8) ideophones. Many words can function as members of more than one class, e.g., both as nominals and verbs. For example:

til 'life; to live';
mul 'star; to shine';
kalag '(being) strong; to be strong; to make strong'.

Nominals

Nominals don't change, and have no visible marks for gender, sex or animateness.

Plural
Number can be marked if desired by reduplication (ḫazin-ḫazin 'axes'; ensi-ensi 'rulers'), by the enclitic -ene (animates only), or by reduplication of the qualifying adjective (ḫazin gal-gal 'mighty axes') or a combination of these (diğir-diğirene 'gods'; diğir galgalene 'great gods'). There are also: mušen didli 'numerous (individual) birds)' (from dili+dili 'one' reduplicated), udu ḫia 'various sheep' ('assorted', from ḫi 'to mix').

Gender
The two genders are called animate (used for human, or divine, persons) and inanimate (for animals and all other things). They are made explicit in person-marking in verbs, and in nominal case and number marking. In later Sumerian we sometimes meet gender mistakes under Akkadian influence.

Compounds
There are many nominal compounds, e.g.:

an-ki 'heaven+earth, world',
gud-udu 'cattle+sheep, domestic animals',
e-gal 'palace' (house+great),
kug-sig 'gold' (precious metal+yellow);

dub-sar 'scribe' (tablet+write),
amar-gi 'freedom' (to mother+return);

a-šu-ğiri 'limbs' (arm+hand+foot);

lu-niğ-tuku 'rich person' (man+possession+have),
lu-du-ḫarrana 'traveller' (man+go+of road);

dub-sar-maḫ 'chief scribe' (tablet+write+senior).

Compounds can also be formed with the noun formants nam-, niğ-, nu-:

namlugal 'kingship' (lugal 'king'),
niğba 'gift' (ba 'give'),
nukiri 'gardener' (kiri 'garden').

Nouns that are originally finite verbal forms include:

unedug 'letter' ('please say to him')
gantuš 'let me dwell' ('tenant').

Specialised 'non-referential' nominals occur only as elements of some phrasal verbs:

mi ... dug 'to treat nicely' (dug 'to do'),
mi zid ... dug 'to treat especially kindly (zid 'good');
ene ... dug 'to play',
ene sud ... dug 'to have sexual intercourse' (sud 'long').

Loanwords
At least as early as the first half of the third millennium Sumerian shared a linguistic area in south Mesopotamia with an early form or relative of Akkadian, resulting in frequent loanwords in each language. Some of the earliest loans from Akkadian end in -a:

tamḫārum 'battle' > damḫara;
rākibum 'emissary, rider' > ragaba.

Others appear without any ending: *šūmum* 'garlic' > šum. Later they often retain the Akkadian nominative -um:

puḫrum 'assembly' > puḫrum, locative puḫruma etc.;
nisqum 'thoroughbred (animal)' > niskum.

Note also that Sumerian borrows from Akkadian the clitic -ma 'and' (> *-ma*); and u 'and' (> *u*; alongside Sum. -bida 'with its': an kibida 'heaven and earth' ('heaven with its earth')).

Loanwords from Sumerian into Akkadian all acquire the Akkadian case endings (nom. sing. *-um*):

agrig > *abarakkum* 'steward, housekeeper';
sağ dili 'single person' > *sagdilûm* 'bachelor';
u-ne-dug (lit. 'please say to them') > *unnedukkum* 'letter';
baḫar > *paḫārum* 'potter', cf. Arab. faḫḫār 'worked clay';
bulug > *pulukkum* 'needle';
papal > *papallum* 'shoot, sprout';
banšur > *paššūrum* 'table', cf. Aram. pāṯūrā, Arab. fāṯūr;
guza > *kussīum/kussû* 'chair', cf. Ugaritic ks', Hebrew kissē, Aramaic kursyā, Arab. kursī;
kisal-luḫ > *kisalluḫḫum* 'courtyard sweeper'.

Nominal cases
The markers for possessives, plural, and cases are all enclitics: they can be attached to whole noun phrases, not only words. The system of eleven cases is:

any noun:

- absolutive (-∅)
- genitive (-ak; intervocalically -k-; in final position -a)
- comitative (-da) (‘in company with’)
- equative (-gin) (‘like’)
- adverbial (-eš) (‘in the manner of’; use is probably restricted to certain lexemes)

animates only:

- ergative (-e)
- dative/directive (-ra)

inanimates only:

- locative/directive (-a)
- dative (-e)
- terminative (-še) (‘towards’, ‘for’ [purpose]; expressed by ki ... -ak-še for animates [ki ‘place’])
- ablative (-ta) (expressed by ki ... -ak-ta for animates).

From these, interlocking phrases can be constructed:

dubsağ ud ulli-ak-ene-gi	‘like the ruler-s of ancient times’
2 6 5 4 3 1	1 2 3 4 5 6
šeš gal-ğu-ne-ra	‘for my elder brother-s’
4 3 2 5 1	1 2 3 4 5
arad šeš abba-n-ak-ak-ene-da	‘with the slave-s of his father’s brother’
2 8 6 5 7 4 3 1	1 2 3 4 5 6 7 8

Noun phrase structure

Noun phrases usually take the form head-modifier-specifier (with some rare exceptions: e.g., kug Inana ‘holy Inana’).

There are three genitive constructions:

a) indefinite: gi duba ‘reed of tablet’ = stylus (word-level category)
b) definite: dumu lugala ‘son of (the) king’ (noun phrase)
c) anticipatory: lugala dumu-ni ‘of the king his son’; ea ğišḫur-bi, lit. ‘of the temple its plan’; lugala e-ani, lit. ‘of the king his house’; this left dislocation moves the genitive noun into the topic position, to emphasise it:

en Ninĝirsuka	nammaḫ-ani	kalame	ḫezuzu
'Of lord Ninĝirsu	eminence-his	by the (whole) Land	let it be known'

'Let the eminence of lord N. (topic) be known by the whole Land'.

Alternatively: nammaḫ en Ninĝirsuka kalame ḫezuzu, without topicalisation of 'Ninĝirsu'.

Adjectives

Almost without exception adjectives follow the noun. Many can be considered 'participial' forms of verbs (e.g., kum 'hot' = 'being hot, which is hot'). There is a fairly small closed class of true adjectives which cannot function as verbs:

didila 'small' (animate plural only)
uru(n) 'high; lofty'
sis 'bitter'
ḫuš(a) 'fierce'
banda 'junior'
libira 'old'
dari / duri 'long-lasting' (Akkadian loanword)
idim 'honoured'
zid 'just, good'
gabu 'left-hand'.

Sumerian appears to be particularly weak in adjectives of the 'human propensity' class, and to lack altogether those of the 'speed' class. In literary Sumerian, various 'substitute' adjectives exist; most are formed as verbal phrases:

niĝnam-zu	'omniscient'	('everything+knowing')
usu-tuku	'powerful'	('power+having')
zid-du	'righteous	(-acting)'
anta-ĝal	'exalted'	('on high+being/having')
gaba-ĝal	'forceful'	('power+being/having')
lala-ĝal	'charming'	('charm+being/having')
saĝki-ĝal	'obstinate'	('forehead+being/having').

Pronouns

Ergative nominal syntax is neutralised in free-standing pronouns, used for topicalised, definite, animate persons. Forms for 1st, 2nd, and 3rd persons, singular and plural, are found, although there is no true free-standing form for 3rd singular inanimate, and the 1st plural and 2nd plural pronouns are really forms of the verb me 'to be' with personal enclitics. (Generally, there is weak marking for 1st and 2nd plural forms.)

	sg.	pl.
1	ğe	menden
2	zae	menzen
3 (animate only)	ane, ene	anene

These can take case markers and other clitics:

ğada 'with me',
enera 'to him (dative)',
mendennanam 'it is indeed us' (-nanam clitic 'it is indeed').

A comparable set of enclitics is found for the possessives:

	sg.	pl.
1	-ğu	-me
2	-zu	-zunene
3 (animate)	-ani	-anene, -bi
3 (inanimate)	-bi	-bi

amağu 'my mother', šešzu 'your (sg.) brother',
šešzura 'for your brother', šešzune 'your (sg.) brothers',
šešzunene 'your (pl.) brother', šeš-šešzunene 'your (pl.) brothers'.

Demonstratives
Nominals which can be used independently are nen ('that'), and ur ('this'); nen can also be used adnominally. Demonstrative clitics are -bi, -re(n), -še, and -e, in increasing order of remoteness (though not exactly understood):

ud-bia 'on that day; at that time, then, next',
ud rea 'in those (distant) days'.

Interrogatives
The interrogative pronouns distinguish animate and inanimate:

aba 'who?', ana 'what?';
mena 'when?';
aname 'how many?'

They can take case markers:

anaš 'why? (for what?)',
anagin 'how? (like what?)',
mea '(at) where?',
meše 'whither?'

Numerals
The numbers from one to ten are formed as a quintal (base 5) system:

1 aš ('one'), diš ('a single')
2 min
3 eš
4 limmu
5 ya
6 yaš (< ya+aš) (5+1)
7 imin (< ya+min) (5+2)
8 uššu (< ya+eš) (5+3)
9 ilimmu (< ya+limmu) (5+4)
10 u
20 niš
30 ušu (< eš+u) (3x10)
40 nimin (< niš+min) (20x2)
50 ninnu (< niš+min+u) (20x2+10)
60 ğiš

There are also traces of a (more ancient?) ternary system (1, 2, 3, 3+1, 3+2, 3+3, 3+3+1 etc.).

Verbs (finite forms)

The verb is the most complicated area of Sumerian syntax. Verbs can be one-, two- or three-participant, meaning that the action or state may involve the participation of only one (broadly, intransitive), two (broadly, transitive), or three (broadly, causative) person(s) or thing(s).

There is a clear distinction between finite and non-finite forms. A finite form can stand as the main verb of an utterance, and it consists minimally of a verbal base preceded by a proclitic. Every finite form must be preceded by a proclitic. There is a tendency to incorporate into the verbal complex other relations – locative, dative etc. – so that the verbal form stands like a summary of the preceding clause, e.g., Old Sumerian enatanied (e-na-ta-ni-ed-∅) 'A caused B to go out from C for D', where a total of four rections are incorporated into the verbal complex (the verb ed = 'to go out').

The verbal bases are essentially invariant, although they can be redoubled or even triplicated to indicate plurality of the associated absolutive:

alanbi i-gulgul 'he destroyed (all) its statues)' (gul 'to destroy')

or intensity of the action:

ki mu-rarara 'the earth trembled' (ra 'to quake').

Pluralic verbs
On some occasions an alternative form of the base, or even a completely different alternative or suppletive base is called for. There are about half a dozen instances of separate pluralic verbs:

de 'to bring (one thing)', laḫ 'to bring (many things)';
gub 'to stand (of one person)', sug 'to stand (of many people)';
tuš 'to sit (of one person)', durun 'to sit (of many people)'
til 'to live (of one person)', sig 'to live (of many people)'
uš 'to die/kill (of one person)', ug 'to die/kill (of many people)' etc.

The plurality is always plurality of the absolutive:

ma-laḫ 'boatman, sailor' (boat + bring (pluralic)) > Akkadian *malāḫum*, Arabic mallāḥ.

Verbal clitics
The proclitics, which stand before the verb, fall into two categories: *initial proclitics* (which precede the base and can stand in initial position) which occupy four ranks; and *non-initial proclitics* (which precede the base but cannot stand in initial position, i.e., must be preceded by an initial proclitic), occupying seven ranks. There is also one rank of verbal *enclitics*, which follow the base, and can be followed by further enclitics.

It would be almost impossible to construct a verbal form in which a clitic of each of the thirteen ranks was present in addition to the verbal base, but it will indicate the great variety of forms possible. For instance there are eleven mutually exclusive proclitics in the first rank alone. With this armoury of forms Sumerian may or may not incorporate into the verbal form the absolutive, the ergative, four or five other case relations and a variety of markers of aspect, direction, modality (intention, desire, ability), causality, relative tense, status (real/unreal), frustration, citation, chaining to previous forms, *Aktionsart*, illocutionary force (such as exhortation, wish, prohibition, command, emphatic declaration, narration), as well as markers which indicate the relation of the whole verbal form to another main verb to which it is subordinate. But however impressive all these technical terms of ours may sound, the reality of the Sumerian verb seems curiously incomplete when we try to consider how each of the categories finds its expression. It's the old problem: the categories are ours. Thus there are no specific markers of tense at all. The only marker of relative tense, if it *is* relative tense, (the prefix u-) marks an action in time by locating it previous to another action to which it is subordinate but whose time is not itself specified:

Ḡirsu ğirizu ku **u**-bi-us ... ğišḫur marapadpadde
'When you reach Ḡirsu, he (will) explain all the plans'

but also:

kisuraindub libira kabi **u-**mide agamabiše si ḫemisa
'After I had led the canal-mouth into the old river-bed, I made it go straight into the marsh.'

The only marker of aspect is the enclitic -ed, which marks actions as 'not yet begun at the moment of contemplation':

izaḫ-**ed-**en
'I am going to run away (in the future)',

but also:

Gutium ḫalam-**ed-**e abi mudanağ
'He ordered me to destroy Gutium (and I have since then destroyed it).'

The only marker of *Aktionsart* is the prefix al-, which can indicate a durative state or process: erinbi **al**-tur 'Their army is small', or a state resulting from an action:

šukubi **al**-gid
'Their rations have been measured out.'

Compare:

dubbi ugu bande **ul**-pad zir-**ed-**am
'Their tablet has been lost; subsequent to when it is in-the-state-resulting-from-being-found (u + al), it is to be destroyed (ed).'

Active and passive
Sumerian has no true passive, but the use of the proclitic ba- (in origin a 3rd person inanimate dative) enables the ergative subject to be deleted:

šulgi	lugal-e	kur	marḫaši-∅	mu-n-ḫul
Šulgi	king.ERG	land	Marḫaši-ABSOL.	PROC.3ERG.destroy

'king Šulgi destroyed the land of Marḫaši'

kur	marḫaši-∅	ba-ḫul
land	Marḫaši-ABSOL.	PROC.destroy

'the land of Marḫaši was destroyed'.

Phrasal verbs
There is a large number of phrasal or 'compound' verbs, in which a verbal base, often of rather general meaning, is closely associated with a noun which carries the verbal idea (but may not be analysable). E.g. sa ... dug 'to reach' (to achieve equality with). Many are derived from parts of the body: gu ... de 'to speak' (to pour the voice), igi ... bar 'to look' (to open the eye). In these verbs the noun usually stands in the absolutive case; the speaker, or looker, is ergative. The indirect object is usually in

the (animate or inanimate) dative; but may be represented by a locative, or a terminative within the verb:

niĝsisa-e	ki	ḫa-ba-aĝ
justice+INAN.DAT.	ki	AFFIRMATIVE.INAN-DAT.aĝ

'I love justice' (ki ... aĝ 'to love')

ama	dumu-ni-ra	igi nu-mu-n-ši-bar-e
mother.ERG.	child.her.DAT.	igi NEG. PROC.3ps.TERM.bar.3ps NOM.

'the mother does not look at her child' (igi ... bar 'to look (at)').

Standard/secondary verbal version

Now comes the confusing bit. The final set of proclitics, occurring immediately before the verbal base ('pronominal clitics'), are generally speaking used to mark the ergative or agent (1st ps. -long vowel- (?), 2nd ps. -e-, 3rd ps. -n-), with the possibility of marking plural if specifically desired by one of the enclitics -enden (1st ps.), -enzen (2nd ps.) or -eš (3rd ps.), e.g.:

mu-na-**n**-šum-**eš** 'They have given (it) to him'.

The set of enclitics -en (1st/2nd ps. sg.), -∅ (3rd ps. sg.), -enden (1st ps. pl.), -enzen (2nd ps. pl.), -eš (3rd ps. pl.) are used to mark the absolutive. This arrangement I call *standard verbal version*, and it can be used either for one-participant verbs (which have absolutive suffixes only) or for two- or three- participant verbs (which have both ergative and absolutive suffixes). It may be what the Babylonians called *ḫamṭu* 'quick'. It's clear enough, although in e.g., mu-na-n-šum-**eš** 'They have given (it) to him' -eš marks the ergative while in mu-un-ši-re-**eš** 'They go to him' it marks the absolutive, and one can detect a straining of the possibilities of the verbal system here.

Now, in *secondary verbal version*, it is the enclitics -en (1st/2nd ps. sg.), -e (3rd ps. sg.), -enden (1st ps. pl.), -enzen (2nd ps. pl.) and -ene (3rd ps. pl.) – in other words, almost the same set of suffixes – which are used to mark the ergative, while the proclitics, in particular -n- and -b-, are used to mark the 3rd ps. animate or inanimate absolutive. In mu-ĝa-ĝa-en, -en marks the ergative ('I [or you] put'). There is good reason for thinking that the suffix position is the more prominent place in which to mark pronominal participation. In secondary verbal version, also, about a quarter of all verbs use a variant verbal base, which may be reduplicated, altered, or (in about five cases) completely different from the standard base. Thus naĝ 'to drink' becomes na-na; ĝar 'to place' becomes ĝa-ĝa; gid 'to extend' becomes gidi; ĝen, the singular verb 'to go', becomes du, while re 'to go (pl.)' becomes sub, and so on. This may be what Babylonian scholars called *marû* 'slow'.

Just what is this secondary version? It is used in a variety of grammatical circumstances where two-participant verbs are used, and while it is impossible to attribute a unified function to it, it does appear to involve the marking of the ergative in a rather more prominent way than in standard verbal version. Whether this is crucial or incidental, I couldn't say. Secondary version is used, for instance, after interrogative words; immediately before direct speech; normally after the prefix na- (prohibitive); with the affix -ed ('not yet begun' aspect: ğišnad-an-a na-mba-nu-**d**-en 'Don't lie on his bed'). It is never used with ga- (1st person volitive) or with the relative future u- or the positive imperative. When used with the positive emphatic and strong denial prefixes ḫe- and bara- respectively, it turns them into an optative and a vetitive/promissory negative instead:

ḫe-ba-n-šum 'He did give (it) to them'
ḫe-ba-b-šum-u 'Let him give it to them' (secondary)

bara-ra-dug 'I certainly did not say to you'
bara-eda-b-e-en 'I undertake not to say that ...' (secondary)

epa-bi šu-bal bara-ag-e 'He is not to destroy the ditch and canal' (secondary).

We are clearly witnessing here a stage in the language's development in some way connected with the specialisation of meaning for the reduplicated base, and the convergence of pairs of originally separate verbs to become grammatically alternating homonymous pairs. It's tempting to feel that it might be in some way connected with the attempt by an ergative language to cope with the increasing prominence of a neighbouring subject-object language, namely Akkadian. But it cannot be as simple as that. Speakers of Hurrian (another ergative language of the region), for example, just get their Akkadian nominative and accusatives mixed up and say in Akkadian 'he took them' for 'they took him'. Besides, the phenomenon of secondary verbal version in Sumerian does appear to be observable from Old Sumerian times for at least 500 years until the death of Sumerian as a mother-tongue. Thereafter, of course, it became fixed anyway, but it must be regarded as a fairly basic aspect of the structure of the language.

In about 70 percent of verbs the verbal base does not vary with the version, but in some instances the variation of the verbal base coincides with the variation of version, as mentioned above. Thus the base may be extended or reduplicated, as in:

ğar > ğağa 'to put',
kur > kuku 'to enter',
nağ > nana 'to drink',
gi > gigi 'to return'.

In other common verbs the two bases are 'suppletive':

de > tum 'to bring',
dug > e 'to speak',
ğen > du 'to go' (sing.), re > sub 'to go' (plur.),
uš > ug 'to die'.

Imperative

The imperative inverts the structure of the finite verb by placing the verbal base first, followed by morphemes which usually appear as proclitics:

ma-b-šum 'he gives to me'
 > šum-ma-b 'give to me', šum-ma-b-zen 'give (pl.) to me'

mu-n-da-ḫulḫul '(he) rejoices (greatly) over him'
 > ḫulḫul-a-mu-n-da 'rejoice greatly over him'

mu-ni-b-pad '(he) makes him swear'
 > pad-mu-ni-b 'make him swear'.

Ideophones

There is a rich class of ideophones or phonaesthetic verbs:

dub-dab ... za 'clatter' (slingstones, hailstones, falling rocks)
bud-bad ... za 'clatter' (slingstones)
pud-pad ... za 'thud' on the ground (slingstones)
suh-sah ... za 'thud' (running feet, dancers)
dum-dam ... za 'growl' (beaten dog) 'rumble' (storm), 'complain, grumble'
zig-zag ... za 'rumble' (drums)
gum-gam ... za 'snarl' (wolf)
ḫun-ḫa ... za 'bark' (dog)
wu-wa ... za 'bleat' (goat)
mur-mara ... ša 'roar' (lion)
dubul-dabal ... za 'glug' (poured beer)
kun-kan ... za 'splash' (beer)
mul-mal ... za 'swish' (boat through water), 'rustle' (woollen garments).

The enclitic copula

Very simple predicative sentences can be expressed using the enclitic copula:

	sg.	pl.
1	-men	-menden
2	-men	-menzen
3	-am, -m, -a	-meš

abam muzu 'what is your name?' (aba, 'what?', mu 'name')
sipadmen 'I am a shepherd'
Ḫammurabimen 'I am Ḫammurabi'
dumu Kiengiramenden 'We are Sumerians (sons of Sumer)'.

The copula may also be used for emphasis: ğakam 'It's mine!' (ğu-ak-am 'it is of me'), or to emphasise a finite verb, as in: lugalanir igi munidu-am 'he actually saw his master', 'it was (that) he saw his master'.

Non-finite verbal forms

The verbal base on its own resembles a participle dependent on a head noun in an ergative relationship with it:

lu dub sar 'a man writing a tablet' (dub, absolutive)
en ni gur 'awe-inspiring lord' (ni, absolutive).

The base with suffix -a forms a participle dependent on a head noun in an absolutive relationship with it:

dub sara 'a written tablet' (sar 'to write')
inim duga 'the spoken word' (dug 'to speak')
inim Ane duga 'the word spoken by (the god) An' (Ane, ergative),
cf. inim duga Ana 'the spoken word of An' (Ana, genitive)
Utu eda 'the rising sun' (Utu = sun god).

These can be extended with the affix -ed, marking an action as 'not yet begun':

e-ani duda (for du-ed-am) ma-n-dug
'He has told me to build his house'
(his house being-about-to-be-built he has told me).

All these forms can be followed by the enclitic copula, e.g., -am/-a/-m, and this, together with -ed-, expresses deontic modality:

dub-bi zir-ed-am
'That tablet is to be destroyed'
(tablet-that destroyed-ought to be-is).

The participial form with -ed- + -a can also occur with the further addition of a personal possessive enclitic (3rd person) or possessive plus suffixed -ne (1st and 2nd person), which often serves as a temporal clause:

kuku-d-a-ni 'When he enters', lit. 'his being-about-to-enter'
kuku-d-a-ğu-ne 'When I was on the point of entering'
or 'When I enter (future)', lit. 'at my being-about-to-enter'.

Complementation ('nominalised' forms)

An entire finite clause can be nominalised by the complementiser -a and can then, by the addition of case-markers, be brought within the structure of the main clause, e.g., as the object of a verb of speaking or swearing. Ablative -ta can have the sense 'from, since (of time)' = 'when', and terminative -še 'to, for (purpose)' = 'because of', etc. This is the commonest type of subordinate construction. Relative clauses are formed as nominalised clauses in apposition to lu 'person', and always follow their head noun.

la-ba-gigi-d-		igi	dikud-ne-še
NEG.LOC.return.PROSP.COMP		front	judge.PL.TERM
Ur-Suenak-e	mu-lugal-bi	i-n-pad	
Ur-Suena.ERG	oath-its	PROC.3ERG.swear	

'Ur-Suena has sworn before the judges that he will not return.'

Finally the evidential or citation form -eše should be mentioned, which can indicate citation of direct speech, or else mark a clause as having proverbial character ('they say'):

lu-ğišḫur-ak-e	ana-š-am	ğa-da-nu-me-a
man-of-drawing.ERG	what-for-COP	me-COM.NEG.be.COMP
i-zig-en-eše	i-n-tud-en	
PROC.rise.2SG.QUOT	PROC.3ERG.beat.1ABSOL	

'Saying, "Why did you get up (from work) in my absence?", the drawing-master beat me'

and the unreal condition (-ğišen):

gaugeden 'I am going to die'
> gaugedenğišen '(if) I were likely to die'.

Variation within Sumerian

Various diachronic and synchronic variations occur within Sumerian, although they are mostly not studied much so far.

Old Sumerian, southern dialect (2500-2350 BC)

The verbal prefixes i- and bi- agree in respect of vowel height with the vowel of the following syllable (so-called 'vowel harmony'): i- and bi- before -i- and -u-; e- and be- before -a- and -e-:

i-gid, i-zig, i-si, i-du, i-dug, i-gu, i-šub;
bi-gi, bi-sig, bi-zig, bi-du, bi-dub, bi-dug, bi-šu, bi-šuš, bi-tuku

but

e-ag, e-ğar, e-la, e-me, e-da-, e-na-, e-ne-, e-še-, e-ta-, e-meğar, e-mesarsar; be-ğareš, ḫe-be-la.

Emesal

The principal linguistic variation is the 'women's language' Emesal. The first attempts to write Emesal (after 2000 BC) used a 'phonetic' orthography. By comparison with the 'normal' dialect called Emegir, it has:

(i) phonetic alteration (dug : zeb 'good');
(ii) lexical substitution (guza : ašte 'chair') ;
(iii) distinctive orthographic features; and
(iv) hardly any grammatical difference.

Emesal was used in literature to characterise the speech of women, and in the religious cult songs of the (male) gala singers.

Emesal	*Emegir*
ka Gašangalada nammigub	ka Ningalada nammigub
me ḫulada idididen	ğe ḫulada iduden
amağu Gašangalra mulu eneğ ḫumunabe	amağu Ningalra lu inimḫumunabe
ušurme a ki desude	usarme a ki ḫesude
kitušani irbi zebam	kitušani irbi dugam
eneğani ağḫulḫulam	inimani niğḫulḫulam

'There he is standing at Ningal's gate, while I am rushing around in excitement. Oh that someone would tell my mother Ningal! Let our neighbour come and sprinkle water on the floor: the fragrance of her dwelling is pleasant, and her words are delightful.'

Conclusion

Sumerian was the principal language of southern Iraq in the earliest periods from which writing survives. It was soon joined by Akkadian (Old Akkadian, then Assyrian and Babylonian). For three thousand years in ancient Iraq it was virtually essential to be literate in Sumerian in order to be a scribe. A vast number of documents were written in the language, and an extensive literature which survived and continued to be copied and studied long after Sumerian had ceased to be a language of everyday communication.

It will be clear that there are quite a few areas where there is further analytic work to be done. In several of these, the study would benefit from the contributions, and in particular the openness to a wide range of possible interpretations, of people with a general training in linguistics, and I think Sumerian is a sufficiently interesting language to attract them. In particular, 'secondary verbal version' has by no means satisfactorily been analysed so far, and possibilities such as marking for pausal forms, changes of focus or introduction of new topic all need to be systematically investigated, perhaps by study of discourse. One could study time adverbials as a way of correlating the possible ways of marking tense. Much work remains to be done on the local variations of Old Sumerian dialects, which have hardly been studied so far; the declarative and emphatic forms, and indirect speech, all need clarification; and the 3000-year lexicographical tradition is a rich field for study, since although a lot of work has been done in reconstructing the texts themselves, the phenomenon as such has not yet been adequately described.

Behind all that we can say about Sumerian, there also lies the question of language death and the extent to which the written forms surviving to us can all be treated as perfectly idiomatic, coupled with the additional difficulty that it was precisely at the time when Sumerian was really being written by people who had learnt it during their studies that the grammatical affixes began to be most completely written out.

Further reading

M.-L. Thomsen, *The Sumerian language* (Mesopotamia 10; Copenhagen, 1984), is a convenient description of Sumerian grammar in more detail.

J.A. Black et al., *The Electronic Text Corpus of Sumerian Literature* (Oxford, 1998-2006) <http://etcsl.orinst.ox.ac.uk> is an extensive searchable collection of Sumerian literary compositions in transliterated Sumerian, with English translations.

J.A. Black et al., *The literature of ancient Sumer* (Oxford, 2004) introduces and presents a selection of 70 literary works from the ETCSL project.

Fig. 2.2a
Statue C of Gudea

Fig. 2.2b
The inscription on the back

Appendix: the ruler of Lagaš dedicates his statue

Gudea, Statue C[2]

Gudea ruled the prosperous city-state of Lagaš in southern Iraq in the late 22nd century BC. Numerous images and inscriptions on stone monuments, and clay cylinders relate how he extended and rebuilt the temples under his control. This particular text, which was inscribed on a standing statue of Gudea (now headless), commemorates the renovation of the goddess Inana's temple E-ana ('House of heaven') in the city of Ğirsu. As the third line shows, Gudea undertook this project only after he had completed the magnificent restoration of E-ninnu, the dwelling of the city's patron deity Ninğirsu, for which he is nowadays best remembered (see C. Suter, *Gudea's temple building: the representation of an early Mesopotamian ruler in text and image* (Styx: Groningen, 2000)).

^{d}nin-ğiš-zid-da diğir gu$_3$-de$_2$-a ensi lagaša^{ki} lu$_2$ e$_2$-an-na in-du$_3$-a-kam
'Ninğišzida is the god of Gudea, the ruler of Lagaš who built the E-ana.'

The whole phrase 'Gudea, the ruler of Lagaš who built the E-ana' is in the genitive, hence the -k- at the end of it.

Grammatically this phrase seems to be unconnected to the following sentence.

^{d}inana nin kur-kur-ra nin-a-ni
'(As for) Inana, the lady of the foreign lands, his lady,'

gu$_3$-de$_2$-a mu gil$_6$-sa ensi$_2$ lagaša^{ki} lu$_2$ e$_2$-ninnu ^{d}nin-ğir$_2$-su-ka in-du$_3$-a
'(and as for) Gudea, for long-lasting years the ruler of Lagaš who built the E-ninnu of Ninğirsu,'

^{d}nin-ğir$_2$-su-ka is a double genitive in -(a)k-a(k) because Nin-ğirsu is already a genitive syntagm, 'lord of Ğirsu'.

Grammatically these two phrases have been brought forward from the following clause; they are attached to 'Inana' and 'him' respectively.

ud ^{d}inana-ke$_4$ igi nam-til$_3$-ka-ni mu-ši-bar-ra-a
'When Inana looked upon him with her look of life,'

ud ... -a 'when' (lit. 'on [locat.] the day that ...') with nominalised clause (in -a) inside.

---

[2] Text follows K. Volk, *A Sumerian reader*, no. 23, with commentary from Jeremy Black's teaching files. The hyphenated transcription follows the conventional system designed to identify the cuneiform signs when presented in the Latin alphabet. For a variant translation, see D.O. Edzard in *Royal Inscriptions of Mesopotamia, Early Periods*, Vol. 3/1 (Toronto 1997), pp. 38-40.

igi ... bar 'to look upon s.o. (terminative)'.

nam-til_3 'life' formed from nam- (abstract formant) + til_3.

gu_3-de_2-a $ensi_2$ lagaša^{ki} ğeštug$_2$ dağal-a-kam arad nin-a-ni ki ağ$_2$-am$_3$ pisağ u_3-šub-ba-ka ğiš ba-ḫur

'Gudea, ruler of Lagaš (he is of broad wisdom) (he is the slave beloved by his lady) designed the frame of the brick-mould.'

ğiš ... ḫur 'to plan, design (+ locative)'

arad nin-a-ni ki ağ$_2$-am$_3$ is a so-called 'Mes-Ane-pada construction' ('hero chosen by An': An is ergative, the verb is a non-finite participial form), except that in this case the verb (ki ağ$_2$) is a compound verb.

zu_2 al-ka urin ba-mul

'With (Sum.: locative) the prong (lit. tooth) of the hoe (i.e. by digging), he made the standard shine' (or 'made it shine on the standard').

mul 'star', as verb 'to shine'.

im-bi ki dadag-ga-a im-mi-lu

'He mixed its clay in (Sum.: locative) a pure place.'

dadag (wr. UD.UD) 'pure, shining, bright' (distinguished from bar_6-bar_6 by final consonant).

lu 'to mix' (here).

im-mi- stands for i+m+bi: bi is locative; im- probably indicates the prefix mu-: mu-bi- is an impossible combination, so is replaced by i+m(u)+bi.

sig_4-bi ki sikil-a im-mi-du_8

'He had its bricks made in a pure place.'

du_8 'to make bricks' (here).

im-mi- stands for i+m+bi.

uš-bi mu-kug

'He sanctified its foundations.'

kug 'holy, pure', as verb 'to make holy, pure'.

izi im-ta-la_2

'He purified (it) with fire.'

izi ... la_2 'to purify with fire'; 'fire' is an underlying ablative, hence -ta- in the verb.

temen-bi i_3 ir nun-ka šu tag ba-ni-dug_4

'He smeared its foundation deposits with oil of superior fragrance.'

i_3 ir nun (gen.) 'oil of superior fragrance' i.e. aromatic oil.

šu tag ... dug$_4$ 'to decorate, smear, sprinkle with (loc.)', double compound verb (šu ... tag 'to decorate' is already a compound verb).

-ni- indicates locative.

e$_2$ ki ağ$_2$-ğa$_2$-ni e$_2$-an-na šag$_4$ ğir$_2$-su^{ki}-ka mu-na-ni-du$_3$
'He built her beloved temple, E-ana, for her within Ğirsu.'

šag$_4$ ... -a cf. Akkadian *ina libbi-*.

-ni- indicates locative

kur ma$_2$-gan^{ki}-ta na$_4$ esi im-ta-ed$_3$
'He had diorite brought up from the land of Magan.'

esi(KAL) is a hard black stone.

-ta- indicates ablative.

alan-na-ni-še$_3$ mu-tud
'He had (it) fashioned as his statue.'

tud 'to give birth; to fashion (a work of art)'.

-še$_3$ terminative, here 'for, as'.

gu$_3$-de$_2$-a lu$_2$ e$_2$ du$_3$-a-ka nam-til$_3$-la-ni ḫe$_2$-sud mu-še$_3$ mu-na-sa$_4$
'For her (Inana) he named (it) "May the life of Gudea who built the temple be prolonged" as a name.'

The statue is given a sentence name.

-še$_3$ terminative, here 'for, as'.

anticipatory genitive 'of Gudea who built the temple, his life'.

ḫe$_2$- optative prefix.

sud 'long', as verb 'to be long'.

e$_2$-an-na-ka mu-na-ni-kur$_9$
'He had (it) brought into E-ana for her.'

kur$_9$ (KU$_4$, later identical with TU, but separate at this period) 'to enter; to bring in', usually with locative.

-ni- indicates locative.

e$_2$-an-na-ka is a genitive ('House of Heaven') followed by locative.

Curse formula

lu$_2$ e$_2$-an-na-ta ib$_2$-ta-ab-ed$_2$-ed$_2$-a
'The man who removes (it) from E-ana,'

-bta- indicates 'from (ablative) + inanimate (temple)'.

-b- before the base indicate 3 ps. inanimate absolutive (the statue).

ed$_2$ 'to go out; to take out'.

ib$_2$-zi-re-a
'who destroys (it)'

zir 'to destroy, vandalise'.
-b- before the base indicate 3 ps. inanimate absolutive (the statue).
-e marks 3rd ps. ergative (the man) after the verb.

mu-sar-a-ba šu bi$_2$-ib$_2$-ur$_3$-a
'(or) who erases its inscription'

mu-sar-a 'inscription', lit. 'written name'.
šu ... ur$_3$ 'to erase' + locative.
bi- indicates locative.
-b- before the base indicate 3 ps. inanimate absolutive (the statue).

^{d}inana nin kur-kur-ra-ke$_4$ sağ-ğa$_2$-ni unken-na nam ḫe$_2$-ma-kud-e
'may Inana, lady of the foreign lands, curse his head in the assembly,'

unken 'assembly'.
nam ... kud 'to curse' + inanimate dative sağ-ğa$_2$-ni (= sağ+ani+e). Note that this is written the same way as nam ... tar 'to determine the destiny' (distinguishable only by final consonant where written).
ḫe$_2$- optative prefix.
-ma- probably stands for -mma- < -mba- = -m- + -ba-.
-e marks 3rd ps. ergative (Inana) after the verb.

^{ğiš}gu-za gub-ba-na suḫuš-bi na-an-gen$_6$-[ne$_2$]
'may she not make his established throne firm,'

^{ğiš}gu-za gub-ba 'established throne' +ani +ak gub 'to stand (intrans.); to establish'.
anticipatory genitive ('of his established throne, its foundation').
gen$_6$ (GI) 'to be/make firm'.
na- vetitive prefix 'may ... not ...'.
-e marks 3rd ps. ergative (Inana) after the verb.

numun-a-ni [ḫe$_2$-til]
'may his seed be ended'

distinguish til (BAD) 'to end' from til$_3$ (TI) 'to live'.

bal-[a-ni ḫe$_2$-kud]
'(and) may his reign be cut short.'

kud 'to cut, cut off'.

Babylonian and Assyrian: A history of Akkadian

Andrew George

School of Oriental and African Studies
University of London

Introduction

Akkadian is the name now given to the ancient dialects of East Semitic. Semitic is the family of western Asiatic languages that includes, among other West Semitic tongues, Hebrew, Ugaritic, Aramaic, Arabic, Ethiopic and Amharic (all conveniently described by Bergsträsser 1983, Hetzron 1997). Because the first substantial discoveries of written Akkadian were made in the remains of Assyrian cities, Akkadian was known to its first decipherers as Assyrian. In due course scholars recognized two important facts that led to a change in terminology. First, it was seen that in the 2nd and 1st millennia an ancient descriptor of Mesopotamian Semitic was *akkadûm,* fem. *akkadītum* "Akkadian". Second, it became apparent that for most of ancient history there were two principal varieties of Mesopotamian East Semitic, one spoken in Babylonia, the south of Iraq, and the other in Assyria, on the middle Tigris valley. These were then identified as Babylonian and Assyrian respectively and paired off on linguistic grounds as twin dialects of a single language, which for want of a better term was named Akkadian. Ancient Assyrian is not the same language as modern Assyrian, a term that denotes the eastern dialects of spoken Aramaic (neo-Syriac) still used by Assyrian Christians from Iraq and elsewhere.

A pairing of the dialects of Babylonia and Assyria, whether under the former name Assyrian or the current name Akkadian, does not reflect native usage, which knows no such common word for them. The ancients thought in terms of two separate languages. The term *akkadûm* "Akkadian" was used to refer to the East Semitic of south Mesopotamia, i.e. Babylonian, often in specific contrast to Sumerian, Assyrian or Aramaic. The ancient Assyrians called their tongue *aššurû* or *aššurāyu* "Assyrian", often in opposition to *armāyu* "Aramaic".

Though Babylonian and Assyrian are today treated as variant forms of Akkadian, they are sufficiently distinct in grammar and vocabulary that one could make a good case for speaking of them as separate languages, as the ancients did. On the other hand, they exhibit a parallel history in several aspects of their grammatical

Table 1. The range of documents written in Akkadian

1. Archival documents
   - a. Administrative lists and inventories
   - b. Receipts
   - c. Disbursements
   - d. Accounts
   - e. Business letters and memoranda
   - f. Private letters

2. Legal documents
   - a. Contracts, title deeds and wills
   - b. Juridical documents
   - c. Collections of laws

3. Royal documents
   - a. Building inscriptions
   - b. Royal annals
   - c. Royal grants and decrees
   - d. Treaties and diplomatic correspondence

4. Chronological and related texts
   - a. Date lists, king lists, eponym lists
   - b. Chronicles
   - c. Other historiographic documents

5. Commemorative and monumental inscriptions
   - a. Votive inscriptions
   - b. Funerary inscriptions

6. Liturgical and religious texts
   - a. Cult songs, hymns and laments
   - b. Temple rituals
   - c. Prayers

7. Divination literature
   - a. Omen compendia
   - b. Rituals, oracle questions and reports
   - c. Liver models

8. Astrological and astronomical literature
   - a. Omen compendia
   - b. Astrological reports
   - c. Astronomical diaries
   - d. Astronomical tables and almanacs

9. Exorcists' lore
   - a. Apotropaic and prophylactic rituals
   - b. Charms, spells and incantations
   - c. Prognostic and diagnostic omens
   - d. Medical recipes and compendia
   - e. Calendrical omens, hemerologies and almanacs

10. Mathematics and surveying
    - a. Mathematical problem texts
    - b. Numerical tables
    - c. Maps and plans

11. Craft-related texts
    - a. Technical manuals
    - b. Horse-training texts

12. Pedagogical texts
    - a. Sign lists
    - b. Vocabularies
    - c. Encyclopedic lists
    - d. Glossaries
    - e. Grammatical tables
    - f. Commentaries and other scholia
    - g. Scribal exercises

13. Belles lettres
    - a. Mythological, epic and narrative poetry
    - b. Literary hymns and devotional poetry
    - c. Lyric and other poetry
    - d. Didactic poetry and prose
    - e. Wisdom literature

14. Folk literature
    - a. Proverbs and fables
    - b. Folk tales

development. This is especially noticeable in the declension of the noun and adjective, where first a loss of mimation and later a reduction in case marking occur at approximately the same time in both Babylonian and Assyrian. Synchronic evolution of this kind speaks for a close historical relationship.

In lexical terms Akkadian is one of the largest Semitic languages. It possesses a vast vocabulary of Semitic words augmented by borrowings from other languages, both Semitic and unrelated. During its long history the various dialects of Akkadian absorbed many foreign words from the several tongues with which, at one or other time and place, they shared speakers and writers. These were chiefly Sumerian, Amorite, Hurrian, Aramaic, Old Persian and Greek. The first four, especially, were much spoken in parts of the Akkadian linguistic area. Bilingualism in Akkadian and one of these other languages is a conspicuous feature of the linguistic history of ancient Mesopotamia.

The vocabulary of Akkadian is still in the process of elucidation, for while we now possess either complete or nearly so two exhaustive modern dictionaries (Wolfram von Soden's *Akkadisches Handwörterbuch* and the *Assyrian Dictionary* of the University of Chicago), the exact meaning of many words last spoken two millennia ago continues to give difficulty. The process of refinement of our understanding of the Akkadian lexical stock will continue to exercise linguists and philologists for many generations. Akkadian was also a very long-lived language. Varieties of Akkadian were spoken in what is now Iraq from at least the middle of the 3rd millennium to the middle of the 1st millennium BC, and a written form of the language continued in use until the 1st century AD, perhaps even later.

A consequence of the long history of Akkadian, and the durability of the clay tablets on which it was written, is that we possess an enormous body of Akkadian texts. These texts fall into of all kinds of different categories and document a huge range of human activities and intellectual pursuits (Table 1). Three principal avenues of research stretch out before the Assyriologist as a result. First, the superabundance of letters and other archival documents permits the reconstruction of ancient institutions and societies with a detail that is impossible for many periods of more recent civilizations, including much of medieval Europe. The existence of multiple manuscripts of texts passed down in the scribal tradition holds out hope for the eventual recovery of the entire corpus of 1st-millennium Babylonian literature and Sumero-Babylonian scholarly achievement, alongside the earlier 2nd-millennium Sumerian corpus. Finally, the considerable variation in dialects of Akkadian over time and space (Table 2) offers lexicographers and historical grammarians almost unlimited scope for diachronic and synchronic linguistic study.

These prospects of new knowledge make competence in Akkadian an exciting tool to possess. It is not possible here to describe all avenues of research in Akkadian, nor to cover every aspect of Akkadian as a language. Others have written brief summaries of Akkadian grammar (Bergsträsser 1983: 25-49, Campbell 1991: 32-6, Buccellati 1997, Huehnergard and Woods 2004). One more would seem superfluous. Instead of adding to their number, it is enough here to draw attention to three salient

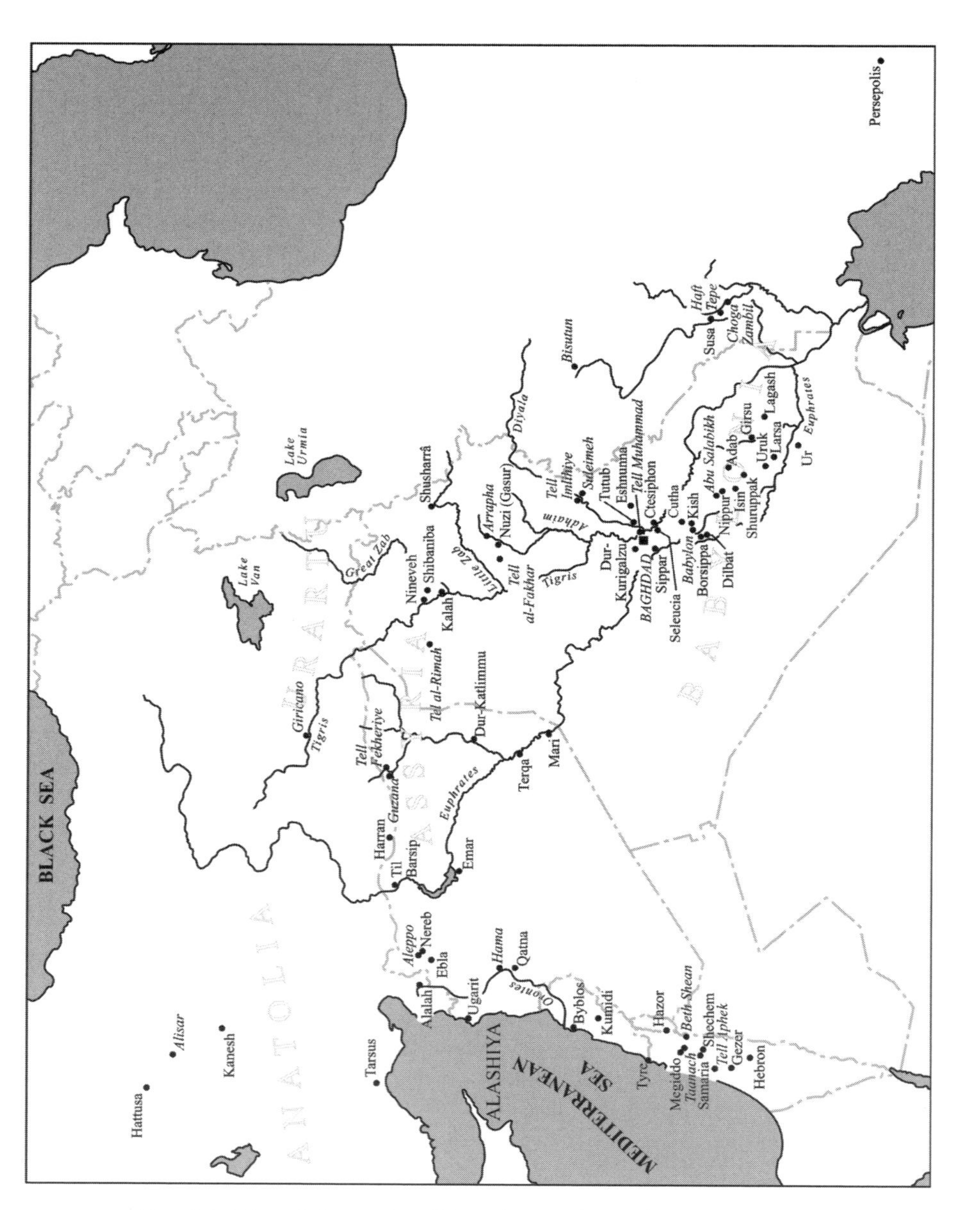

Fig. 3.1 Map of the ancient Near East to show places mentioned

features of Akkadian that distinguish it from most other Semitic: (a) the range of consonants is sharply reduced, probably under the influence of Sumerian, (b) word order in prose is subject - object - verb (SOV) as in Sumerian (Semitic is usually VSO), and (c) the verbal conjugations are put to uses different from their counterparts in other Semitic. Here the purpose is rather to examine the history and development of Akkadian based on current knowledge. What emerges is an account of the spread and usage of Akkadian: who spoke it, who wrote it, where, when and for what purpose.

This history is not definitive, however, for there is a caveat. Even in later periods, written forms of language tend to favour one variety of the language over another and so hide from us the full picture of dialectal diversity. When we also take into account the sporadic and uneven nature of the extant documentation, both in time and space, it will be obvious that any current history of Akkadian and its dialects will be provisional. New discoveries will force regular revisions.

Akkadian and Akkade

The adjective *akkadûm* "Akkadian" derives from the place name Akkade (in older literature Agade). Akkade was the ancient capital of the dynasty founded by Sargon, whose kings were the first to make extensive use of written Akkadian. Its exact site has not yet been located on the ground but there is strong documentary evidence that it lay on the Tigris in the vicinity of modern Baghdad (McEwan 1982: 11-12, Wall-Romana 1990). Some have sought it further upstream (e.g. Westenholz 1999: 31-4) but an unpublished Old Babylonian letter from Mari records an itinerary that places Akkade (*[a-kà]-dè*^{ki}) between the towns of Sippar (modern Abu Habba and Tell ed-Der) and Tutub (Khafajah) on the route to Eshnunna (Tell Asmar) (Charpin 1988: 150 fn. 68).[1] The direct route from Sippar to Eshnunna heads north-east to the Tigris and then up the river Diyala. This suggests a location for Akkade a little downstream of Baghdad, near the confluence of the two rivers. Since other evidence from Mari places Akkade at a river-crossing, it seems the strategic importance of Akkade lay in its control of a vital ferry over the Tigris.

Akkade gave its name to the area around it, *māt Akkade* "the land of A."; in Sumerian this country was called *ki-Uri* "the land of Uri". Uri is a toponym that in Old Babylonian Akkadian appears as *Wari'um*. Warium was the land east and north of the confluence of the Tigris and Diyala rivers, later centred on the important city of Eshnunna. In the 18th-century royal archives of Mari the gentilic adjective *akkadûm* "Akkadian" refers most often (but not exclusively) to people from the kingdom of

[1] The alternative restoration *[ú]-pi*$_5^{ki}$ is orthographically improbable in this period, when the toponym Upi (Greek Opis) was written *ú-pí-(i)*^{ki}.

Table 2. Time-chart showing the development of Akkadian

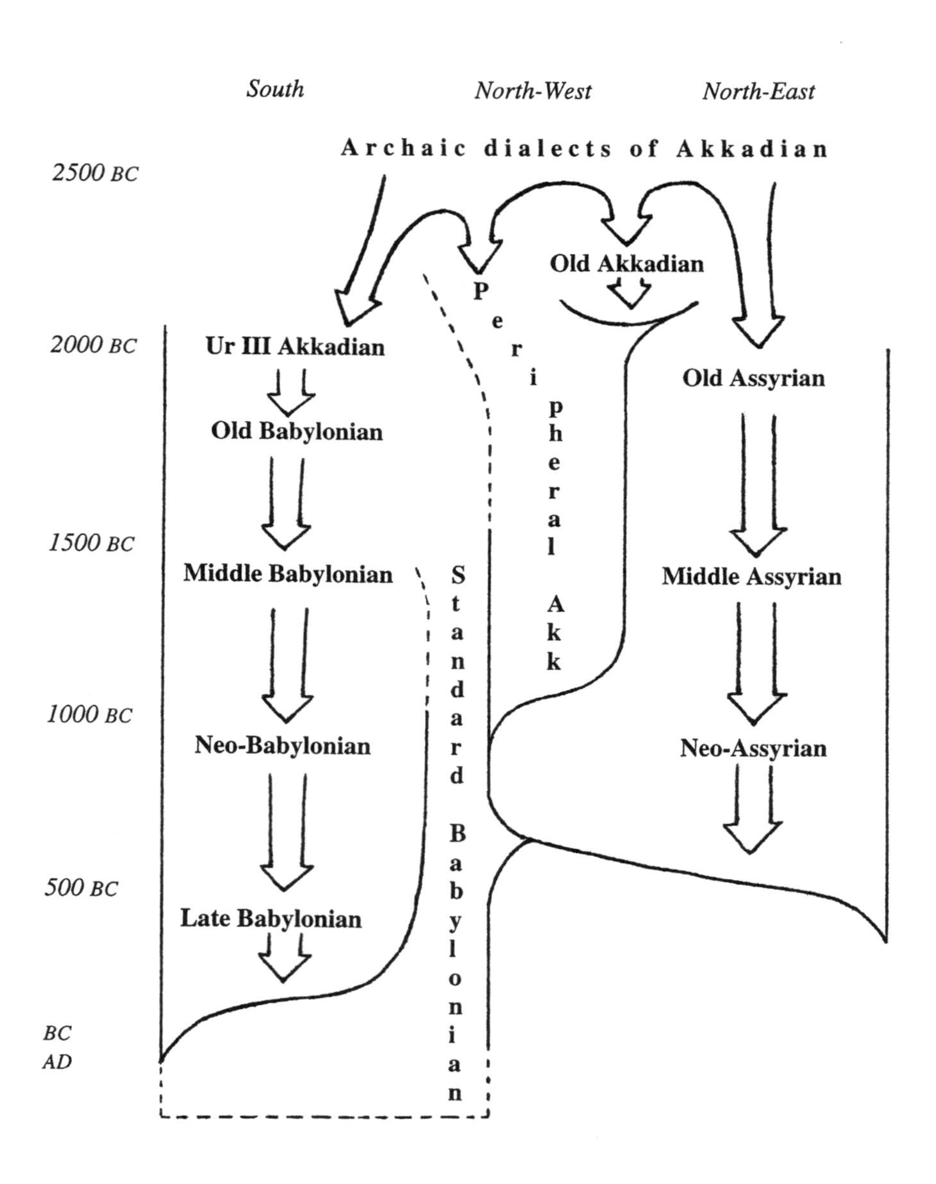

Eshnunna, i.e. the Tigris-Diyala basin (e.g. Durand 1992: 123, Birot 1993: 224). Similarly a year-name of Samsuiluna of Babylon refers to the troops of Eshnunna as the "army of Akkade" (year 11, see Charpin 2004: 341). This usage demonstrates a correct understanding of the historical geography. As already noted, however, when the ancients used the adjective *akkadûm* with reference to language, they meant the Semitic language of wider southern Mesopotamia, i.e. Babylonian. The ancient nomenclature suggests that the people of ancient Iraq considered the area around Akkade, broadly speaking the north-eastern fringe of Babylonia, to be the historical heartland of the Babylonian language. As we shall see, this was not exactly the case, but the notion reflects the special place occupied by the era and legacy of the kings of Akkade in the intellectual culture of later Babylonia.

In traditional surveys of the history and periodization of Akkadian it has been conventional to speak of Old Akkadian until the end of the 3rd millennium, and then a division into Assyrian in the north and Babylonian in the south, each neatly subdivided into three stages, Old, Middle and New (Neo-Assyrian and Neo-Babylonian), all six roughly synchronized in pairs, with a prolongation of the southern dialect as Late Babylonian (Reiner 1966: 20-1, Ungnad 1992: 4-6, von Soden 1995: 2-5, Buccellati 1996: 1-2, Caplice 1988: 3, Huehnergard 1997: xxiii-xxv). This picture is over-simplistic (as many of these scholars intimate), especially in the light of increasing evidence, particularly from the 3rd millennium. A detailed survey yields a much more complex history.

Akkadian and East Semitic in the mid-3rd millennium

The earliest traces of Akkadian are found predominantly in texts written in Old Sumerian, the principal written language of southern Iraq in the Early Dynastic period. Mid-3rd-millennium tablets from such Sumerian towns as Shuruppak (Fara) and Tell Abu Ṣalabikh attest the existence of individuals bearing names of East Semitic derivation, in a society where personal names were predominantly Sumerian. At Abu Ṣalabikh some of the scribes who wrote the famous Early Dynastic literary tablets bore East Semitic names, demonstrating that such names were part of the onomastic repertoire drawn on by the educated élites. These names do not, therefore, necessarily represent the infiltration into southern society of foreign elements from north Babylonia, but instead speak for a long history of linguistic symbiosis stretching back several centuries, perhaps well into prehistory. Many loanwords from East Semitic appear in Old Sumerian and reinforce the impression of what has been called a *Sprachbund*, a Sumerian-Akkadian linguistic area (Edzard 2003: 173-8). Interaction between Sumerian and Akkadian has also been documented in morphology and syntax; this is evidence of linguistic convergence, implying a growing similarity over time (Pedersén 1989).

Alongside the evidence for early Akkadian embedded in Sumerian texts are documents that seem to have been drawn up in an early form (or forms) of Akkadian.

Contemporaneous with the Old Sumerian tablets from Fara and Abu Ṣalabikh, they are predominantly written in Sumerian logograms but the presence of Semitic prepositions, pronouns, numbers and other particles betrays the language of composition. These documents include land deeds, votive inscriptions, a sale contract and administrative documents, and come predominantly from Kish and elsewhere in northern Babylonia, but also from as far north as Mari and Terqa on the middle Euphrates and as far south as Abu Ṣalabikh. On the basis of orthography, language, system of dating, names of months and persons, this Semitic cultural tradition of the mid-3rd millennium has been termed the "Kish civilization" (Gelb 1981, 1992).

The votive inscriptions of northern kings of the pre-Sargonic era document the use of the Semitic language of the Kish civilization in the wielding of political power at the very beginning of history. An instructive example is the short inscription from Girsu, in the deep south of Sumer, on a macehead dedicated to Ningirsu by Mesalim, "king of Kish", who was overlord of much of Sumer about 2600 BC. The inscription is ostensibly written in Sumerian, but the order of the signs shows that they are logograms to be read in an East Semitic dialect, presumably an early form of Akkadian (Wilcke 1993: 35 fn. 32). In this era we must reckon with a situation in which the south of Babylonia (Sumer) was predominantly Sumerian-speaking, and the north predominantly Semitic-speaking. Central towns like Nippur and Abu Ṣalabikh were widely bilingual. Probably this pattern of distribution was already established in late prehistory. Among the East Semitic languages of 3rd-millennium and earlier Mesopotamia were ancestral dialects of Akkadian; indeed, much more is now known of the early history of East Semitic than was the case a few decades ago.

The use of Semitic language in administration, law and displays of royal power was complemented by literary creativity. Among the many Early Dynastic literary tablets from Abu Ṣalabikh was a text written not in the conventional Sumerian, as were the huge majority of extant early literary compositions, but in East Semitic. Knowledge of this text was much improved by the discoveries at Ebla (Tell Mardikh, south of Aleppo in Syria). At this site were found copies of late Early Dynastic-period literature that to some extent replicate the literary corpus attested in Babylonia, including two important compositions in Semitic, one of them a duplicate of the text from Abu Ṣalabikh (Lambert 1989, 1992, Krebernik 1992). Between them these early works of East Semitic literature offer a glimpse of the literary traditions of northern Babylonia in the pre-Sargonic era, that is, of the literature of the Kish civilization.

By the mid-3rd millennium these literary traditions had spread from north Babylonia upstream to Mari and thence further into Syria. It appears probable that a pattern familiar from later eras was already in place: "a written Babylonian-based Semitic 'high language' with local variations was used and understood throughout Syro-Mesopotamia, and local spoken Semitic dialects [were] arrayed along a linguistic continuum stretching from Babylonia across upper Mesopotamia to Ebla, varying from the written 'high language' to greater or lesser degrees" (Cooper 2000: 69). A Semitic language of south Mesopotamia, whether we know it as East Semitic,

Akkadian or Babylonian, remained the predominant language of writing in Syria for the best part of a millennium and a half.

The local dialect of Ebla, called Eblaite or Eblaic, is only partly visible to us because the writing system was predominantly logographic. Most scholars now consider it to have been an East Semitic language closely related to Akkadian (e.g. Huehnergard 1995: 2120, Huehnergard and Woods 2004). The language of Ebla has much in common with what may be called "Mariote", the contemporaneous but little-known language of pre-Sargonic Mari (Gelb 1992). Some suppose that Eblaite was imported from Mesopotamia, specifically from Kish and northern Babylonia, where a "linguistic heterogeneity" is suspected (Michalowski 1987). Others view it as a local, Syrian variety of Akkadian that speaks for an early distribution of East Semitic outside Mesopotamia proper (Krebernik 1996).

The later 3rd millennium: Old Akkadian and Ur III Akkadian

Old Akkadian was the term once used to signify all 3rd-millennium Akkadian, and some choose still to use the phrase thus, despite the increasing evidence for diversity in the Semitic of pre-Sargonic Mesopotamia. Others use the label to refer only to the best-known East Semitic of the 3rd-millennium, which can be defined in historical terms as the official language of the empire established by Sargon of Akkade. The latter position is taken here: for present purposes Old Akkadian is the Akkadian of the Sargonic state (otherwise known as Sargonic Akkadian).

Apart from Eblaite, Mariote and the literary East Semitic of the Kish civilization, little has survived of the linguistic diversity postulated in the preceding section. Nevertheless, against such a background it would be foolish to assume that as the 3rd millennium wore on East Semitic was represented in Mesopotamia proper only by the ancestor of Old Akkadian. The existence of other dialects, contemporary with Old Akkadian and near relatives of it, can also be postulated on the grounds that, in linguistic terms, neither the Babylonian nor the Assyrian form of the language is a direct, lineal descendant of Old Akkadian (Sommerfeld 2003). The two main varieties of Akkadian evidently had other ancestors.

Old Akkadian. The prominence of Old Akkadian in linguistic history is owed to a particular circumstance: its use as a written language in the chanceries of Sargon of Akkade and his successors. Old Akkadian was the official language of record of the Sargonic state, the vehicle of its monumental inscriptions, administrative texts, and official correspondence (Text sample 1). It also occurs in private letters and a little literature. Presumably it was chosen because it was the common tongue of Sargon and the men of Akkade who governed his dominions. Accordingly it can be defined in geographical terms as an East Semitic dialect of Uri (Warium) in the Tigris-Diyala basin, which was the land around Akkade. This marks it as a peripheral dialect (Sommerfeld 2003). Many other earlier and contemporaneous dialects of East

Semitic surely remain unknown for want of being written down. Among these are the ancestors of Assyrian and Babylonian.

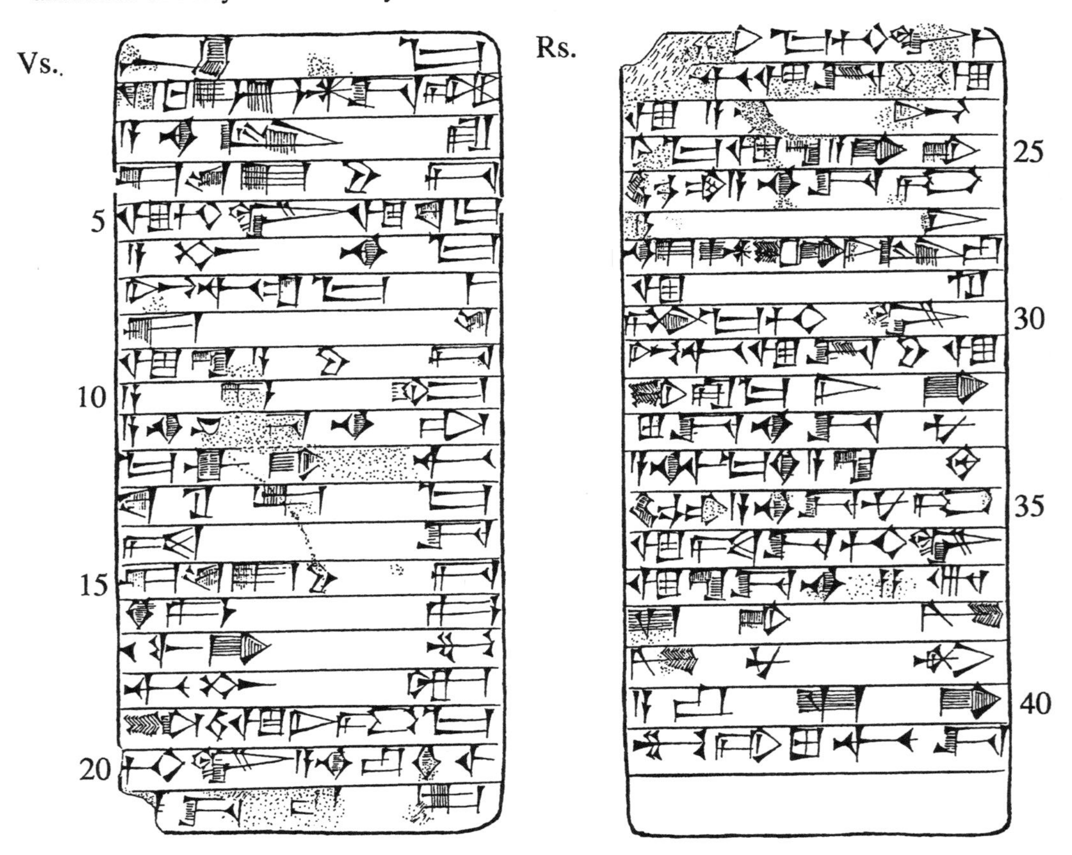

Fig. 3.2. Old Akkadian letter (BM 121205), copied by A. Westenholz
Lines 4-21 are transcribed as Text sample 1.

Our sight of Old Akkadian is confined by definition to the period of the Sargonic dynasty, when Sargon and his successors, most famously Naram-Sîn, carved out an empire in Mesopotamia and then lost it again (2334-2154 BC in the conventional chronology). Old Akkadian archival texts come from, in order north-west to south-east, the Habur triangle, Ashur on the Tigris, Gasur (Yorgan Tepe near Kirkuk), Suleimeh and the Diyala towns, Kish, Nippur, Adab, Ur and Lagash-Girsu in Babylonia, and Susa in Elam (modern Khuzistan). This is a geographical spread that matches the extent of the Sargonic empire. It speaks only for the use there of Old Akkadian as a bureaucratic tool, not for the area in which it was a vernacular. In most of these places writing in Old Akkadian ceased abruptly with the end of the empire. Nevertheless, to the east, in places where Old Akkadian took cuneiform writing for the first time, there were lasting consequences. When Elam became independent of Akkade under Puzur-Inshushinak, Akkadian continued in use as an official language, and the cuneiform script it brought with it in due course replaced the old Proto-Elamite script (Galter 1995: 34-6). Rulers of eastern highland tribes also emulated Old Akkadian monumental inscriptions in vaunting their power, first in Gutium and then in Lullubum.

Text sample 1. Old Akkadian. Letter of Ishkun-Dagan to LUGAL.RA

ḥaqlam ḥaruth u būlam 'uṣur 'appunnāma Quti'ummami ḥaqlam 'ulā aḥruth ay taqbi ana mithil bēr maqqātī sūsibma 'atta ḥaqlam ḥaruth kī 'eṭlūtim yuwakkamū tibûtam lisse'ūnikkumma būlam ana 'ālim suta'rib[2]

Kienast and Volk 1995: Gir 19

Till the land and guard the livestock. And don't you dare say, "There were Gutians about, so I couldn't till the land!" Position *detachments of scouts* at half-league intervals and get on with tilling the land. If they spy men coming, they can attack on your behalf, while you get the livestock safely into town.

In Old Akkadian letters the verb is always in final position, with the exception of two instances in letters from the north (Gasur and probably Eshnunna) where a verb is followed by the same adverb of degree (*danniš*).[3] In Sargonic monumental inscriptions and the similar text of Erridupizir of Gutium (c. 2200) verbs in non-final position are commoner. This deviation from normal word order sets the language of royal display apart from the vernacular of the letters, and allows one to distinguish a literary register of Akkadian prose for the first time in its history. Much later the placing of the verb in penultimate position in its clause is a common mark of literary style. Very little survives of Old Akkadian poetry. The grammar of Old Akkadian and

[2] The transcription of Old Akkadian dialect is not an exact science. In this passage I have followed the new system proposed by Hasselbach 2005, but with the use of *th* for the interdental θ ($š_3$). Others would no doubt render some words differently.

[3] *HSS* X 5: 19 *li-ṣú-ru da-ni-iš* and *MAD* I 298: 6-7 and 15-16 *a-ṣi-ḫa-mì da-ni-iš da-ni-iš*; cf. *CT* 50 69: 4-5 *da-ni-iš-mì da-ni-iš a-ṣi-ḫa-am* (southern?).

its writing conventions were described by Gelb, who also compiled a dictionary dedicated to the dialect (Gelb 1957, 1961; now also Hasselbach 2005).

Ur III Akkadian. Following the eclipse of the Sargonic kingdom, kings of the Gutian interregnum emulated Sargonic monumental inscriptions. Power was prised from the Gutians by a dynasty from Uruk in the Sumerian-speaking south. Choosing as their capital the nearby city of Ur, they presided over a Sumerian cultural swansong. In the administration of their state Sumerian took preference over Akkadian, which was little used in official communication, even if, as many suspect, it was rapidly ousting Sumerian as the vernacular in the deep south as well as further north. The Akkadian of this, the Ur III period, used to be considered a continuation of Old Akkadian. Recent study of what little survives, however, has revised that view, and the current consensus is that, beneath a mask of 3rd-millennium spelling conventions, Ur III Akkadian exhibits much greater continuity with what came afterwards than with what went before. Some describe it as "essentially an archaic version of Old Babylonian" (Westenholz 1999: 33), even as the "earliest, precisely identifiable developmental stage of the Babylonian dialect" (Hilgert 2003: 11). Many historians now judge the interval between the Sargonic and Ur III periods, the Gutian interregnum, to have endured for perhaps only a single generation, so that Sargonic and Ur III Akkadian can be considered nearly contemporaneous. The conclusion has been drawn that Old Akkadian, originating in northern Babylonia, and Ur III Akkadian, known mostly from the far south, are geographical variants of Akkadian, rather than diachronic or sequential forms of the language (Buccellati 2004: 108). The Akkadian of the Ur III period is now studied by Hilgert 2002.

Archaic north-west Akkadian. From the middle Euphrates region we get a glimpse of Akkadian as it had developed outside Babylonia. At Mari (Tell Hariri) and Terqa (Tell al-'Ashara), near Deir ez-Zor, tablets and clay models of livers are extant from what is known as the period of the military governors (Akk. *šakkanakku*), formerly dated after the fall of Ur. These military governors were a succession of local rulers initially subservient to Akkade but soon independent of first Akkade and then Ur (Durand 1995). The texts (administrative records and liver omens) exhibit a form (or forms) of early Akkadian sometimes identified as Old Akkadian (e.g. Edzard 1985). What is meant by this term is not, however, the specific dialect of Warium used by Sargon and Naram-Sîn. The language written at Mari was already distinctively East Semitic in the Early Dynastic period (see above), and evidently evolved as an Akkadian dialect. Study of the language of the *šakkanakku*-period at Mari shows that it still exhibits little evidence of West Semitic influence. This indicates that Akkadian was more entrenched on the middle Euphrates in the 3rd millennium than it was in the early 2nd millennium, when Amorite became the regional vernacular. The dialect of the *šakkanakku*-period is nevertheless distinct from the Akkadian of the south and represents a marginal, north-western form of the language (Westenholz 1978). Archaic north-west Akkadian would be a better term for this and other early forms of the language from this area.

The early 2nd millennium: archaic Old Babylonian and Old Assyrian

At the turn of the 3rd millennium the kingdom of Ur collapsed under the onslaught of Amorite nomads and Elamite invaders. In Babylonia itself, increasing numbers of written sources enable us to observe the local Akkadian in the period immediately following the fall of Ur. On the middle Tigris Assyrian emerged as a distinctive local form of Akkadian.

Archaic Old Babylonian. In the south, the bureaucrats of the successor states of Ur III continued to use Sumerian as the written language of administration and government, but in the north Akkadian texts became common again. The principal evidence comes from Eshnunna in the Diyala basin, where two groups of private letters document the transition from "archaic Old Babylonian" to classical Old Babylonian (Whiting 1987). The earlier letters show that here the southern dialect of Akkadian had ousted the local Old Akkadian by the turn of the millennium. They use a form of the language barely distinguishable from that written further south in the Ur III period; in some respects it seems slightly older (Heimpel 2004). The later letters indicate that this language quickly developed into the classic Old Babylonian dialect, for they display a form of it found in other corpora of early Old Babylonian texts (Whiting 1987, 16-19). Very early Old Babylonian royal inscriptions, such as those of Ashduniarim of Kish, exhibit an archaic subjunctive that may be a mark of an elevated, literary style.

Old Assyrian. A much larger and more productive body of material is the tablets from Cappadocia, which hold texts written in an early form of the Assyrian dialect of Akkadian that we call Old Assyrian. These tablets have been dug up in their thousands and, as excavations proceed, the number continues to grow at a steady rate. More than 21,500 are now extant (Michel 2001: 30). They constitute the private archives of members of Assyrian merchant colonies based mostly at Kanesh, modern Kültepe, near Kayseri (Text sample 2). Similar tablets have been found in smaller numbers elsewhere in Anatolia, at Hattusa (Boğazköy) and Alişar, and in and around Assyria, at Ashur itself and at Gasur, and illustrate the use of Old Assyrian by businesses across a wide area. Local rulers in Cappadocia could also use Old Assyrian as a medium of communication. However, documents of an Assyrian merchant based at Sippar in Babylonia, though dated in Assyrian style, are written in Old Babylonian (Walker 1980).

Text sample 2. Old Assyrian. Letter of Lamassi to her husband, Pushu-ken

tašammēma tanēštum iltemin aḫum ana aḫim ana ḫalātim izzaz kutabbitma u alkamma kurṣīka parrir . . . aḫatka amtam ana šīmim taddinma anāku ana arbešarat šiqil apṭurši Šalim-aḫum šina bētēn ištu atta tūṣ'u ētapaš nīnūma ana mati neppaš

Garelli 1965: 159

You know, of course, how bad folk here have got. One fellow stands ready to eat the other alive! Treat yourself right: come home [to Ashur] and throw off your shackles! . . . . Your sister went and sold one of the slavegirls, so I had to get her back at a cost of fourteen shekels. Since you went away that Shalim-ahum has set himself up with *two* houses. How about us? When shall we ever do that?

Letters and memoranda predominate in the archives of the colony at Kanesh, but rare copies of royal texts, spells and literary compositions offer a glimpse of other registers of Old Assyrian. A few Old Assyrian royal inscriptions also survive from Assyria itself. The Old Assyrian dialect is nearer to Old Akkadian than to Ur III Akkadian, unsurprisingly given Assyria's northerly location on the middle Tigris, but a closer kinship has been observed between Assyrian and the pre-Sargonic language of Ebla and Mari (Parpola 1988). Old Assyrian can be seen as a local development of one of the East Semitic dialects postulated as spoken in northern Mesopotamia and Syria in the mid-3rd millennium. Assyrian as a whole differs considerably from Babylonian in grammar and vocabulary, and maintains many of these distinctions throughout its history. Orthography, as well as dialect, was distinctive: Old Assyrian scribes used a restricted syllabary of only about one hundred and thirty signs and avoided all but a few common logograms. Old Assyrian language and writing have been well described by Hecker 1968.

The Old Babylonian period

The period when Babylonia, and for a time all Mesopotamia, was dominated by Babylon under its 1st dynasty is known as the Old Babylonian period (1894-1595 BC in the conventional chronology), and the Akkadian of the time is called Old Babylonian.

Old Babylonian. Old Babylonian is considered the classic manifestation of Akkadian, and is the dialect usually taught to beginners. This is because in its southern form it shows great regularity, exhibits little contamination by other Semitic languages, and is the vehicle for a very extensive body of texts. Most famous of these is the laws of King Ḫammurapi (18th century), inscribed on a great stone stele found in 1901 at Susa, where it had been taken as booty in antiquity. Ḫammurapi's monument is widely celebrated as the world's first law code, though it is neither a code nor the oldest collection of laws. It is certainly the Akkadian text most widely read in the original language, for beginners in Akkadian customarily grapple with it in universities worldwide. Old Babylonian is the normative form of Akkadian described in most standard reference grammars (Ungnad 1992, von Soden 1995, Buccellati 1996) and teaching manuals (Marcus 1978, Caplice 1988, Huehnergard 1997). It also presents a useful corpus for linguistic research (e.g. Kaplan 2002).

Alongside the many building inscriptions and several edicts of Ḫammurapi's dynasty are masses of archival documents (letters, memoranda, legal and administrative documents) from the same period (Text sample 3). These come especially from Sippar, Ur and Larsa (Senkereh). Twenty-five years ago they were thought already to number nearly fifteen thousand texts (Lieberman 1977: 10-11), but this was probably too conservative an estimate. Extant in far smaller numbers are monumental texts, both royal and private, e.g. funerary and votive inscriptions, and other genres of text that use plain Old Babylonian: compendia of omens for use in divination, astrology etc., with their associated ritual texts; vocabularies and other pedagogical lists; and other practical texts, such as mathematical problems, medical therapies, culinary recipes etc.

Text sample 3. Old Babylonian. Letter of Huzalum to his sister, Nishi-inishu

šumma ina kinātim atḫūtam tarammī eqlam ašaršani lā tanaddinīma lā anazziq eqlam idnimma anāku lūpuš eli qātim aḫītim ša ṭūb libbīki lūpuš u dummuqī amrī

Altbabylonische Briefe XI 41

If you truly have a sister's love for me, don't give the land away to somebody else, don't make me upset! Give the land to me and let me work it. I'll do what pleases you better than any stranger. You just see how well I'll do!

Literary Old Babylonian. Literary forms of Akkadian begin to be better attested in the Old Babylonian period, though the number of extant tablets and texts remains very small. The scarcity of Old Babylonian literature, and of narrative poetry in particular, is explained by the fact that in scribal schools Sumerian remained the language of instruction to the late 18th century. It was still the old literature in Sumerian that provided most of the copy-books and was most written down. The Old Babylonian literary corpus includes magic spells and incantations; omen compendia of all kinds; hymns, prayers and laments; proverbs, fables and other wisdom literature, love poetry, and mythological and narrative poetry. Enough survives of the last to show that the poems of Atram-hasis, Gilgamesh, Anzû and Etana were already present, alongside compositions about the ancient kings of Akkade. Literary texts in Old Babylonian display a vibrant poetic language unburdened by the scholasticism that came later, and give us an inkling of the style and content of what must have been a very extensive oral literature in Old Babylonian. The most recent studies of literary Old Babylonian style are Metzler 2002, Wasserman 2003, Izre'el and Cohen 2004.

Some Old Babylonian literary texts use an elevated register of the poetic language that is often known as "hymno-epic dialect" (Text sample 4). This is not a true dialect but literary Old Babylonian embellished with archaizing features, especially of morphology and vocabulary (von Soden 1931-3, Groneberg 1971, 1978-9). Some of these features are observed in older forms of Akkadian, not only Old Akkadian but also the archaic Old Babylonian of the earlier group of letters from Eshnunna (Whiting 1987: 18).

Text sample 4. Old Babylonian. From a hymn to Ishtar on behalf of King Ammiditana

šaptīn duššupat balāṭum pīša
simtišša iḫannimā ṣīḫātum
šarḫat irimmū ramû rēšušša
bani'ā šimtāša bitrāmā īnāša šit'ārā

Thureau-Dangin 1925: 172

Syrup-sweet her lips, her mouth is life itself,
upon her complexion bloom the smiles.
So noble she, that charms of love do dwell upon her head,
beauteous her colouring, iridescent her eyes and lustrous.

Old Babylonian literary texts in Akkadian come not only from Babylonia but also, in smaller quantities, from peripheral areas. The Sumero-Babylonian scribal tradition is well attested at Susa in Elam, so the presence there of a few Akkadian literary texts is unsurprising. More revealing is group of late Old Babylonian omen tablets, whose spellings attest to a peripheral orthographic tradition (Labat 1974). Some of these texts' curious spelling conventions also occur in the roughly contemporaneous omen tablets from Tigunanum on the upper Tigris below Diyarbakir, which were certainly not composed in Babylonia. Fragments of late Old Babylonian omen texts recovered at Hazor in modern Israel show just how far abroad this typically Akkadian genre travelled. Another text composed in the periphery was a Babylonian heroic poem to the glory of king Zimri-Lim of Mari. The discovery of Old Babylonian cuneiform outside Babylonia sheds light on the diffusion of Babylonian intellectual culture to peripheral areas, on its reception and adaptation there, and on Babylonian Akkadian as a vehicle of original literary expression outside Babylonia. It also reveals the varieties of Akkadian used in peripheral areas at this time.

Provincial and barbarized Old Babylonian. Visible in the extant records for a timespan of three centuries, Old Babylonian is not monolithic: differences in phonology, grammar, syntax and spelling do arise from era to era, place to place and register to register (viz. literary *vs.* vernacular), but they are comparatively small and the dialect can be said to be a coherent, though evolving, whole. For the most part local and diachronic variants of vernacular Old Babylonian remain to be studied in detail; a good example of one such local variant is the provincial Akkadian written in this period in Elam, where a significant Akkadian-speaking population may have been descendants of immigrants from southern Babylonia (Lambert 1991). The Akkadian of Old Babylonian Elam has been studied by De Meyer 1962 and Salonen 1962.

A special place, however, is occupied by the Old Babylonian dialects of the middle Euphrates and beyond. The extensive royal archives of Mari, excavated in the 1930s and since, number about twenty thousand pieces, and have been supplemented by smaller finds at Tell al-Rimah and other sites in upper Mesopotamia. These texts exhibit a form of provincial Old Babylonian also current in the Diyala region but more affected by the local West Semitic vernacular, Amorite, especially in vocabulary. Possibly it was never spoken, but used only as a written language in chancery. It has been described by Finet 1956 and Charpin 1989. A variety of Old Babylonian similar to that current in Mari was also written in the southern Levant, as demonstrated by tablets from Hazor, Shechem and Hebron in Palestine (Rainey 1999: 154*-5*). A purer form of Old Babylonian was used for royal building inscriptions by kings of Mari, notably Yaḫdun-Lim, and by other upper Mesopotamian kings of this period, especially Shamshi-Adad I.

More barbarized forms of Akkadian undoubtedly existed on the periphery. At Shusharrâ (Tell Shemshara), in the upland valley of the Lesser Zab in Iraqi Kurdistan, was found a modest archive of letters and administrative texts left by a local ruler who was a correspondent of Shamshi-Adad I. The letters from Shamshi-Adad exhibit a dialect close to that written at Mari. Those of more local origin display another provincial dialect of Old Babylonian (Kupper 2001). Personal names indicate the predominance here of Hurrian, a regional vernacular increasingly found across a large area of upper Mesopotamia, north Syria and Kurdistan. An early glimpse of Hurrianized Akkadian can be seen in the older group of texts excavated by Woolley at Alalaḫ (Tell Açana) in the Turkish Hatay. The chancery of Yarim-Lim of Alalaḫ (17th century) could write excellent formal Old Babylonian, but the imprint of Hurrian is increasingly observed in archival documents (Aro 1954-6, Giacumakis 1970).

In its variety the Babylonian written in the western and eastern peripheries early in the 2nd millennium conforms to the pattern already noted for the mid-3rd millennium. Provincial chanceries imported the technology of cuneiform writing from Babylonia, and with it texts of the scribal tradition written in good Babylonian. These provided a linguistic model for official inscriptions and international correspondence. Less permanent documents exhibited a greater influence of vernacular forms, whether West Semitic (Amorite) or Hurrian. The language of writing, whatever the register, was not a local vernacular. Later in the 2nd millennium the Akkadian of the western periphery is exposed in still greater variety.

The later 2nd millennium: Middle Babylonian, Middle Assyrian and international Akkadian

The end of Ḫammurapi's dynasty came when Babylon fell to a raid by the Hittite adventurer Mursili I, a date conventionally fixed at 1595 BC. This was a cataclysmic event: the city was abandoned and probably remained so for many years. In the current scheme of linguistic history the fall of Babylon marks the end of the Old Babylonian dialect. The political vacuum was filled by a dynasty of kings of Kassite origin and by the little-known rulers of the Sealand, already established as a power in the far south. After an interval of uncertain length the Kassite dynasty imposed their dominion over all Babylonia and remained in power until the twelfth century. The throne then fell into the hands of a sequence of rulers known as the 2nd dynasty of Isin (1157-1026 BC). The language of Babylonia under these three dynasties, especially the Kassite era, is called Middle Babylonian.

Middle Babylonian. The development of Old into Middle Babylonian was a slow evolution, at least in southern Mesopotamia. The application of a different term for Babylonian as it appeared in the latter part of the 2nd millennium arose not because Middle Babylonian is radically different from late Old Babylonian but because a long gap intrudes between the fall of Babylon and the reappearance in the south of documentation on a large scale. This interval is often characterized as a Dark Age. The darkness is gradually dispersing, however, for several large caches of tablets of the period immediately following the fall of Babylon have recently come to light and await publication. As the gap in documentation fills, so more will be known of the development of Akkadian in the mid-2nd millennium. It is already apparent that many of those traits thought characteristic of Middle Babylonian appear sporadically in later Old Babylonian (Lieberman 1977: 8-9 fn. 21). Legal texts from Tell Muhammad in the Diyala basin that post-date the fall and resettlement of Babylon are reported to continue Old Babylonian traditions. Clearly the transition was gradual.

The corpus of texts in Middle Babylonian has been estimated at fifteen thousand documents but the vast majority still awaits publication (Brinkman 1976: 3). Finds from 14th and 13th-century Nippur predominate, numbering about twelve thousand. These are mostly letters and legal and administrative documents, some of them connected with the personnel of the temple of Enlil at Nippur and with the management of its estates and income. Smaller groups of Middle Babylonian archival documents come from Ur, Dur-Kurigalzu and Babylon and date mostly to the 13th and 12th centuries. Other well-known Babylonian cities have yielded isolated finds; from provincial Tell Imlihiye on the Diyala comes the small 13th-century archive of a farming family (Kessler 1982). Letters of diplomacy sent by two 14th-century Kassite kings, Kadashman-Enlil I and Burnaburiash II, turned up in the Egyptian royal archives found at El-Amarna in the 1880s and '90s. Letters of other Kassite kings survive in later copies. Royal building and votive inscriptions in Akkadian are comparatively rare, for an artificial form of Sumerian was favoured here, but a typical product of the royal chancery of this period are land grants written in Middle Babylonian and inscribed on beautiful stone monuments called *kudurru*s. Middle Babylonian has been described by Aro 1955.

The late 2nd millennium is known as a time of considerable literary creativity and also of scholarly editorial work that brought old compositions up to date and standardized them. Very little literature of the period has survived on Middle Babylonian tablets, however, and it is best known from 1st-millennium copies. Pedagogical texts and other tablets from scribal schooling preserve scraps of the standard Kassite-period copy-books, enough to show that the old Sumerian texts had largely been abandoned and their place taken by works in Akkadian, some of them new compositions, others already known in the Old Babylonian period. These, again, are mostly from Nippur, with a smattering from Ur and Babylon. Narrative poetry is represented by Gilgamesh and Atram-hasis, professional literature by an increasing number of omen compendia and medical tablets. The vehicle for some of this corpus is Middle Babylonian similar to the contemporaneous letters, but the poetic compositions, especially, were written (or rewritten) in a literary register of the language that English-speaking scholars call Standard Babylonian (*Jungbabylonisch* in German). The chief evidence for Standard Babylonian is 1st-millennium copies of literary texts and the royal inscriptions composed for the Sargonid kings of Assyria, and it will be discussed below, in the section on the early 1st millennium.

Middle Assyrian. Akkadian continued to be spoken and written in Assyria, where it is known in the late 2nd millennium as Middle Assyrian. Here there is a much longer hiatus between the Old and Middle forms of the local dialect. Middle Assyrian documents come principally from Ashur, excavated before the 1st world war. The many archives of letters, legal and administrative documents found there stem from the 14th to 11th centuries, with a predominant number dating to the 13th. Other such texts come from Shibaniba (Tell Billa) near Nineveh, Tell al-Rimah and other sites in the Jezirah, where they document the presence of Assyrian officials posted locally.

From about the time of Adad-narari I (1307-1275) the royal inscriptions of Assyrian kings are mostly written in slightly Assyrianizing Middle Babylonian, demonstrating the continuing prestige of the Babylonian dialect in Assyria first observed when the region was ruled by Shamshi-Adad I. Middle Babylonian copies of southern literary compositions were imported to Assyria, especially as booty by Tukulti-Ninurta I when he sacked Babylon (about 1230 BC). From this time on Assyria, so often mightier than Babylonia in war and political influence, was under the cultural domination of its southern neighbour. More or less the entire Babylonian scribal tradition seems to have been known in 11th-century Assyria. Narrative poetry such as the poem of Etana, Ishtar's Descent and the Sumerian *Lugale* and

Angimdimma (by this time in bilingual Sumero-Babylonian format), other literary compositions and scholarly texts - hymns, omens, incantations, rituals, medical texts, hemerologies, Ḫammurapi's laws, lexical lists - were handed down in Assyrian copies that survive today. Over generations some of this Babylonian literature became more or less Assyrianized. New literature in praise of Assyrian might was composed locally, also in Babylonian; this includes the Tukulti-Ninurta epic.

The great Middle Assyrian law code, the unique palace edicts that regulate conduct at the Assyrian court, the Assyrian coronation ritual, however, all these had no literary pretensions and were written in pure Middle Assyrian, as was one of King Ashur-uballiṭ's two letters to pharaoh, found at El-Amarna. Middle Assyrian has been studied by Mayer 1971.

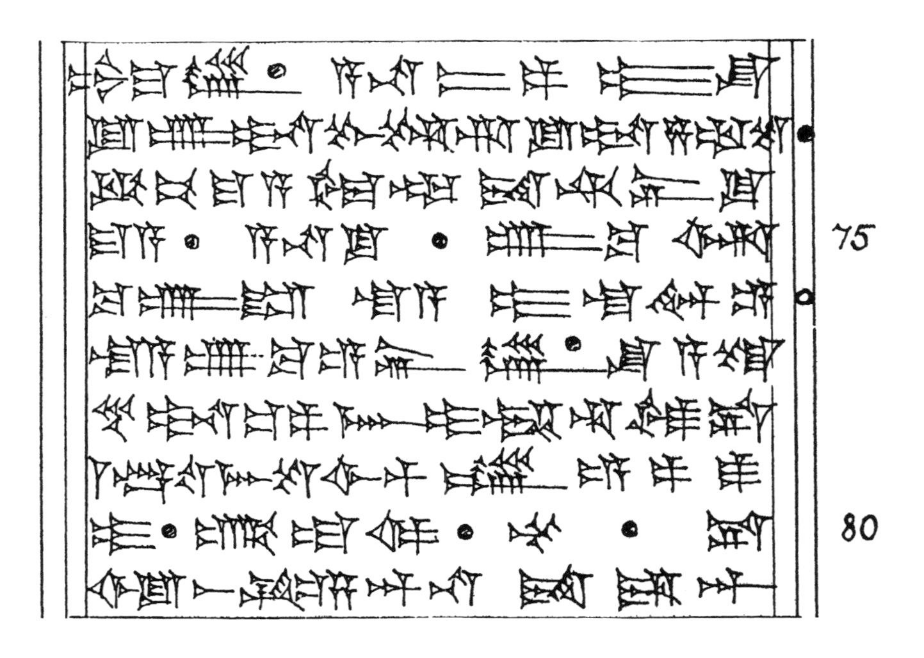

Fig. 3.3 The Middle Assyrian Laws, Tablet A §18, copied by O. Schroeder

Text sample 5. Middle Assyrian. From the laws

šumma a'īlu ana tappā'ēšu lū ina puzre lū ina ṣalte iqbi mā aššatka ittinikkū mā anāku ubâr ba''ura lā ila''e lā uba''er a'īla šu'ātu arbâ ina ḫaṭṭāte imaḫḫuṣūš iltēn uraḫ ūmāte šipar šarre eppaš igaddimūš u iltēt bilat annaka iddan

MA Law §18

If a man says to his friend, whether in private or in a fight, "Your wife sleeps around," and adds, "I shall prove it," but he cannot prove it and does not prove it, that man shall be flogged forty strokes of the rod, shall do the king's labour for a full month, have his head shaved and pay a fine of one talent of tin (*or* lead).

Peripheral Akkadian. Akkadian continued to be employed beyond the bounds of Babylonia and Assyria proper. In the latter part of the 2nd millennium there is extensive evidence for peripheral dialects of Akkadian and for the continuing spread of literary Babylonian outside Mesopotamia. Legal documents from Terqa on the middle Euphrates and private archives from Ekalte (Tell Munbaqa) further upstream exhibit a continuation of Old Babylonian traditions of writing. However, by the early Kassite period (16th century) the Babylonian written at Terqa contained provincial traits, including loans from West Semitic and the occasional Assyrianism (Podany 1991-3). Middle Assyrian eventually prevailed here as the language of writing.

Archives excavated at Gasur, at this time known as Nuzi, in the 1920s and '30s yielded about seven thousand tablets distributed among perhaps as many as forty archives, institutional and private. Similar tablets also came from nearby Arrapha (Kirkuk) and Tell al-Fakhar. They hold legal and juridical documents, letters and administrative texts written in a form of Akkadian much influenced by the local Hurrian vernacular and dating to the 15th and 14th centuries. This is the period just before the rise of the Middle Assyrian state under Ashur-uballiṭ I, who was probably responsible for Nuzi's destruction. The local suzerain was the king of Arrapḫa, a vassal in turn of Mittanni, at that time a greater power than Assyria. The use of Akkadian by kings of Mittanni is well documented (Adler 1976) and speaks for the continuing dominance of Babylonian as a written means of communication in upper Mesopotamia, outside Assyria proper. Unsurprisingly, therefore, the Hurrianized Akkadian of Nuzi is more akin to early Middle Babylonian than to Assyrian, though it shows occasional Assyrianisms. The language of the Nuzi texts has been studied by Berkooz 1937 and Wilhelm 1970.

Our knowledge of the Akkadian written in Levantine Syria in the same period formerly rested on 15th-century tablets from Alalaḫ, treaties involving the local rulers, Idrimi and his son Niqmepa, and Idrimi's autobiographical statue inscription. The Hurrianized Akkadian of these texts is described by Rowe 1998. Also extant, but less informative linguistically, was an archive of inventories unearthed by a pre-war

French expedition at Qatna (Tell Mishrife), further up the Orontes valley in Syria. The evidence has been much augmented by the discovery of an important 14th-century royal archive during the new excavations at Qatna. This archive of letters and administrative documents will shed fascinating new light on the political relations of this small Syrian city-state with the major powers, at a time when Mittanni was retreating before the expansion of the Hittite empire. As regards the study of language, the epigraphists deciphering the archive report the use of a new variety of Hurrianized Akkadian (Richter 2002). Extensive glossing in Hurrian shows very clearly that Hurrian was the local vernacular.

Further south, at Taanach (Tell Ti'innik) near Megiddo in Palestine, 15th-century letters and administrative documents are early evidence for a form of local Babylonian under West Semitic influence (Rainey 1999). In Elam, east of Babylonia, scribes were briefly writing Akkadian again, as shown by 14th-century archives from Kabnak (Haft Tepe), near Susa (Glassner 1991). The texts are mostly administrative but an omen list is evidence for the Babylonian scribal tradition and curious orthographies again speak for a local tradition of cuneiform scholarship (Herrero and Glassner 1996). The local vernacular of Elam at this time was Middle Elamite, but the prestige of Babylonian is also seen in its use in several monumental inscriptions of King Untash-napirisha (13th century). This ruler was evidently what might be called a Babylonophile, for he gave his new ceremonial cult-centre an Akkadian name, Al-Untash "Untash-town" (now Choga Zambil). A century later, however, Shutruk-Nahhunte and his sons Kutir-Nahhunte and Shilhak-Inshushinak, the vanquishers of Babylon (sacked in 1157 BC), had their inscriptions written in Elamite alone.

By the floruit of the Nuzi and Qatna archives scribes were writing Akkadian in Anatolia again. As elsewhere in the West the Babylonian scribal tradition had been imported wholesale to the Hittite capital at Hattusa along with the technology of cuneiform writing. This was most probably not a single event but a continuing process. One reason for suspecting this is that texts of the scribal tradition can be seen there at several stages in their development. For example, the Babylonian Epic of Gilgamesh occurs first in an early 14th-century copy very close to an Old Babylonian version known from Babylonia, then as a partly garbled Akkadian paraphrase (13th-century copy), probably composed locally or in north Syria, and also as a story retold in Hittite and in Hurrian.

International Akkadian. Already employed at Hattusa during the Hittite Old Kingdom, when royal texts of Hattusili I were furnished with Akkadian translations (Galter 1995: 36-7), Akkadian is most visible there as an international language for diplomatic correspondence and treaty-writing in the service of the Hittite state (described by Labat 1932, Durham 1976, Marazzi 1986). In this the Hittites were falling into line with the rest of the East Mediterranean. What might be called "international" Akkadian is best known from the Egyptian royal archives of El-Amarna (ancient Akhetaten), the short-lived capital of the 14th-century pharaoh

Akhenaten (Amenophis IV), from smaller archives of the same period, such as that at Kumidi (Kamid el-Loz) in Lebanon, and from isolated finds such as those of Sidon, on the Lebanese coast, and of Hazor, Tell Aphek, Gezer and Beth Shean in modern Israel. These demonstrate that during the Late Bronze Age a very extensive network of diplomatic links was in place between the major and minor powers of the Near East and their vassals, and Akkadian was the medium of international communication. The Hittite monarch and the kings of Babylonia and Assyria, the ruler of Alashiya (Cyprus), Egyptian vassals like Abdi-Ashirta of Amurru, Rib-Hadda of Byblos and Abi-Milku of Tyre: all wrote to pharaoh in forms of Akkadian and received his reply in Akkadian.

Royal letters from kings of the Kassite dynasty of Babylon have already been mentioned in discussing Middle Babylonian, and the Middle Assyrian letter of an Assyrian ruler has also been noted. The language of most of the Amarna correspondence, however, was far from these pure Mesopotamian dialects, exhibiting many provincial archaisms and very considerable influence of local tongues. It was not homogeneous. Letters from Hittite, north Syrian and Egyptian chanceries indicate greater or lesser influence of Hurrian, and are held to represent a northern, Hurro-Akkadian tradition of writing and language. In the southern Levant various forms of pidgin-Akkadian were used, more or less combining Babylonian vocabulary with local West Semitic (Canaanite) grammar (Moran 1992: xviii-xxii, Rainey 1996, Izre'el 1998). Akkadian dialects of the Amarna period have lately been given renewed attention (Sivan 1984, Gianto 1990, Izre'el 1991, Moran 2003, Cochavi-Rainey 2003).

Like the cuneiform scribes of Hattusa, the writers of the letters of the Amarna archives learnt to master cuneiform in the traditional way, so that texts of the Babylonian scribal tradition have been recovered from El-Amarna. These are mostly lexical texts but include also poems on mythological and heroic subjects, such as Adapa, Nergal and Ereshkigal, and Sargon King of Battle. The Egyptians were taught cuneiform writing by Hittites of the Old Kingdom (16th-15th centuries), and some Akkadian literature found at Amarna bears a Hurro-Hittite cultural imprint. This means that though in Egypt cuneiform writing has so far only turned up at 14th-century Amarna, older finds are to be expected. Other compositions, handed down at Amarna in good Middle Babylonian recensions, imply continuing influence, either directly from Mesopotamia or through Syro-Mesopotamian intermediaries. There was certainly a tradition of cuneiform learning in the southern Levant well before the tablets from Amarna. The presence of Old Babylonian at Hazor has already been mentioned, as has the early Middle Babylonian archive from Taanach. Megiddo can also be cited, where a Middle Babylonian paraphrase of Gilgamesh was already known in perhaps the 15th century. So in writing Akkadian, Akhenaten's chancery at Amarna was following the trend, not leading it. While we talk of the Amarna period as exemplifying the widespread use of international Akkadian in the eastern Mediterranean region of the 14th century, it should be remembered that this was not an innovation of this period, even in Egypt.

Later evidence reveals the full extent of cuneiform learning and Akkadian writing in the West. Towards the end of the 2nd millennium much of the Near East, particularly around the eastern Mediterranean, suffered in the catastrophes that brought the Late Bronze Age to an end. Among cities that fell at that time were Alalaḫ, Ugarit (Ras Shamra) on the Mediterranean seaboard, and Emar (Meskene) on the Euphrates downstream of Carchemish. Destruction levels at Ugarit and Emar, especially, have yielded many archives of cuneiform tablets, large and small, ranging across the 14th to 12th centuries. Their texts demonstrate again the use in the periphery of local forms of written Akkadian for practical communication and documentation - the familiar combination of letters, legal, juridical and administrative texts - built on an education in the scribal tradition imported from Babylonia. The latter is represented by lexical texts, scholarly compendia, fables and wisdom literature, Middle Babylonian Gilgamesh and an account of the flood, no doubt a fragment of the poem of Atram-hasis. The Akkadian of Ugarit has been much researched (Swaim 1962, Huehnergard 1989, van Soldt 1991), and linguistic studies of Emar Akkadian are fast catching up (Ikeda 1995, 1998, Seminara 1998, Pentiuc 2001).

The end of the Late Bronze Age in the eastern Mediterranean brought with it a breakdown in international communications that spelled the termination of local traditions of Akkadian writing in Mediterranean Syria, Egypt and Anatolia, and, after perhaps 1500 years, the end in the west of the cultural domination of Babylonian language and scribal traditions.

The early 1st millennium: Neo-Assyrian, Standard and Neo-Babylonian

The transition to the Iron Age coincides with a loss of documentation that intervenes in the history of Akkadian. The turn of the millennium marks the beginning of a period of confusion in Mesopotamia, as a flowing tide of Arameans overran the north, for all the earlier efforts of Tiglath-pileser I (1114-1076) to stem it, leading to the eventual collapse of Assyrian power. Recovery lay two centuries away. Babylonia, already weakened by Assyrian invasion, succumbed first to famine and then to more Arameans.

Until recently this interval of silence was a convenient point to divide Middle Babylonian and Middle Assyrian from the later dialects, but new discoveries sharpen the picture. A ninth-century diplomatic letter, sent to the king of Hama in Syria from Anat (now Ana) on the middle Euphrates, gives a rare glimpse of the southern language late in the evolution of Middle to Neo-Babylonian (Parpola 1990). The transition from Middle to Neo-Assyrian was explored by Postgate 1997. Evidence from provincial centres adds to the picture, demonstrating that the evolution of Middle to Neo-Assyrian had already begun in the early 11th century. Inscriptions of Ashur-ketti-leshir, a king of Mari and vassal of Tiglath-pileser I, are couched in heavily Assyrianized Babylonian, and some of their Assyrianisms anticipate Neo-Assyrian grammar and spelling (Maul 1992: 18-19). A small archive of legal documents excavated in south-eastern Turkey at Giricano, on the upper Tigris (ancient Dunnu-sha-Uzibi), dates to the same era, and exhibits what is clearly a transitional dialect, already partly Neo-Assyrian (Radner 2004: 53-4).

The darkness lifts gradually: as the nation states of Mesopotamia reasserted their authority, economic stability increased and written sources grow in number. Assyria was the first to recover its political and military might, especially under kings Ashurnasirpal II (883-859) and Shalmaneser III (858-824), who campaigned vigorously and successfully pushed back the frontiers of the Assyrian state on all sides. In this era of renewed Assyrian strength it is significant that the long inscriptions that report these kings' campaigns are written in a form of Babylonian under heavy Assyrian influence (Deller 1957a, b). Further west and north, the local ascendancy of Assyrian over Babylonian is clearer still. A statue of Hadad-yis'i, an Aramean who became Assyrian provincial governor of Bit-Bahiyani in the mid-9th century, was found at Tell Fekheriye in the Habur triangle, inscribed with text in both Akkadian and Aramaic. The Akkadian is partly Assyrian and partly an Assyrianized literary Babylonian (Fales 1983). In Urartu, a short-lived but troublesome kingdom based near Lake Van, royal inscriptions of the late 9th century were couched in Assyrian, though this experiment soon gave way to Assyrian-Urartian bilingualism and monolingual Urartian texts (Wilhelm 1986, Galter 1995: 37-9).

Neo-Assyrian. In Assyria itself archival documents appear again in the 9th century (at Shibaniba) and become more common in the late 8th century, turning into a flood by the reigns of Sargon II (721-705), Esarhaddon (680-669) and Ashurbanipal (668-627). Private and public documents occur, but texts from the great institutions of state predominate, especially archives from the successive royal capitals of Kalaḫ (Nimrud) and Nineveh (Kuyunjik). Among the twenty thousand tablets and fragments excavated at Nineveh in the 1850s and subsequently, it is estimated that archival documents - letters, legal and administrative documents, royal grants and decrees, officials' reports, especially from diviners, astrologers and other scholars, and oracular questions on matters of state - add up to more than 5,500 (Parpola 1986: 228). These derive overwhelmingly from the period 721 to 645 and document the history and politics of imperial Assyria in extraordinary detail (Text sample 6).

Smaller quantities of tablets come from other Assyrian cities, especially Ashur, and from provincial centres across the Jazira (Guzana-Tell Halaf, Til-Barsip, Dur-Katlimmu etc.). Isolated discoveries from more distant provinces of the empire are the Neo-Assyrian tablets found at Tarsus in Cilicia (Goetze 1939), at Samaria, the capital of Israel taken by Shalmaneser V in 722 BC (Pedersén 1998: 225), and further south at Gezer (Macalister 1911: 22-30). These document the activities of expatriate bureaucrats and are legacies of imperial administration and practice. They do not speak for any re-establishment in the west of cuneiform and Akkadian as media of local communication and intellectual activity.

The language of all these documents is Neo-Assyrian. In Neo-Assyrian the influence of Aramaic on Akkadian is seen for the first time. In the written form of the language Aramaisms are very limited but Aramaic notes written on many tablets indicate the growing currency of Aramaic as the vernacular language. In a multi-ethnic empire where natives of Assyria were hugely outnumbered by Aramaic-speakers from upper Mesopotamia and Levantine Syria, many of them forcibly resettled in the heartland of Assyria itself, the native dialect was fast losing ground as a spoken language. It continued to be written, however, where tradition dictated that it was the proper medium of communication. This was so even after the collapse of the empire, for legal texts from Dur-Katlimmu (Tell Sheikh Hamad) on the river Habur, dated to the reign of Nebuchadnezzar II of Babylon, document the survival of written Assyrian a little after the fall of Nineveh and the demise of the imperial Assyrian government (Radner 2002). The Neo-Assyrian scribal tradition lived on at Harran, one of the old imperial cities, to influence the monumental inscriptions of Nabonidus (555-539) (Schaudig 2001: 72-3). Neo-Assyrian letters were early the subject of special grammatical study (Ylvisaker 1912) and the dialect has met with renewed attention more recently (Hämeen-Anttila 2000, Luukko 2004).

Fig. 3.4. Neo-Assyrian letter (SAA XVI 105= K 11; © Trustees of the British Museum)

Text sample 6. Neo-Assyrian. Letter of Ubru-Nabû to the king of Assyria, probably Esarhaddon

ina pānēya izakkar abū'a ina māt nakire mēt mā ḫanšā ṣābē ša qātēšu šinšerat sīsê ina qātēšunu iṣṣabtūni ittalkūni ina battibatti ša Ninūa kammusū mā anāku aqṭibâššunu mā abū'a lū mēt maṣṣartu ša šarre atâ turamme'ā tallikāni ūmâ annurig ina pān šarre bēlēya ussēbilaššu šarru bēlī liš'alšu kī ša abutūni ana šarre bēlēya liqbi

State Archives of Assyria XVI 105

(Shumma-ilu) declared in my presence, "My father died in enemy territory. The fifty men who were under his command took twelve horses and came back. They are staying near Nineveh. I told them, 'My father may be dead, but why did you forsake the king's duty and come back?'" I am sending him right now to the king my lord. Let the king my lord question him, so he tells the king my lord how the matter stands.

Alongside the masses of archival documents in the Neo-Assyrian dialect, the early 1st millennium also bears witness to a brief flowering of Assyrian court literature and religious poetry. The long tradition of native scholarship in Sumero-Babylonian textual analysis began also to spawn academic works in the Neo-Assyrian dialect. Though short-lived, these are further signs of the growing prestige of Assyrian in intellectual culture during the hegemony of the Assyrian empire.

Standard Babylonian. Notwithstanding the Assyrians' literary creativity in their own dialect, Babylonian maintained its position as the foremost language of literary expression. The Sargonid kings, especially, opted to produce royal building inscriptions and annals in the literary register of Babylonian, introduced above as Standard Babylonian. This is the dialect of Akkadian in which was phrased much of the literature handed down in the scribal tradition of the 1st millennium, ranging from mythological and other narrative poetry, through hymns and poetic prayers, fables and wisdom literature, pseudo-autobiography and didactic poetry, and the occasional folktale, to scholarly compendia (e.g. omens), professional literature (e.g. exorcistic and therapeutic texts), calendar lore and technical treatises. Some of this literature was very old, being traceable back to Old Babylonian recensions. Examples are narrative poems in comparatively plain style: Anzû, Atram-hasis, Etana, Ishtar's Descent to the Netherworld and Gilgamesh (Text sample 7). Other compositions derived from later in the 2nd millennium, often displaying the more recherché vocabulary and learned touches of Middle Babylonian scholar poets. The Creation epic (*Enūma eliš*) comes under this category, as does the poem of the Righteous Sufferer (*Ludlul bēl nēmeqi*).

Text sample 7. Standard Babylonian. From the Epic of Gilgamesh

Gilgāmeš ana Enkīdu ibrīšu
ṣarpiš ibakkīma irappud ṣēra
anāku amâtma ul kī Enkīdu-mā
nissatu īterub ina karšīya
mūta aplaḫma arappud ṣēra
ana lēt Ūta-napišti mār Ubār-Tutu
urḫa ṣabtākūma ḫanṭiš allak

SB Gilgamesh IX 1-7

For his friend Enkidu Gilgamesh
was weeping bitterly as he roamed the wild:
"I shall die, and shall I not then be like Enkidu?
Sorrow has entered my heart.
I became afraid of death, so go roaming the wild,
to Uta-napishti, son of Ubar-Tutu,
I am on the road and travelling swiftly."

Almost all of Standard Babylonian literature is currently known only from 1st-millennium copies. These derive from Assyrian royal, temple and private libraries of the 8th to 7th centuries and from Babylonian private and temple libraries of later centuries. Isolated finds at Hama in Syria (Laessøe 1956) and Tarsus in Cilicia (Goetze 1939: No. 8) demonstrate that agents of the Assyrian empire had such tablets in the west, but these were surely exports and not evidence of any local engagement with Babylonian culture. The practice of copying texts from the Sumero-Babylonian scribal tradition was in this period restricted to Mesopotamia proper, and from the 6th century confined to Babylonia alone. By this era, and probably for some time before, the Standard Babylonian corpus was no longer living literature, but the preserve chiefly of the scholars and students engaged in teaching and learning cuneiform and in writing ceremonial texts in traditional literary language. At the Assyrian and Babylonian courts and in the market place the more vital language of literary expression and oral literary tradition was undoubtedly Aramaic.

Nevertheless, Standard Babylonian remained a productive dialect throughout the 1st millennium, alongside new developments in style that were less successful (Lambert 1968). Most inscriptions of Nabopolassar and his successors display Standard Babylonian language and word order, even if they are often falsely characterized as Neo- or Late Babylonian. The prose of Nabonidus (555-539) exults in a particularly high literary Standard Babylonian that occasionally reads almost as poetry. Among later rulers, Cyrus of Persia (538-530) and the Seleucid Antiochus Soter (281-261) both put out commemorative inscriptions in the traditional style.

Standard Babylonian is not a homogeneous dialect. The modes of expression range from self-consciously ornate and highly archaizing, reminiscent of the "hymno-epic" style of some Old Babylonian poetry, to much plainer modes of expression that are nevertheless old. For example, a stylistic device favoured especially by the composers of the Sargonid annals was the placing of the verb in penultimate position in its clause, a feature of prose style met above in Old Akkadian monumental texts. The grammar of all forms of Standard Babylonian, allowing for variations in spelling and the occasional intrusion of vernacular, exhibits a recognizable affinity with Old Babylonian. Perhaps its greatest unifying feature is that this was always elevated, old-fashioned language, distinct from any kind of vernacular Akkadian in lexicon, phrasing and word order. The standard treatment is Reiner 1966. Studies of different kinds of Standard Babylonian have concentrated on the epic poetry (Hecker 1974), "hymnic" literature (Groneberg 1987) and royal inscriptions (Stein 2000, Schaudig 2001).

Neo-Babylonian. The vernacular form of the southern dialect, Neo-Babylonian, was also used at the imperial Assyrian court, for after the final annexation of Babylonia under Sennacherib in 689 BC, many Babylonian officials, scholars and administrators employed it in their dealings with the government and received letters back in the same dialect (Text sample 8). The language of the Neo-Babylonian letters from Nineveh has been explored in Woodington 1982 and de Vaan 1995.

Text sample 8. Neo-Babylonian. Letter of King Sargon II of Assyria to Sîn-iddina

[ša tašpura umma . . .] kī pān šarri maḫru ina libbi sipri armāyi luspirma ana šarri lušēbila mīnamma ina šipirti akkadattu lā tašaṭṭarma lā tušebbila kitta šipirtu ša ina libbi tašaṭṭaru kī pî agannītimma idat lū šaknat

State Archives of Assyria XVII 2

Regarding the message you wrote . . . , "If it is acceptable to the king I will write a letter to the king in Aramaic style," why can you not write a letter to me in Akkadian style? Be sure that the document you write is like this one [i.e. in cuneiform]. It is the custom. Let it remain so!

In the south, a glimpse of early Neo-Babylonian is given by the governor's archive from 8th-century Nippur, which contains a mix of letters with texts from the Sumero-Babylonian scribal tradition. Neo-Babylonian archival documents begin to become common in the late 7th century. As Babylon gained economic power as the seat of a new empire, and other southern cities such as Sippar, Cutha, Borsippa, Dilbat, Nippur, Ur and Uruk prospered with it, the extant documentation increases. Twenty years ago it was estimated that more than thirteen thousand archival documents - letters, economic, business, juridical and legal documents - dating to the Neo-Babylonian and Persian periods had already been published (Dandamayev 1986:

274). This is only a small fraction of the extant whole, however: the administrative archive of the temple of Shamash at Sippar excavated by Rassam between 1878 and 1882 numbers at least twice that quantity of pieces on its own. At perhaps ten thousand tablets even the archive of Eanna at Uruk (7th to 5th centuries) looks small by comparison. Alongside huge institutional archives of this kind are extensive dossiers that document over several generations the activities of families of businessmen, such as the Murashû family at Nippur and the Egibi family at Babylon. Here attempts to understand the form and function of the archives have taken precedence over grammatical research. The language of the business documents was studied by Tallqvist 1890. More recently scholars have concentrated on individual aspects of the dialect (e.g. Dietrich 1969, Streck 1995).

The empire of Nabopolassar (625-605) and his successors took many Babylonians abroad, in the service of the imperial administration and on private ventures. Tablets from expatriates' archives have surfaced in several Levantine cities but, as in the Neo-Assyrian period, they speak only of the use there of Akkadian cuneiform by people of Mesopotamian origin, not of any local revival of cuneiform writing (Dalley 1993: 141-3). One Babylonian family left an archive of Neo-Babylonian legal documents at Nereb (Neirab), near Aleppo, where they lived in the mid-6th century. Some of their tablets were glossed with Aramaic notations. This practice became more common in Babylonia itself in the 5th century, when it speaks for a growing reliance on Aramaic among the record-keeping classes. As in Assyria, Aramaic was strongly entrenched in the Babylonian south early in the imperial period, boosted by a large population of Aramean and Chaldean descent. The prevalence of Aramaic surely had a greater effect on spoken Babylonian than on the written language, which remained remarkably impervious to Aramaic loanwords. The loss of inflected endings on nouns was probably a development speeded up by analogy with Aramaic. The writing of cuneiform was also affected by the advent of bilingual literacy. Changes in spelling conventions can be attributed to the influence of Aramaic writing practices.

It was not all one-way traffic: Babylonian had some influence on Aramaic too (Kaufman 1974), but the suspicion is that it was steadily losing ground as a vernacular, spoken language when Nebuchadnezzar II (604-562) made Babylon great again. The strength of the cuneiform tradition kept it alive as a written language for centuries more.

The end of Akkadian: Late Babylonian and cuneiform scholarship

Babylon fell to Cyrus the Great of Persia in 539 BC. This date marks the end in ancient history of independent nation states in Mesopotamia, but Babylonian civilization was far from spent. Religious life and intellectual culture continued much as before, perpetuating by many centuries the ancient languages that were their vehicles (Oelsner 2002b). Under the Achaemenid Persians, Akkadian found use as one of several languages of state display, most famously in the trilingual rock inscription of Darius I (521-486) at Bisutun (Behistun) in Iran. Only a single Neo-Babylonian tablet was found among the large archive excavated in the fortification wall at Darius' capital, Persepolis, for this king's use of Akkadian was ceremonial not practical. Imperial Aramaic was the official *lingua franca* of the Persian empire. From the time of Xerxes I (485-465) there is across Babylonia generally a marked decrease in the number of Neo-Babylonian archival documents now extant. It seems that increasingly more communication and record-keeping were being done in Aramaic alone. The great temple of Shamash at Sippar abandoned cuneiform writing early in Xerxes' reign, presumably in favour of the alternative technology. Private letters become very rare after about 450 BC, a development that signals for most scholars the final extinction of a vernacular Babylonian tongue, after a long decline.

The death of the Akkadian language was much prolonged, however, for it was bound up with the death of cuneiform writing. The persistence of the ancient script kept Akkadian alive among the scribal classes long after it ceased to be anybody's first language. From the extant documentation the general trend of the later 1st millennium is clear: as in private life Aramaic writing was adopted more widely, and as in public life successive non-native governments demanded expertise first in Aramaic and then in Greek, so cuneiform was used for an ever more restricted set of purposes. This in turn steadily diminished the number of those who had occasion to learn and use the Akkadian language.

Late Babylonian. The convention is to divide the vernacular Babylonian of the 1st millennium into Neo-Babylonian and Late Babylonian. There is no consensus as to where in time the division should occur. Some place it at the accession of Nabopolassar, others at the capture of Babylon by Cyrus eighty-six years later. Both are manifestly dates of political rather than linguistic significance and neither marks a clear discontinuity in the history of the southern dialect. However, the Babylonian written under Alexander the Great, his successors the Seleucid kings, and then the Parthian dynasty of Iran, shows a definite evolution from 7th-century language, and rightly deserves the label Late Babylonian.

At Babylon and Uruk legal documents composed in Babylonian on clay continue through the reigns of Alexander the Great (330-323 BC), his short-lived dynasty and the Seleucid kings that succeeded it, but are little in evidence after the Parthian conquest (140 BC). The same can be said for texts that capture in writing the daily rituals of the great temples, a genre of Late Babylonian writing whose rise is symptomatic of anxiety about the future of these venerable institutions. At Borsippa an archive of letter-orders (memoranda from temple administrators) records the activities of the temple brewers' office at the beginning of the Hellenistic era. The last surviving archives from the great temples of Uruk date from the early to mid-2nd century, but an isolated tablet records the temples' existence as late as 108 BC. Administrative records are more plentiful at Babylon, where they continue beyond the Seleucid domination into the early 1st century BC. In reporting the continuing existence of several temples at the old capital, they document the careers of individual astronomers maintained out of temple funds (Text sample 9). Astronomical diaries written at Babylon straddle the Persian and Seleucid periods but fail in the mid-1st century BC.

Text sample 9. Late-Babylonian. Protocol of the temple assembly of Babylon (127 BC)

ultu ūmi annâ ša šattussu šina mana kaspu kurummat Itti-Marduk-balāṭu ā abīšunu ana Bēl-aḫ̮ḫ̮ē-uṣur u Nabû-mušētiq-uddi ultu ḫ̮išiḫ̮tīni ninamdin libbû mimma ša Itti-Marduk-balāṭu abūšunu iššû ša naṣāri inaṣṣarū u tērsêti ša šattussu inamdinū itti Bēlšunu Lâbâši Mūrānu Iddin-Bēl Bēl-nāṣiršu ṭupšar Ud-An-Enlilla *u ṭupšar* Ud-An-Enlilla *šanûti*

Pinches 1889-90: 132

The pronunciation of this passage, based on the evidence of roughly contemporaneous Greek transcriptions of Akkadian, might be something like this:
ultu ūw annâ sa sattus sina mana kasap kuruwat Ittiwardukbalāṭ ā abīsun ana Bēlaḫ̮ḫ̮uṣur u Nabûwusētiqud ultu ḫ̮isiḫ̮tīn ninamdin libbû miwa sa Ittiwardukbalāṭ abūsun issû sa naṣār inaṣṣarū u tērsêt sa sattus inamdinū itti Bēlsun Lâbās Wūrān Iddinbēl Bēlnāṣirs ṭupsar Ud-An-Enlilla *u ṭupsar* Ud-An-Enlilla *sanût*

From this day forth, every year, we shall pay from our resources two shekels of silver, the expenses of the aforementioned Itti-Marduk-balaṭu, their father, to Bel-aḫ̮ḫ̮e-uṣur and Nabû-mushetiq-uddi, in accordance with what their father Itti-Marduk-balaṭu drew. They will make [diaries of] observations and produce the yearly astronomical tables together with the astronomers Belshunu, La-abash, Muranu, Iddin-Bel, Bel-naṣirshu, and other astronomers.

Cuneiform scholarship. The number of extant cuneiform tablets of the Hellenistic period has been estimated at more than two thousand, of which well over one thousand are of astronomical content (Oelsner 1986: 138). This gives a good indication of the predominant use to which Akkadian was put in the last centuries of the cuneiform tradition. Astrologer-astronomers must have formed the majority of scholars still writing the language at this time. Akkadian in the Seleucid and Parthian periods was, like Sumerian before it, a scholars' language that had to be learned by a long apprenticeship. The art of writing it was inextricably bound up with the survival of the ancient temples and the duties of their personnel, especially the astronomers. As populations moved away from the old cities to the new royal capitals at Seleucia and then Ctesiphon, and royal patronage and funding came to an end, these buildings became increasingly difficult to maintain. At the same time the people that staffed them and otherwise relied on them for support must have decreased rapidly.

Alongside the diminishing archival documentation of the Persian, Seleucid and Parthian periods, production of new copies of texts of the old Sumero-Babylonian scribal tradition continued, especially at Babylon, Borsippa and Uruk. Much of this was carried out as part of their education by boys and young men learning to write in order to enter the literate professions. Though few new texts were written, there is plentiful evidence that in the 4th century BC Akkadian was still the vehicle for a flourishing intellectual culture, particularly in the exegesis of professional lore (Frahm 2002). By the Parthian era, however, cuneiform learning was much less widespread. It was the preserve only of a few families of learned scholars, mostly astronomers, clinging to the ancient ways in cities that history had passed by. The latest dated copy of a text of the old scribal tradition known at present was written at Babylon in 35 BC (Oelsner 2002a: 12). It is an apprentice's manuscript of a literary prayer to Marduk. Undated copies of literary texts far outnumber dated exemplars and it is not improbable that we possess many other literary tablets of the same period. Some may even date from as late as the astronomical almanacs. These almanacs are, at present, our very last dated cuneiform documents. The most recent of them contains predictions of planetary movements and other events for AD 75. The almanacs are ostensibly written in Akkadian and prefaced with a standard scribal prayer in Babylonian, but whether they had to be read in that language is uncertain: the stereotyped and abbreviated formulae in which they are couched is a kind of scholarly code, readable in any language by anyone with a little training.

Whoever wrote the almanacs, however, must have had some grasp of the Akkadian language, for they were surely trained to write cuneiform in the time-honoured way, by exposure to the Sumero-Babylonian scribal tradition. Relics from their education may even survive in the form of school tablets from Babylon that hold passages of Sumerian and Akkadian texts in cuneiform accompanied by Greek transcriptions. These have been dated on the basis of palaeography mostly to the two centuries either side of the turn of the era, but one or two examples may be later still. Partly on this evidence it has been argued that cuneiform culture, and thus written Babylonian, survived to the 2nd century AD and even into the 3rd, when many old traditions were finally extinguished by the religious reforms of the Sasanian Persians, who had put an end to Parthian rule in Mesopotamia by AD 230 (Geller 1997).

Without a breakthrough in cuneiform palaeography it remains to be seen whether any of the many undated cuneiform copies of texts from the Late Babylonian scribal tradition could be as late as the 2nd century AD. As matters stand, this seems unlikely but it would be unwise completely to discount it. Two events, perhaps interconnected, contributed greatly to the end of the cuneiform tradition of native scholarship in Babylonia, and so to the final demise of Akkadian. The transfer of astronomical writing to a medium other than cuneiform was one (Brown forthcoming). The decline of the venerable cult-centres was the other. Though there is evidence that the cults of some of the old gods survived into the 3rd century AD, they must by then have been relocated. Archaeological excavation shows that the great temple buildings of Uruk were abandoned and built over soon after about 100 BC, at all events early in the Parthian period. At Babylon the ancient cult-centre of Marduk (Bel) and other sanctuaries endured longer. Marduk's temple was ruined, levelled into a mound and redeveloped as a residential quarter some time before the Parthian era closed in the early 3rd century AD.

Some have speculated that a tradition of Sumero-Babylonian scholarship — and with it a reading knowledge of Akkadian — survived the death of the cuneiform script in Greek and Aramaic transcriptions written on scrolls of papyrus and leather, now perished (e.g. Oelsner 2002a: 30-1). Late allusions to Babylonian language and learning, for example by the scholiast who credits the Greek novelist Iamblichus (fl. AD 200), a native-speaker of Syriac, with a knowledge of the "Babylonian language" (Geller 1997: 50), might speak for a continuing endurance of learned Akkadian, whether read from cuneiform tablets or from scrolls. Others have argued, however, that allusions to Mesopotamian learning in the Roman period refer not to the old Sumero-Akkadian tradition but to a contemporaneous "pagan Aramaic literature" that is now lost (Houston *et al.* 2003: 456). We will probably never know. The end of written Akkadian, then, is not clearly visible in history.

Further reading and references

Adler, Hans-Peter 1976. *Das Akkadische des Königs Tušratta von Mitanni*. Alter Orient und Altes Testament 201. Kevelaer and Neukirchen-Vluyn.
Aro, Jussi 1954-6. Remarks on the language of the Alalakh texts. *Archiv für Orientforschung* 17: 361-5.
- 1955. *Studien zur mittelbabylonischen Grammatik*. Studia Orientalia 20. Helsinki.
Bergsträsser, Gotthelf 1983. *Introduction to the Semitic Languages. Text Specimens and Grammatical Sketches*. Transl. Peter T. Daniels. Winona Lake.
Berkooz, Moshé 1937. *The Nuzi Dialect of Akkadian: Orthography and Phonology*. Philadelphia.
Birot, Maurice 1993. *Correspondance des gouverneurs de Qaṭṭunân*. Archives royales de Mari 27. Paris.
Brinkman, John A. 1976. *Materials and Studies for Kassite History* 1. Chicago.
Brown, David forthcoming. Increasingly redundant: The growing obsolescence of the cuneiform script in Babylonia from 539 BC on. In J. Baines, J. Bennet and S. Houston (eds.), *Last Writing*. Papers of a conference on the Disappearance of Writing Systems, Oxford, 27 March 2004. London.
Buccellati, Giorgio 1996. *A Structural Grammar of Babylonian*. Wiesbaden.
- 1997. Akkadian. In Hetzron 1997: 69-99.
- 2004. Review of Hilgert 2002. *Zeitschrift für Assyriologie* 94: 106-8.
Campbell, George L. 1991. *Compendium of the World's Languages*. 2 vols. London and New York.
Caplice, Richard 1988. *Introduction to Akkadian*. 3rd edn. Studia Pohl (Series Maior) 9. Rome.
Charpin, Dominique 1988. Première partie. In Charpin, Francis Joannès, Sylvie Lackenbacher and Bertrand Lafont, *Archives épistolaires de Mari* 1, 2. Archives royales de Mari 26, 2. Paris.
- 1989. L'akkadien des lettres d'Ilân-ṣûra. In Marc Lebeau and Philippe Talon (eds.), *Reflets des deux fleuves: volume de mélanges offerts à André Finet*. Akkadica Supplementum 6. Leuven: 31-40.
- 2004 Histoire politique du Proche-Orient amorite (2002-1595), part 1 of D. Charpin, D. O. Edzard & M. Stol, *Mesopotamien. Die altbabylonische Zeit*. Orbis Biblicus et Orientalis 160/4. Fribourg & Göttingen.
Cochavi-Rainey, Zipora 2003. *The Alashia Texts from the 14th and 13th Centuries BCE: A Textual and Linguistic Study*. Alter Orient und Altes Testament 289. Münster.
Cooper, Jerrold S. 2000. Sumerian and semitic writing in most ancient Syro-Mesopotamia. In K. Van Lerberghe and G. Voet (eds.), *Languages and Cultures in Contact*. Rencontre Assyriologique Internationale 42, Orientalia Lovaniensia Analecta 92. Leuven: 61-77.
Dalley, Stephanie 1993. Nineveh after 612 BC. *Altorientalische Forschungen* 20: 134-47.
Dandamayev, M. A. 1986. The Neo-Babylonian archives. In Klaas R. Veenhof (ed.), *Cuneiform Archives and Libraries*. Rencontre Assyriologique Internationale 30. Leiden and Istanbul: 273-7.
Deller, Karlheinz 1957a. Zur sprachlichen Einordnung der Inschriften Assurnasirpals, (883-859). *Orientalia* NS 26: 144-56.
- 1957b. Assyrisches Sprachgut bei Tukulti-Ninurta II (888-884). *Orientalia* NS 26: 268-72.

De Meyer, Léon 1962. *L'accadien des contrats de Suse*. Suppléments à Iranica antiqua 1. Leiden.

Dietrich, Manfried 1969. Untersuchungen zur Grammatik des Neubabylonischen. I. Die neubabylonischen Subjunktionen. In W. Röllig and M. Dietrich (eds.), *Lišān mitḫurti. Festschrift Wolfram Freiherr von Soden zum 19.4.1968 gewidmet von Schülern und Mitarbeitern*. Alter Orient und Altes Testament 1. Kevelaer and Neukirchen-Vluyn: 65-99.

Durand, Jean-Marie 1992. Unité et diversité au Proche-Orient à l'époque amorrite. In Dominique Charpin and Francis Joannès (eds.), *La circulation des biens, des personnes et des idées dans le Proche-Orient ancien*. Rencontre Assyriologique Internationale 38. Paris: 97-128.

- 1995. La situation historique des *šakkanakku*: Nouvelle approche. *Mari, Annales de recherches interdisciplinaires* 4: 127-72.

Durham, John W. 1976. Studies in Boğazköy Akkadian. PhD thesis, Harvard University.

Edzard, Dietz Otto 1985. Die 3. Person M. Pl. *tiprusū* im Altakkadischen von Mari. In J.-M. Durand and J.-R. Kupper (eds.), *Miscellanea babylonica. Mélanges offerts à Maurice Birot*. Paris: 85-6.

- 2003. *Sumerian Grammar*. Handbuch der Orientalistik 71. Leiden and Boston.

Fales, Frederick M. 1983. Le double bilinguisme de la statue de Tell Fekherye. *Syria* 60: 233-50.

Finet, André 1956. *L'accadien des lettres de Mari*. Académie Royale de Belgique, Mémoires (Lettres) 51, 1. Brussels.

Frahm, Eckart 2002. Zwischen Tradition und Neuerung: Babylonische Priestergelehrte im achämenidenzeitlichen Uruk. In R. G. Kratz (ed.), *Religion und Religionskontakte im Zeitalter der Achämeniden*. Gütersloh: 74-108.

Galter, Hannes D. 1995. Cuneiform bilingual royal inscriptions. In Shlomo Izre'el and Rina Drory (eds.), *Israel Oriental Studies* 15. *Language and Culture in the Near East*. Leiden: 25-50.

Garelli, Paul 1965. Tablettes cappadociennes de collections diverses (suite). *Revue d'assyriologie* 59: 149-76.

Gelb, Ignace J. 1957. *Glossary of Old Akkadian*. Materials for the Assyrian Dictionary 3. Chicago.

- 1961. *Old Akkadian Writing and Grammar*. Materials for the Assyrian Dictionary 2. 2nd edn. Chicago.

- 1981. Ebla and the Kish civilization. In L. Cagni (ed.), *La lingua di Ebla. Atti del convegno internazionale (Napoli, 21-23 aprile 1980)*. Naples: 9-73.

- 1992. Mari and the Kish civilization. In G. D. Young (ed.), *Mari in Retrospect: Fifty Years of Mari and Mari Studies*. Winona Lake: 121-202.

Geller, M. J. 1997. The last wedge. *Zeitschrift für Assyriologie* 87: 43-95.

Giacumakis, George 1970. *The Akkadian of Alalaḫ*. Janua linguarum 59. The Hague and Paris.

Gianto, Agustinus 1990. *Word Order Variation in the Akkadian of Byblos*. Studia Pohl 15. Rome.

Glassner, J.-J. 1991. Les textes de Haft-Tépé, la Susiane et l'Élam au 2ème millénaire. In L. De Meyer and H. Gasche (eds.), *Mésopotamie et Élam: Actes de la XXXVIème Rencontre Assyriologique Internationale*. Mesopotamian History and Environment, Occasional Publications 1. Ghent: 109-26.

Goetze, Albrecht 1939. Cuneiform inscriptions from Tarsus. *Journal of the American Oriental Society* 59: 1-16.

Groneberg, Brigitte R. M. 1971. Untersuchungen zum hymnisch-epischen Dialekt der altbabylonischen literarischen Texte. PhD thesis. University of Münster.

- 1978-9. Terminativ- und Lokativadverbialis in altbabylonischen literarischen Texten. *Archiv für Orientforschung* 26: 15-29.

- 1987. *Syntax, Morphologie und Stil der jungbabylonischen "hymnischen" Literatur.* 2 vols. Freiburger altorientalische Studien 14. Stuttgart.

Hämeen-Anttila, Jaakko 2000. *A Sketch of Neo-Assyrian Grammar.* State Archives of Assyria Studies 13. Helsinki.

Hasselbach, Rebecca 2005. *Sargonic Akkadian. A Historical and Comparative Study of the Syllabic Texts.* Wiesbaden.

Hecker, Karl 1968. *Grammatik der Kültepe-Texte.* Analecta Orientalia 44. Rome.

- 1974. *Untersuchungen zur akkadischen Epik.* Alter Orient und Altes Testament, Sonderreihe 8. Kevelaer and Neukirchen-Vluyn.

Heimpel, Wolfgang 2004. Ur-III-Babylonisch. *Orientalia* 73: 245-54.

Herrero, Pablo and Jean-Jacques Glassner 1996. Haft-Tépé: choix de textes IV. *Iranica Antiqua* 31: 51-82.

Hetzron, Robert (ed.) 1997. *The Semitic Languages.* London.

Hilgert, Markus 2002. *Akkadisch in der Ur III-Zeit.* Imgula 5. Münster.

- 2003. New perspectives in the study of third millennium Akkadian. *Cuneiform Digital Library Journal* 2003, 4 online at http://cdli.ucla.edu/pubs/cdlj/2003/cdlj2003_004.html, version 26 August 2003).

Houston, Stephen, John Baines and Jerrold Cooper 2003. Last writing: Script obsolescence in Egypt, Mesopotamia, and Mesoamerica. *Comparative Studies in Society and History* 43: 430-79.

Huehnergard, John 1989. *The Akkadian of Ugarit.* Harvard Semitic Studies 34. Atlanta, Ga.

- 1995. Semitic languages. In Jack M. Sasson (ed.), *Civilizations of the Ancient Near East.* 4 vols. New York: 2117-34.

- 1997. *A Grammar of Akkadian.* Harvard Semitic Studies 45. Atlanta, Ga.

- & Christopher Woods 2004. Akkadian and Eblaite. In Roger D. Woodard, *The Cambridge Encyclopedia of the World's Ancient Languages.* Cambridge: Chapter 8.

Ikeda, Jun 1995. A Linguistic Analysis of the Akkadian from Emar: Administrative Texts. PhD dissertation, Tel Aviv University.

- 1998. The Akkadian language of Emar: Texts related to a diviner's family. In S. Izre'el, I. Singer and R. Zadok (eds.), *Israel Oriental Studies* 18. *Past Links: Studies in the Languages and Cultures of the Ancient Near East.* Winona Lake: 33-61.

Izre'el, Shlomo 1991. *Amurru Akkadian: A Linguistic Study.* 2 vols. Harvard Semitic Studies 40-1. Atlanta, Ga.

- 1998. *Canaano-Akkadian.* Languages of the World: Materials 82. Munich.

- and Eran Cohen 2004. *Literary Old Babylonian.* Languages of the World: Materials 436. Munich.

Kaplan, Golda H. 2002. *Use of Aspect-Tense Verbal Forms in Akkadian Texts of the Hammurapi Period.* LINCOM Studies in Afroasiatic Linguistics 9. Munich.

Kaufman, Stephen A. 1974. *The Akkadian Influences on Aramaic.* Assyriological Studies 19. Chicago.

Kessler, Karlheinz 1982. Kassitische Tontafeln vom Tell Imlihiye. *Baghdader Mitteilungen* 13: 51-116.

Kienast, Burkhart and Konrad Volk 1995. *Die sumerischen und akkadischen Briefe des III. Jahrtausends aus der Zeit vor der III. Dynastie von Ur*. Freiburger altorientalische Studien 19. Stuttgart.

Krebernik, Manfred 1992. Mesopotamian myths at Ebla: *ARET* 5, 6 and *ARET* 5, 7. In P. Fronzaroli (ed.), *Literature and Literary Language at Ebla*. Quaderna di semitistica 18. Florence: 63-149.

- 1996. The linguistic classification of Eblaite: Methods, problems, and results. In J. S. Cooper and G. M. Schwartz (eds.), *The Study of the Ancient Near East in the 21st Century: The William Foxwell Albright Centennial Conference*. Winona Lake: 233-49.

Kupper, Jean-Robert 2001. L'akkadien des letters de Shemshara. *Revue d'assyriologie* 95: 155-73.

Labat, René 1932. *L'akkadien de Boghaz-Köi, étude sur la langue des lettres, traités et vocabulaires trouvés à Boghaz-Köi*. Bordeaux.

- 1974. *Textes littéraires de Suse*. Mémoires de la Délégation Archéologique en Iran 57. Paris.

Laessøe, Jørgen 1956. A prayer to Ea, Shamash, and Marduk from Hama. *Iraq* 18: 60-7.

Lambert, W. G. 1968. Literary style in first-millennium Mesopotamia. *Journal of the American Oriental Society* 88: 123-32.

- 1989. Notes on a work of the most ancient Semitic literature. *Journal of Cuneiform Studies* 41: 1-33.

- 1991. The Akkadianization of Susiana under the *sukkalmaḫs*. In L. De Meyer and H. Gasche (eds.), *Mésopotamie et Élam: Actes de la XXXVIème Rencontre Assyriologique Internationale*. Mesopotamian History and Environment, Occasional Publications 1. Ghent: 53-7.

- 1992. The language of *ARET* V 6 and 7. In P. Fronzaroli (ed.), *Literature and Literary Language at Ebla* . Quaderna di semitistica 18. Florence: 41-62.

Lieberman, Stephen J. 1977. *The Sumerian Loanwords in Old-Babylonian Akkadian* 1. *Prolegomena and Evidence*. Harvard Semitic Studies 22. Missoula, Montana.

Luukko, Mikko 2004. *Grammatical Variation in Neo-Assyrian*. State Archives of Assyria Studies 16. Helsinki.

Macalister, R. A. S. 1911. *The Excavation of Gezer*. London.

Marazzi, Massimiliano 1986. *Beiträge zu den akkadischen Texten aus Boğazköy in althethitischer Zeit*. Bibliotheca de ricerche linguistiche e filologiche 18. Rome.

Marcus, David 1978. *A Manual of Akkadian*. New York and London.

Maul, Stefan M. 1992. *Die Inschriften von Tall Bderi*. Berliner Beiträge zum Vorderen Orient, Texte 2. Berlin.

Mayer, Walter 1971. *Untersuchungen zur Grammatik des Mittelassyrischen*. Alter Orient und Altes Testament, Sonderreihe 2. Kevelaer and Neukirchen-Vluyn.

McEwan, G. J. P. 1982. Agade after the Gutian destruction: The afterlife of a Mesopotamian city. In H. Hirsch and H. Hunger (eds.), *Vorträge gehalten auf der 28. Rencontre Assyriologique Internationale in Wien, 6.-10. Juli 1981*. Archiv für Orientforschung, Beiheft 19. Horn: 8-15.

Metzler, Kai A. 2002. *Tempora in altbabylonischen literarischen Texten*. Alter Orient und Altes Testament 279. Münster.

Michalowski, Piotr 1987. Language, literature, and writing at Ebla. In Luigi Cagni (ed.), *Ebla 1975-1985: Dieci anni di studi linguistici e filologici. Atti del convegno internazionale (Napoli, 9-11 ottobre 1985)*. Naples: 165-75.

Michel, Cécile 2001. *Correspondance des marchands de Kanish au début du IIe millénaire avant J.-C.* Paris.

Moran, William L. 1992. *The Amarna Letters*. Baltimore and London.

- 2003. *Amarna Studies: Collected Writings*, ed. J. Huehnergard and S. Izre'el. Harvard Semitic Studies 54. Winona Lake.

Oelsner, Joachim 1986. *Materialien zur babylonischen Gesellschaft und Kultur in hellenistischer Zeit*. Budapest.

- 2002a. *"Sie ist gefallen, sie ist gefallen, Babylon, die große Stadt" Vom Ende einer Kultur.* Sitzungsberichte der Sächsischen Akademie der Wissenschaften, philogisch-historische Klasse 138, 1. Leipzig.

- 2002b. Babylonische Kultur nach dem Ende des babylonischen Staates. In R. G. Kratz (ed.), *Religion und Religionskontakte im Zeitalter der Achämeniden*. Gütersloh: 49-73.

Parpola, Simo 1986. The royal archives of Nineveh. In Klaas R. Veenhof (ed.), *Cuneiform Archives and Libraries*. Rencontre Assyriologique Internationale 30. Leiden and Istanbul: 223-36.

- 1988. Proto-Assyrian. In H. Waetzoldt and H. Hauptmann (eds.), *Wirtschaft und Gesellschaft von Ebla: Akten der internationalen Tagung Heidelberg, 4.-7. November 1986*. Heidelberger Studien zum alten Orient 2. Heidelberg: 293-8.

- 1990. A letter from Marduk-apla-uṣur of Anah to Rudamu/Urtamis, king of Hamath. In P. J. Riis and M.-L. Buhl (eds.), *Hama. Fouilles et recherches de la Fondation Carlsberg 1931-1938*, II/2. Copenhagen: 257-63.

Pedersén, Olof 1989. Some morphological aspects of Sumerian and Akkadian linguistic areas. In Hermann Behrens, Darlene Loding and Martha T. Roth (eds.), *DUMU-E$_2$-DUB-BA-A. Studies in Honor of Åke W. Sjöberg*. Occasional Publications of the Samuel Noah Kramer Fund 11. Philadelphia: 429-38.

- 1998. *Archives and Libraries of the Ancient Near East 1500-300 B.C.* Bethesda.

Pentiuc, Eugen J. 2001. *West Semitic Vocabulary in the Akkadian Texts from Emar*. Harvard Semitic Studies 49. Winona Lake.

Pinches, Theophilus G. 1889-90. A Babylonian tablet dated in the reign of Aspasinē. *Babylonian and Oriental Record* 4: 131-5.

Podany, Amanda H. 1991-3. A Middle Babylonian date for the Ḫana kingdom. *Journal of Cuneiform Studies* 43-5: 53-62.

Postgate, John Nicholas 1997. Middle Assyrian to Neo-Assyrian: The nature of the shift. In Hartmut Waetzoldt and Harald Hauptmann (eds.), *Assyrien im Wandel der Zeit*. Heidelberger Studien zum Alten Orient 6, Rencontre Assyriologique Internationale 39. Heidelberg: 159-68.

Radner, Karen 2002. *Die neuassyrischen Texte aus Tall Šēḫ Ḥamad*. Berlin.

- 2004. *Das mittelassyrische Tontafelarchiv von Giricano/Dunnu-ša-Uzibi*. Subartu 14. Turnhout.

Rainey, Anson 1996. *Canaanite in the Amarna Tablets: A Linguistic Analysis of the Mixed Dialect used by the Scribes from Canaan*. 4 vols. Handbuch der Orientalistik I, 25. Leiden.

- 1999. Taanach Letters. *Eretz-Israel* 26:153*-162*.

Reiner, Erica 1966. *A Linguistic Analysis of Akkadian*. Janua linguarum, Series practica 21. The Hague.

Richter, Thomas 2002. Bericht über die 2001 in Qatna gemachten Inschriftenfunde. *Mitteilungen der Deutschen Orient-Gesellschaft* 134: 247-55.

Rowe, Ignacio Marquéz 1998. Notes on the Hurro-Akkadian of Alalaḫ in the mid-second millennium B.C.E. In S. Izre'el, I. Singer and R. Zadok (eds.), *Israel Oriental Studies* 18. *Past Links: Studies in the Languages and Cultures of the Ancient Near East*. Winona Lake: 63-78.

Salonen, Errki 1962. *Untersuchungen zur Schrift und Sprache des Altbabylonischen von Susa*. Studia Orientalia 27, 1. Helsinki.

Schaudig, Hanspeter 2001. *Die Inschriften Nabonids von Babylon und Kyros' des Grossen samt den in ihrem Umfeld entstandenen Tendenzschriften: Textausgabe und Grammatik*. Alter Orient und Altes Testament 256. Münster.

Seminara, Stefano 1998. *L'accadico di Emar*. Materiali per il vocabolario sumerico 6. Rome.

Sivan, Daniel 1984. *Grammatical Analysis and Glossary of the Northwest Semitic Vocables in Akkadian Texts of the 15th-13th C.B.C. from Canaan and Syria*. Alter Orient und Altes Testament 214. Kevelaer and Neukirchen-Vluyn.

Soden, Wolfram von 1931-3. Der hymnisch-epische Dialekt des Akkadischen. *Zeitschrift für Assyriologie* 40: 163-227, 41: 90-183.

- 1995. *Grundriss der akkadischen Grammatik*. 3rd edn. Analecta Orientalia 33. Rome.

Soldt, Wilfred van 1991. *Studies in the Akkadian of Ugarit. Dating and Grammar*. Alter Orient und Altes Testament 40. Kevelaer and Neukirchen-Vluyn.

Sommerfeld, Walter 2003. Bemerkungen zur Dialektgliedurung Altakkadisch, Assyrisch und Babylonisch. In G. J. Selz (ed.), *Festschrift für Burkhart Kienast: zu seinem 70. Geburtstage dargebracht von Freunden, Schülern und Kollegen*. Alter Orient und Altes Testament 274. Münster: 569-86.

Stein, Peter 2000. *Die mittel- und neubabylonischen Königsinschriften bis zum Ende der Assyrerherrschaft: Grammatische Untersuchungen*. Jenaer Beiträge zum Vorderen Orient 3. Wiesbaden.

Streck, Michael P. 1995. *Zahl und Zeit. Grammatik der Numeralia und des Verbalsystems im Spätbabylonischen*. Cuneiform Monographs 5. Groningen.

Swaim, Gerald G. 1962. A Grammar of the Akkadian Tablets Found at Ugarit. PhD thesis, Brandeis University.

Tallqvist, Knut Leonard 1890. *Die Sprache der Contracte Nabû-nâ'ids (555-538 v.Chr.), mit Berücksichtigung der Contracte Nebukadrezars und Cyrus'*. Helsinki.

Thureau-Dangin, François 1925. Un hymne à Ištar de la haute époque babylonienne. *Revue d'assyriologie* 22: 169-77.

Ungnad, Arthur 1992. *Akkadian Grammar*. 5th edn., rev. Lubor Matouš, trans. Harry A. Hoffner, Jr. Atlanta, Ga.

Vaan, J. M. C. T. de 1995. *"Ich bin ein Schwertklinge des Königs". Die Sprache des Bēl-ibni*. Alter Orient und Altes Testament 242. Kevelaer and Neukirchen-Vluyn.

Walker, C. B. F. 1980. Some Assyrians at Sippar in the Old Babylonian period. *Anatolian Studies* 30: 15-22.

Wall-Romana, Christophe 1990. An areal location of Agade. *Journal of Near Eastern Studies* 49: 205-45.

Wasserman, Nathan 2003. *Style and Form in Old-Babylonian Literary Texts*. Cuneiform Monographs 27. Leiden and Boston.

Westenholz, Aage 1978. Some notes on the orthography and grammar of the recently published texts from Mari. *Bibliotheca Orientalia* 35: 160-9.
- 1999. The Old Akkadian period: History and culture. In Walther Sallaberger and Aage Westenholz, *Mesopotamien: Akkade-Zeit und Ur-III Zeit*. Orbis Biblicus et Orientalis 160, 3. Freiburg and Göttingen: 15-117.
Whiting, Robert M., Jr. 1987. *Old Babylonian Letters from Tell Asmar*. Assyriological Studies 22. Chicago.
Wilcke, Claus 1993. Politik im Spiegel der Literatur, Literatur als Mittel der Politik im älteren Babylonien, in K. Raaflaub (ed.), *Anfänge politischen Denkens in der Antike, die nahöstlichen Kulturen und die Griechen*. Schriften des historischen Kollegs, Kolloquien 24. München: 29-75.
Wilhelm, Gernot 1970. *Untersuchungen zum Ḫurro-Akkadischen von Nuzi*. Alter Orient und Altes Testament 9. Kevelaer and Neukirchen-Vluyn.
- 1986. Urartu als Region der Keilschriftkultur. In V. Haas (ed.), *Das Reich Urartu: Ein altorientalischer Staat im 1. Jahrtausend v. Chr.* Xenia 17. Constance: 95-116.
Woodington, Nancy R. 1982. A Grammar of the Neo-Babylonian Letters of the Kuyunjik Collection. PhD thesis, Yale University.
Ylvisaker, S. 1912. *Zur babylonischen und assyrischen Grammatik, eine Untersuchung auf Grund der Briefe aus der Sargonidenzeit*. Leipziger semitistische Studien 5, 6. Leipzig.

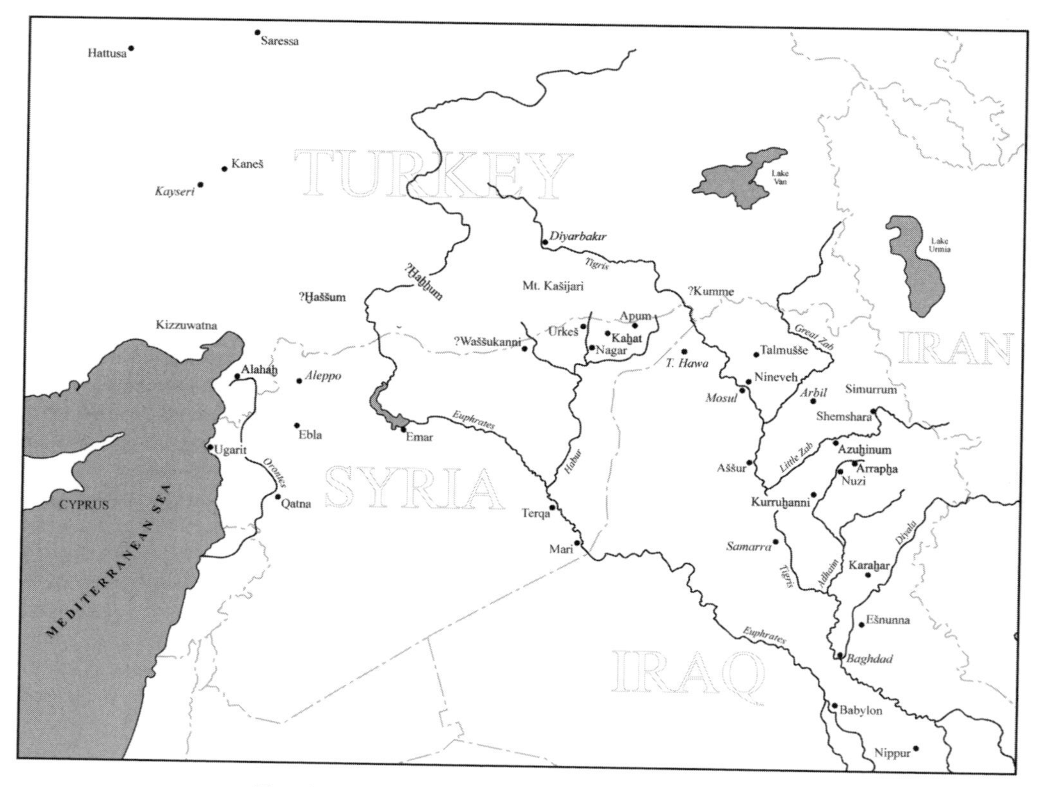

Fig. 4.1 Hurrian: Map to show places mentioned

Hurrian

David Hawkins

School of Oriental and African Studies

University of London

The Hurrians were a people of the Ancient Near East known principally from texts written in their language but also from their personal names and the names of their gods. Their floruit was the IInd millennium B.C., although they can now be seen to have been important already in the IIIrd millennium, and traces of their presence persist into the Ist millennium. Geographically their heartland seems to have been Upper Mesopotamia, the scene of their greatest political dominance, the Hurrian kingdom of Mittani, but their influence at its greatest extent spread across the Euphrates westwards into Anatolia to the Hittite kingdom of Hattusa and eastwards across the Tigris to the Zagros mountains. Very little of their written language has been found within the political boundaries of modern Iraq, yet there is ample evidence for their presence there from a number of notable sites, and this justifies the inclusion of Hurrian among the languages of Iraq. In the present overview it will be seen that most of what is known of the Hurrian language comes from the West, specifically the cuneiform archives of the Hittite capital Boğazköy-Hattusa, and even their political prominence is best seen from sources from areas west of Iraq. In the context of the present symposium however, emphasis is placed on the evidence for the Hurrians in the east in Iraq itself.

The language: sources and identification

As early as 1881 it was noted that Akkadian synonym lists included some non-Akkadian words glossed *su*(-*bir*$_4$)^{KI}, later identified as the land *Subartu*. With the discovery of the Amarna letters, among the Akkadian correspondence of Tušratta King of Mittani was a very long letter (494 lines) in an unknown language thereby named "Mittanian" (publ. 1889), and it was then noted that this language contained some *subir*-words. The discovery of the Boğazköy archives from 1906 onwards produced Akkadian documents (e.g. the treaties of Suppiluliuma I with Šattiwaza son of Tušratta, publ. 1916) referring to the "land" and "men of Hurri" (at first read

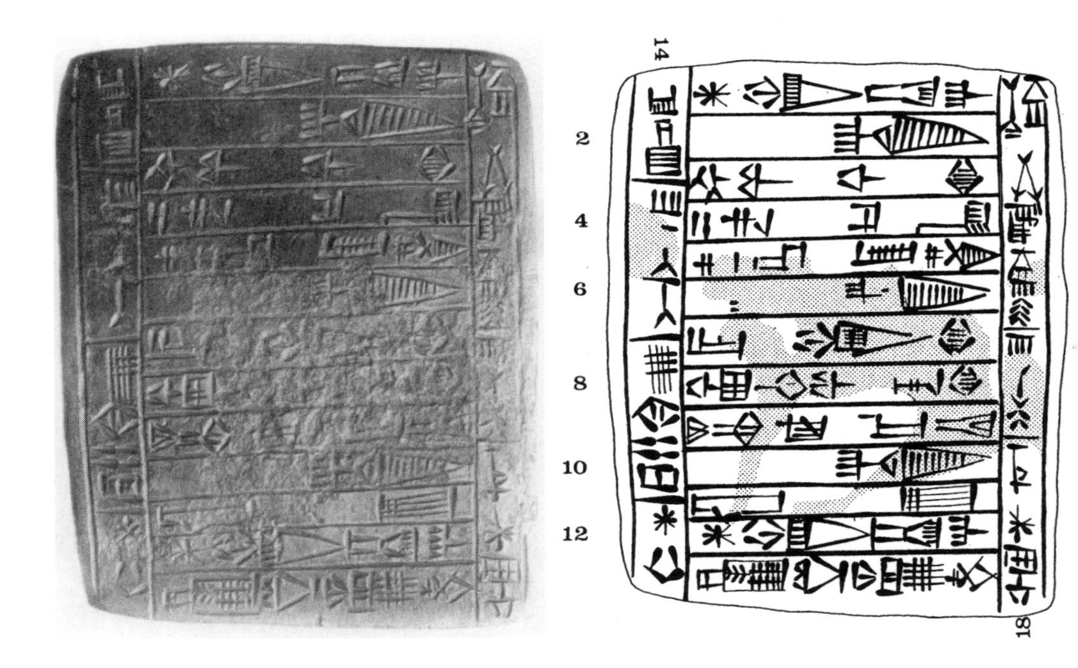

Fig. 4.2. The inscription of Atalšen on the bronze "Samarra tablet"

Harri, written with the sign HAR/HUR). They also produced a group of texts written in a language designated *hurlili*, "(in) the language of Hurla", recognized as the Hittite ethnicon for *Hurri* and the same language as that of the Mittani letter. After some hesitation between "Subarian", "Mittanian" and "Hurrian" as the proper term for this language, scholars finally settled on the last.

Before and after the Second World War new Hurrian material became available from Ugarit (Hittite Empire period) and Mari (Old Babylonian). At the same time the Alalah texts, especially those of level IV, showed a marked Hurrianization in terms of the onomastics and provided new historical and dynastic information on Mittani. More recently Emar with a heavily Hurrianized population in the Late Bronze Age has yielded similar material to that of Ugarit. In general, Hittite Empire evidence on contemporary Syria shows a largely Hurrian governing class as well as population all across the map. Indeed extremely recently excavations at Qatna have produced some remarkable texts in Hurrianized Akkadian belonging to the period of Suppiluliuma's conquest.

Hurrians in Iraq
While almost no actual Hurrian texts have been found in Iraq, evidence suggests that already in the later IIIrd millennium B.C. there was a presence of Hurrians in the areas east of the Tigris. Campaigns of Naram-Sin of Akkad and Shulgi of the Ur III dynasty into the Zagros mountains encountered chieftains with Hurrian names, and similar names occur at Drehem, presumably captives of Shulgi. Old Akkadian texts from Yorgan Tepe near Kirkuk show that the city at this date was called *Gasur* (later Nuzi), and that the largely Akkadian names of the population already contain an admixture of Hurrian.

A unique marble tablet from Nippur of late or post-Akkadian date bears a list of clothes, some recognizably Hurrian, and some Hurrian names, and might almost be considered a Hurrian document. Another Hurrian document (but not text - it is written in Akkadian) is the bronze "Samarra tablet" which appeared in that city but without provenance and was published in 1912 (see now Wilhelm *apud* Haas 1988: 46-50). It is an inscription of Atalšen, king of Urkiš and Nawar, recording his building of the temple of Nergal of Hawalum, and is probably to be dated post-Akkadian - early Ur III. It must stand in some relationship to the Lion of Urkiš text, a

Fig. 4.3. The bronze lion and stone tablet of Tišatal of Urkiš

stone tablet held by a small bronze lion and bearing a cuneiform inscription, the oldest known Hurrian text, recording the building of the temple of Nergal by Tišatal *endan* of Urkiš (see now Wilhelm *apud* Buccellati 1998: 117-143). The provenance of this monument, which is doubtless the foundation deposit of the temple, should be Urkiš itself, now securely identified as Tell Mozan in north-east Syria currently under excavation (see below). The site of Nawar joined to Urkiš as Atalšen's kingdom remains problematic (see also below). As to the person and date of Tišatal, a possible identity with "Tišatal man of Nineveh" named on two Ešnunna tablets dated to Šu-Sin year 3 would give a date which would fit well with the style and palaeography of the inscription, but not with an archaeological date proposed by the excavator of Tell Mozan (see below). Similarly the relationship of Atalšen king of Urkiš and Nawar and Tišatal *endan* of Urkiš with their respective Akkadian and Hurrian inscriptions now has an archaeological dimension arising from the Mozan excavations.

Fig. 4.4. Impressions from seals of members of the royal household at Urkiš

Tell Mozan excavations

This site in north-east Syria right on the frontier with Turkey has been under excavation for over fifteen seasons, and has been securely identified as ancient Urkiš on the basis of the seal inscriptions of the ruler. The "Storehouse" building low on the west side of the mound has produced impressions of the seals of Tupkiš the *endan* of Urkiš, of his wife and of several domestics including the nurse and the cook, all carved with charming scenes of domestic life. All the seal-holders have Hurrian names except the queen whose name is Akkadian. This royal family of Urkiš may be dated to the early Akkadian period, since the subsequent level of the building has yielded impressions of the seal of Taram-Agade, daughter of Naram-Sin, whose presence in Urkiš may be explained by marriage to the ruler or possibly by her installation as priestess. Atalšen and Tišatal of the Samarra and Urkiš Lion tablets have been viewed as later rulers, perhaps of the same dynasty. It should however be noted that the excavator of Tell Mozan proposes the dating of Tišatal to *before* Tupkiš on the basis of a postulated provenance of the Urkiš Lion foundation deposit from the early Sargonic levels of the Temple of Mozan. However this may turn out, these documents show the existence of a substantial and enduring Hurrian kingdom in the area of the upper Habur in the later IIIrd millennium B.C. As for the city Nawar linked to Urkiš by Atalšen, pieces of evidence are accumulating that Tell Brak was ancient Nawar or, in a variant form, Nagar. Other evidence however suggests the possible existence of a more northerly second Nawar, perhaps the same as later Nabula, which at Girnavaz north of Kamishliye is much closer to Mozan. For a discussion of this problem, see D. Matthews & G. Eidem 1993; also *Reallexikon der Assyriologie* vol. 9, s.v. Nagar (Eidem), and Nawar (Kessler).

For the excavations of Mozan and the discoveries discussed here, see G. Buccellati and M. Kelly-Buccellati, items in Bibliography.

Mittani and Nuzi

In the IInd millennium B.C., sources from Upper Mesopotamia extending from west of the Euphrates (Kültepe, Alalah) through the central area (Mari, Tell Brak, Tell Leilan, Tell al Rimah, Tell Chagar Bazar) up to east of the Tigris (Tell Shemshara) by the increasing number of Hurrian personal names occurring attest to the expansion of the Hurrian population and the assumption of power by Hurrian community leaders. Yet almost none of the documents from these scattered archives are written in Hurrian (only a tiny number from the enormous collection from Mari), any more than they are written in Amorite, the language of the other main population group. To the newly founded kingdom of Hattusa the states of the Euphrates frontier and beyond were the "Hurri lands", and they represented the enemies with whom the Hittite kings contended here in the later 17th and 16th centuries B.C.

This is the milieu in which the Hurrian political entity Mittani took shape. Its origins are poorly attested, and in the absence of any central archive from any site in its core area, even the identity and location of its political capital Waššukkanni remains uncertain - but probably Tell Fekheriyeh on the upper Habur. The rise of Mittani is best documented in the Hittite historical references to their struggles with Hurrian kings for ascendancy in the Euphrates states and Kizzuwatna, and also the Alalah tablets of level IV, which provide tantalizing glimpses of Mittanian domination.

Just as Mittanian power pushed westwards across the Euphrates into north Syria including Halab and Alalah, and the Taurus states, so too it crept eastwards over the Tigris in even less well documented circumstances. Occasional references show that the city of Assur, though preserving its own line of kings as recorded in the Assyrian King List and their own contemporary inscriptions, lay under Mittanian overlordship. Even beyond Assur, Mittanian influence extended to the Kingdom of Arrapha (mod. Kirkuk) and its subordinate city of Nuzi (mod. Yorgan Tepe).

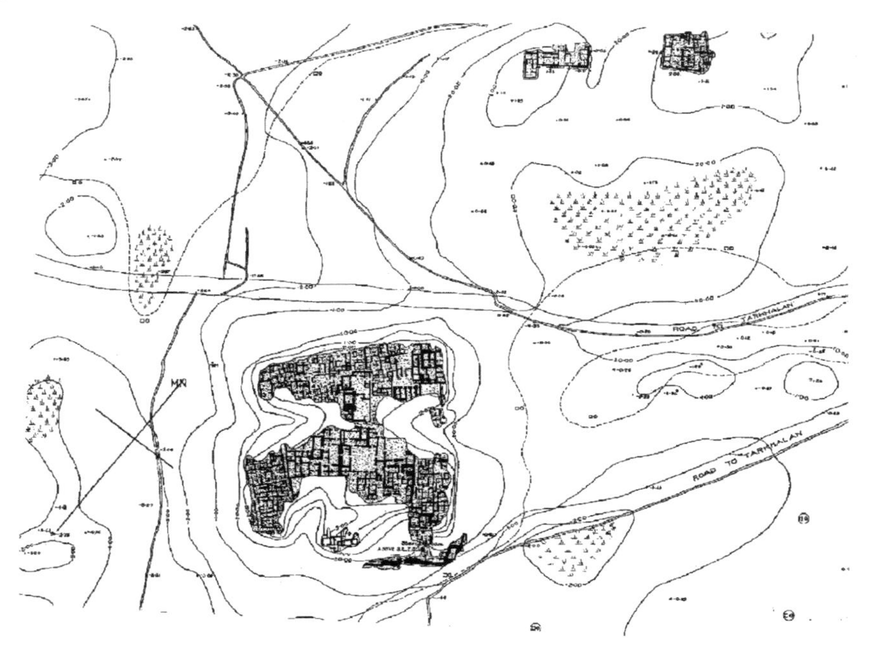

Fig. 4.5. Plan of the Palace and outlying houses at Nuzi (Starr 1939, Plan 2)

Nuzi is the site in Iraq which has indeed yielded an extraordinary amount of information on the Hurrians of the east. The city lies some 13 km. south-west of its local capital Arrapha. Excavated in the years 1925-1931 by the American Schools of Oriental Research and the Iraq Museum, Nuzi has presented a unique picture of a Hurrian provincial town of the mid-IInd millennium B.C. On the main mound two civic centres have been uncovered, the government building (É.GAL) and the temple together with their surrounding residential quarters; and outside in the country two rich princes' houses have also been excavated. All sectors have produced tablet archives, a total of some 7000 tablets, which are enormously informative on the daily lives and businesses of the citizens.

The great majority of the attested Nuzians bear Hurrian names, and this justifies the designation of the city as a Hurrian settlement and reveals the extent of the Hurrian penetration of the trans-Tigridian zone. Yet the copious documentation from the city is entirely composed in Akkadian, albeit a Hurrianized form of the Middle Babylonian dialect, with a plethora of Hurrian loan words, and grammatical constructions influenced by Hurrian. Not a single text written actually in Hurrian has been found.

Politically Nuzi appears to have been under the authority of the Kings of Arrapha, who themselves bore Hurrian names, and they in their turn seem to have been vassals of Mittani. The floruit of Nuzi is difficult to date exactly. Family archives in the city extend over five generations. The terminal destruction of Nuzi by fire may be linked to the fall of Mittani and the rise of the Middle Assyrian dynasty. An approximate 1500-1350 B.C. looks most probable for the city's span. The latter date indeed can be seen as an important turning point for the Hurrians across the Tigris as in their heartland of Upper Mesopotamia, since the Hurrian tide which had been running strongly for centuries began to ebb. The Middle Assyrian dynasty established a land of Assur east of the Tigris, and gradually conquered the former Mittani, now Hanigalbat, pushing their frontiers westwards to the Euphrates. Into this Assyrian *Reich* the Hurrians were absorbed linguistically as well as politically, so that by c. 1000 B.C. they had effectively disappeared.

Hurrian texts and language

But if in the east and centre Hurrians and their language declined to extinction with the fall of Mittani, in the west they enjoyed another century and a half of prominence. Indeed most of what we know about their language and culture comes from this phase. Hurrian political and religious influence on Hattusa under its Empire Period dynasty is well attested in the onomastics of the royal family, the syncretism of the pantheon, the mythology and the cult. The largest corpus of Hurrian texts was already that of Hattusa (Laroche, 1971), when in 1983 a large Hurrian-Hittite bilingual series was excavated at Boğazköy (bibliography, The Bilingual). Entitled the "Song of Releasing", this composition consists of a number of tablets the order of which is not yet clearly established. Nevertheless this bilingual (or bilinguals - there might indeed be more than one composition involved) marked a significant step forward in the process of understanding Hurrian.

Actually it is not only the Hittite capital which has yielded Hurrian texts from this period. The site of Ortaköy (anc. Sapinuwa) currently under excavation is said to have produced substantial Hurrian material, but this remains unpublished. The Hittite Empire sites in Syria, Ras Shamra-Ugarit and Meskene-Emar, have already been noted as sources with polyglot vocabularies and rich Hurrian onomastics, as also the Hurrianized Akkadian of Mishrife-Qatna. All this was taken to point to a strong Hurrian element in the Syrian ruling classes.

Hurrian shows some dialectal divergences, principally Old Hurrian (Tišatal) and the dialect of the Mittani letter. As a language it is agglutinative, and shows pronounced ergativity in its verbal system, a feature of interest to philologists. A

Fig. 4.6. Bilingual tablet from Boğazköy

close relationship has been demonstrated between Hurrian and Urartian, a corpus of largely monumental royal inscriptions from the Kingdom of Urartu in the early Ist millennium B.C. A further attempt to link Hurro-Urartian with a Caucasian language group is not regarded as clearly established.

For a good summary of the main features of the Hurrian language, I append that of G. Wilhelm given to an Erasmus Seminar in Cambridge in 1995 (revised version, by kind permission).

Selected features of Hurrian grammar

1. Hurrian is an agglutinative language. It exclusively uses monofunctional suffixes, arranged in a strict sequential order.
2. The "roots" are usually, if not always, monosyllabic.
3. The "stem" is formed by the root and one, two or possibly three optional root-complements, e.g. *ar-i* "give!", *ar=ann=i* "let give!" (causative).
4. Most nominal stems have a final vowel *-i*, which apparently has a nominalizing force. A small group of nouns end in *-a* (*šēna* "brother", *ēla* "sister" and other relative terms; Šavuška (name of a goddess) and other names of gods; *tiža* "heart").
5. Hurrian grammars distinguish the following word classes: nouns, adjectives (mostly derived from nouns), pronouns, numbers, verbs, and particles (including enclitic ones). Nouns, numbers and verbs may easily change their word class by derivational suffixes and root-complements: *eman* "ten", *eman=am-* "to make tenfold", *eman=d=i* "group of ten", *eman=d=o=ġ=li* "decurio"; *ḫan-* "to give birth", *ḫan=i* "child", *ḫan=o/u=mb=a=s=ḫe* "fertility"(?).
6. As to nouns, there are two numbers (sg., pl.), but no grammatical genders. At least 10 cases have been observed so far: absolutive (Ø), ergative (*-ž*), genitive (*-ve*), dative (*-va*), directive (*-da*), comitative (*-ra*) ablative-instrumental (*-ne/i*), ablative (*-dan*), directive(-locative?) (*-ē*), and essive (*-a*). Several more suffixes have also been defined as case endings, though their syntax seems to be somewhat different and they apparently do not have a plural in *-až-*: instrumental (*-ae*), equative (*-ož*), associative (*-nni*) and associative-essive (*-nna*).
7. Between nouns and case-endings (except the last-mentioned group) a relator *-ne* (sg.) or *-na* (pl.) appears (not with all names, however). It seems to be incompatible with possessive-suffixes (see below 9.). *-ne* does not occur in the absolutive, whereas *-na* does, forming the normal plural (*tive* "word" vs. *tive=na* "words"). The suffixes have been called "articles", but they do not refer to the categories of definiteness or indefiniteness. They also play a significant role in *Suffixaufnahme* (copying of case-endings at attributes, including genitive attributes and nominalized verbal forms: *šēn(a)=iffu=we=nē=ž ašt(i)=i=ž* "the wife (Erg.) of my brother", *šēn(a)=iffu=we=nē=va ōmīn(i)=nē=va* "to the country of my brother"; *tive=na tān=ož=āw=šše=na* "the things which I did").
8. Hurrian has only a few postpositions. They occur, however, rather frequently (e.g. *ed(i)=ī=da* "concerning", lit. "to its body") and require the dative of their head.
9. The possessive suffixes are directly linked to the stem, and they are followed by the case endings. There are three persons (1st: *-iffə*, *-iffe-*, *-iffu-*, 2nd: *-v*, 3rd: *-ī*) and two numbers. The plural forms are distinguished from the singular forms by a pluralizer -

až- which follows the possessive suffix. Since the same pluralizer *-až-* precedes the case-ending of nouns in the plural, *ēn(i)=iff=až=už* ("god"=poss. 1 Ps=pl.=erg.) indiscriminately means "our gods" and "our god" (and perhaps "my gods"(erg.); "my gods" in the absolutive, however, is *ēn(i)=iff=a=lla*).

10. There are independent personal pronouns which appear in various case-forms, and enclitic personal pronouns which are restricted to the absolutive.
11. The verb in the Mittani letter distinguishes tenses (pres. -∅-, pret. *-ož-*, fut. *-ed-*): *tān=i=a* "he makes", *tān=ož=a* "he made", *tān=ed=a* "he will make".
12. Both dialects have suffixes which presumably refer to modes of action (*-ar-* iterative, *-ill-* inchoative, *-uva-* durative: *talm=uva=b* "he grew up", *pid=uva* "she danced", *šīn(i)=a ḫapš=ar=uva* "it constantly looked at").
13. Construction is ergativic: The agent is encoded as an ergative and the patient as an absolutive; the subject of an action or state without patient is encoded as an absolutive. Transitivity is marked by the so-called "class-marker" *-i-* in a number of forms, intransitivity by *-a* (*tad=i=o* "you love (him / her)" - *un=a(=lla)* "they come"). At Boğazköy and in older texts, there is a third "class-marker" *-o-* for transitive verbs in ergativic construction, *-i-* being restricted to transitive verbs in non-ergativic construction ("anti-passive"). In rare cases the agent is encoded in the absolutive and the patient in the essive.

    In the Mittani dialect, verbal forms in ergativic construction contain a pronominal suffix referring to the ergative, whereas verbal forms in non-ergativic construction (both, transitive and intransitive) have no obligatory reference to person. The subject, however, in the latter case is frequently and repetetively referred to by the enclitic absolutive personal pronouns, which may or may not be attached to the verbal form.
14. Hurrian has a complex system of non-indicative forms, which has not yet been fully understood. Most of these forms do not contain personal suffixes.
15. Finite verbal forms may be nominalized and treated like adjectives (cf. above 7.). In this case, the head of the attributive nominalized verb is always its direct object, regardless of its case form.
16. The word order is usually "(ergative -) absolutive - verb". Participants in the dative or directive may follow the verb, otherwise their position would be between the ergative and the absolutive. In rare cases, presumably as a means of topicalization, the verb may appear in initial position.

Gernot Wilhelm

Further reading

General

Wilhelm, G., 1989. *The Hurrians* (Warminster: Aris and Phillips).

Language and Texts

Laroche, E., 1971. *Catalogue des textes hittites* (Paris: Klincksieck), ch. XI.D Hourrite.
- 1976-1977 *Glossaire de la langue hourrite* (*Revue Hittite et Asianique* XXXIV-XXXV) (obsolescent due to the Bilingual).

Diakonoff, I.M. & Starostin, I.A., 1986. *Hurro-Urartian as an Eastern Caucasian Language* (Munich: Kitzinger).

Wegner, I., 2000. *Hurritisch. Eine Einführung* (Wiesbaden: Harrassowitz).

Wilhelm, G., 2004. "Hurrian", in R.D. Woodard (ed.), *The Cambridge Encyclopedia of the World's Ancient Languages* (Cambridge University Press): 95-118.

The Bilingual

Neu, E., 1988. *Das Hurritische: eine altorientalische Sprache in neuem Licht* (Mainz Academy; Steiner, Wiesbaden)
- 1996. *Das Hurritische Epos der Freilassung* (Studien zu den Boğazköy-Texten 32; Wiesbaden: Harrassowitz)

Wilhelm, G., 2001. "Das hurritisch-hethitische 'Lied der Freilassung'", in O. Kaiser (ed.), *Texte aus der Umwelt des Alten Testament, Ergänzungslieferung* (Gütersloh): 82-91.

Mitanni Letter

Wilhelm, G., 1992. in W.L. Moran, *The Amarna Letters* (Baltimore/ London: Johns Hopkins): 63-71 (EA #24).

Recent Colloquia

Haas, V. (ed.), 1988. *Hurriter und Hurritisch* (Xenia 21; Konstanz).

Owen, D.I.& Wilhelm, G. (eds.), 1999. *Nuzi at Seventy-Five* (Studies on the Civilization and Culture of Nuzi and the Hurrians 10; Bethesda, Maryland).

Durand, J.M. (ed.), 1996. *Amurru 1-2. Mari, Ebla et les hourrites, dix ans de travaux* (Paris).

Buccellati, G. & Kelly-Buccellati, M. (eds.), 1998. *Urkesh and the Hurrians* (Urkesh/Mozan Studies 3; Undena, Malibu)

Sites

See *Reallexikon der Assyriologie* s.v. Kurruhanni, Mōzān, Nagar, Nawar, Nuzi.

Nuzi

Note series *Studies on the Civilization and Culture of Nuzi and the Hurrians* 1 (1981) - 15 (2005), abbr. *SCCNH*

Maidman, M.P., 1995. "Nuzi: Portrait of an Ancient Mesopotamian provincial town", in J. Sasson (ed.), *Civilizations of the Ancient Near East*, vol. II (New York: Scribner): 931-947.

Fincke, J., 1993. *Die Orts- und Gewässernamen der Nuzi-Texte* (*RGTC* 10; Wiesbaden: Reichert).

Tell Shemshara (Šušarra)

Eidem, J., 1992. *The Shemshara Archives* 2. *The Administrative Texts* (Copenhagen: Royal Danish Academy).

Eidem, J. & Læssøe, J., 2001. *The Shemshara Archives* 1. *The Letters* (Copenhagen: Royal Danish Academy).

Tell Mozan (Urkeš)

Buccellati, G. & Kelly-Buccellati, M., 1995-96. "The Royal Storehouse of Urkesh: the glyptic evidence from the southwestern wing", *Archiv für Orientforschung* 42/43: 2-32.

- 1999/2000/2001/2002 "Die 11/12/13/14 Kampagne in Tall Mozan/Urkeš", *Mitteilungen der Deutschen Orientgesellschaft,* 131/132/133/134.

Tell Brak (Nagar/Nawar?)

Reports in *Iraq* 42 (1980) onwards by D. Oates; also *Iraq* 47 (1985) (I.L. Finkel); 50 (1988) (N.J.J. Illingworth); 53 (1991) (G. Wilhelm); 55 (1993) (D. Matthews and J. Eidem)

Mishrife (Qatna)

Richter, T., 2003. "Das 'Archiv des Idanda'", *Mitteilungen der Deutschen Orientgesellschaft* 135: 167-188.

- 2005. "Qatna in the Late Bronze Age. Preliminary Remarks", *SCCNH* 15: 109-126.

Early Aramaic

Alan Millard

University of Liverpool

The three previous contributions deal with languages that were used for long periods of time but were all but dead by the beginning of the Christian era. There is one language whose use can be traced for about three thousand years and is still current in Iraq, Aramaic. This essay offers a simplified survey of the first half of its history, a period for which the information available is meagre.

1. What is Aramaic ?

Aramaic is a Semitic language, that is to say, it belongs to the same family of languages as Akkadian (Assyrian and Babylonian) and so shares many basic features with them, but it differs in some major ways and those place it with Amorite, Ugaritic, Hebrew, Phoenician and others in the West or North-West Semitic branch, rather than in the East Semitic, Akkadian, branch of the family, or the South Semitic, Arabic, branch.

(a) East Semitic : West Semitic

Four simple examples illustrate differences between East and West Semitic.

1. In phonology Akkadian has third person pronoun forms with initial sh, whereas West Semitic has initial h and the same distinction applies to the initial phoneme of the causative stem of the verb (Akkadian III or Š theme, West Semitic Hiph'il).

2. Forms of the verbal system have developed in opposite ways:
Akkadian preterite *ipqid* : West Semitic imperfective *yipqud*;
Akkadian stative *paqid* : West Semitic perfective *pāqad*.

3. Akkadian word order is basically subject-object-verb; West Semitic word order is basically verb-subject-object.

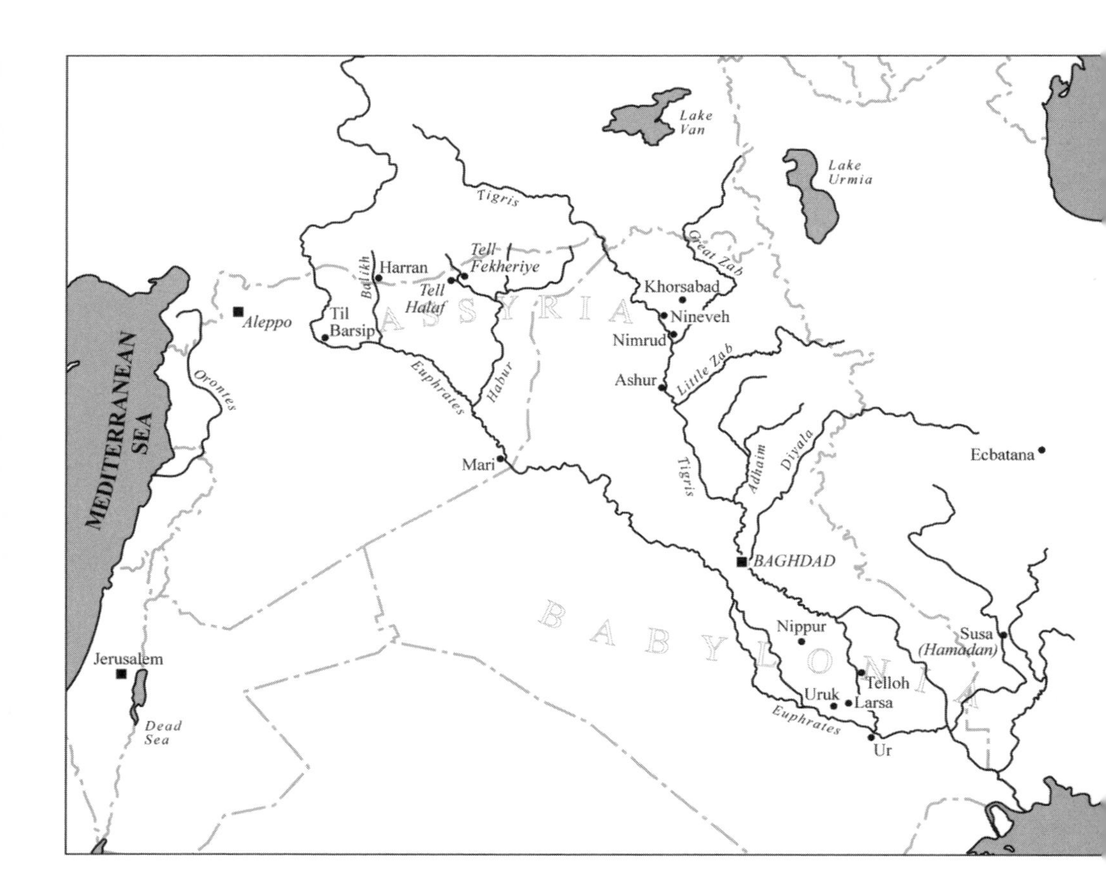

Fig. 5.1 Early Aramaic: map to show places mentioned

4. Some primary vocabulary is different: Akkadian *awēlum* 'man': West Semitic *'îš* 'man'; Akkadian *šaṭārum* 'to write', West Semitic *kathab* 'to write'.

(b) Aramaic : West Semitic

Like the other ancient West Semitic languages, Aramaic is known to us from documents written with the early alphabet, that is, the Canaanite or Phoenician alphabet. Although it is a very simple writing system, it has two disadvantages for understanding ancient Aramaic. Firstly, it only marks a few of the long vowels and no short ones, unlike cuneiform, so restricting knowledge of patterns of vowels and stress to some extent. Secondly, it has only twenty-two consonantal characters and

Aramaic had more than twenty-two consonantal sounds or phonemes. Consequently, the scribes had to use one sign to represent more than one sound. Thus the letter *z* in early Aramaic stands for /z/ and for /th/ as in 'zoo' and 'that', the letter š stands for /sh/ and for /th/, as in 'shrink' and 'think'. (These sound contrasts are rather like the problems some non-English speakers have when they say 'zat' for 'that' and 'sink' for 'think'.)

Aramaic stands apart from the other ancient West Semitic languages in various ways.

1. There are the phonetic distinctions already mentioned, and some others.
2. Short vowels in open, unaccented syllables usually disappear.
3. It has an unusual phonetic shift in the words for 'son, daughter' and 'two'. Where the other West Semitic languages have *ben* and *šina*, Aramaic has *bar* and *tren*.[1]
4. The verbal system has no form with initial *n* (Akkadian IV theme, West Semitic Niph'al).
5. Unlike other West Semitic languages, but like Akkadian, each theme of the verb has an infixed *t* sub-theme with reflexive or passive meaning.
6. The noun can occur with a suffixed *ā'* as the definite article, whereas Akkadian has no definite article and some other West Semitic languages have prefixed *h*.

2. The Use of Aramaic

(a) Early history

The Aramaic language was taking root in Assyria and Babylonia by about 1,000 B.C. It spread into Assyria and Babylonia as tribes from the Habur and mid-Euphrates moved east and southwards, perhaps as a result of drought reducing their pasture-land and causing famine. The threat they posed a little before 1,100 B.C. led Tiglath-pileser I of Assyria to campaign against them repeatedly in the early years of his reign, his forces reaching the Mediterranean coast. Although one of his successors also fought the Aramaeans, soon afterwards they all but overran Assyria. Little more than the capital, Ashur, probably Nineveh and one or two outposts remained under Assyrian control. In the south, Babylonia fell into a period of chaos as the tribesmen settled in many areas. Late in the 10th century, the Assyrians began to re-assert themselves, conquered Aramaean positions east of the Tigris and to the north, then began to re-establish control over the territories of the Jezireh as far as the great bend of the Euphrates, land which had been under Assyrian rule three centuries before. The famous kings Ashurnasirpal II and Shalmaneser III subjugated many Aramaean princes of northern Syria.

Some local rulers submitted to Assyrian suzerainty and were allowed to continue in power, bound by oath to be loyal to Assyria and to pay a regular tribute, in effect a rent for their thrones. Members of a vassal's family might be taken to the

---

[1] D. Testen, 'The Significance of Aramaic r<*n', *JNES* 44 (1985) 143-46.

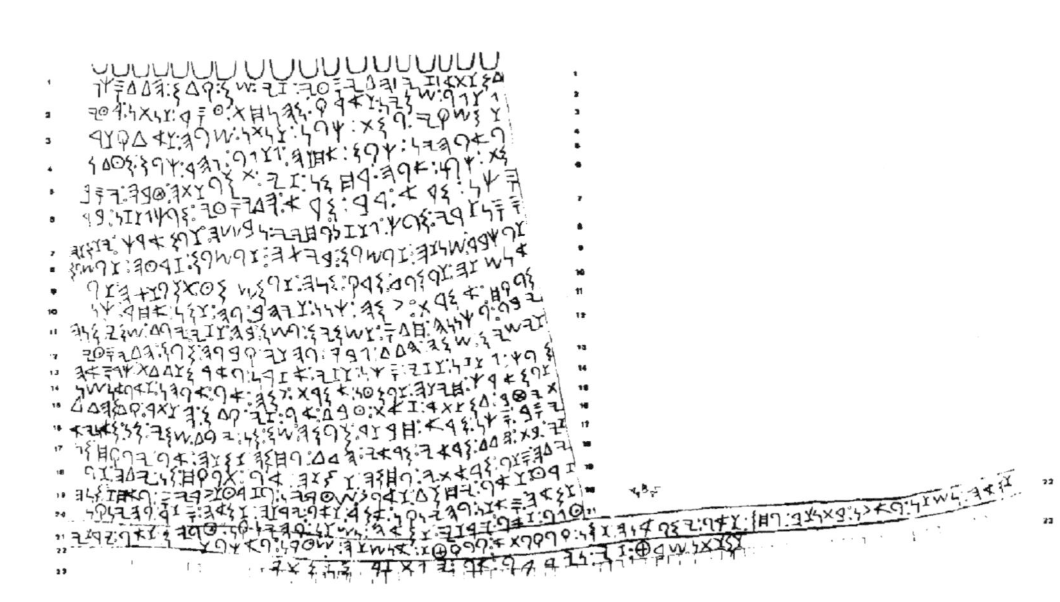

Fig. 5.2 The Aramaic text on the statue of a king of Guzan, from Tell Fekheriyeh

Assyrian court as hostages for his good behaviour. These arrangements brought Assyrian influence into Aramaean courts, as is well shown by the life-size statue from Tell Fekheriyeh, near ancient Guzan, now Tell Halaf, in north-east Syria. Set up during the reign of Shalmaneser III, I believe, this statue represents the local prince and tells of his piety in both Assyrian and Aramaic. This is the oldest Aramaic text of any length and is significant for the history of the language. Its discovery showed the ability of a local scribe, trained in Assyrian, to imitate the inscriptions of the Assyrian kings in cuneiform, then present his composition in his local tongue. The Aramaic text is written in an archaic form of the old Aramaic alphabet and the language displays the impact of Assyria in loan-words and in phraseology. Indeed, the propensity of Aramaic for borrowing words from other languages is already evident in this composition.

The earlier history of Aramaic is obscure. Certain of its distinctive features are present in the Tell Fekheriyeh inscription (such as the definite article *-ā'*), but attempts to trace Aramaic elements in earlier texts have not been successful. It should be noted that there are few documents relating to the Habur, Balikh and mid-Euphrates regions between the Mari archive of c. 1750 B.C. and the Neo-Assyrian annals of the 9th century B.C. The archives of cuneiform tablets from Middle Assyrian levels at a few sites in the area disclose little trace of Aramaeans or Aramaic.[2] Hebrew traditions, in the book of Genesis especially, locate Aramaeans in the Harran district, and that situation would be early in the second millennium B.C., if the narratives are given any credence.[3]

(b) Under Assyria

The Assyrian policy of deporting people from conquered lands and re-settling them in Assyria or in other regions, spread Aramaeans, in particular, across the empire and with them went their language which became such an international tongue that even a prince in north-west Iran used it for his inscription about 700 B.C.[4] Craftsmen used Aramaic letters to mark the order of bricks in a glazed panel in a palace of Shalmaneser III at Nimrud, and we may suppose they were speaking Aramaic.[5] However, not until the latter part of the 8th century does there appear the first clear evidence for writing Aramaic in Assyria and Babylonia. One of the reliefs from Tiglath-pileser III's palace at Nimrud presents a scribe writing on a sheet of flexible material, papyrus or leather, beside another writing on a tablet, and a similar scene was painted in a fresco at the Assyrian palace at Til-Barsip on the mid-Euphrates, which may be dated a few years later.[6] The deduction that these were scribes writing Aramaic is unavoidable. The spread of Aramaic in the Assyrian administration can be deduced from a few references in cuneiform texts to documents in Aramaic. Also from Tiglath-pileser's reign, there is a letter in cuneiform referring to a communication sent in Aramaic, and from Sargon II's reign a letter from the king rejects the request of an official in Ur that he might report to the king in Aramaic.[7]

---

[2] For a small example, see R.M. Whiting, 'A late Middle Assyrian tablet from North Syria', *State Archives of Assyria Bulletin* 2 (1998) 99-101.

[3] A. R. Millard, 'Arameans,' in D. N. Freedman, ed., *The Anchor Bible Dictionary,* New York: Doubleday (1992) I 345-50.

[4] The Bukan Stele, see A. Lemaire, 'Une inscription araméenne du VIIIe s. av. J.-C. trouvée à Bukan,' *Studia Iranica* 27 (1998) 15-30; M. Sokoloff, 'The Old Aramaic Inscription from Bukan: A Revised Interpretation,' *Israel Exploration Journal* 49 (1999) 105-15; K. L. Younger, 'The Bukan Inscription,' in W. W. Hallo, K. L. Younger, eds, *The Context of Scripture* 3, Leiden: Brill (2003) 219.

[5] A. R. Millard, 'The Graffiti on the Glazed Bricks from Nimrud,' Appendix to J. Curtis et al. 'British Museum Excavations at Nimrud and Balawat in 1989,' *Iraq* 55 (1993) 35, 36.

[6] R. D. Barnett, *The Sculptures of Tiglath-pileser III from Nimrud*, London: British Museum (1962), Pl.VI; A. Parrot, *Nineveh and Babylon*, London: Thames & Hudson (1961), p.278, no.348.

[7] H. W. F. Saggs, *Iraq* 17 (1955) 130, no.13,3 = H. W. F. Saggs, *The Nimrud Letters*, London: British School of Archaeology in Iraq (2001), pp. 154-55; M. Dietrich, *The Babylonian Correspondence of*

Note in passing the assumption of leaders in Jerusalem that the Assyrian general could address them in Aramaic when Sennacherib invaded Judah in 701 B.C.[8] Seals with their owners' Assyrian names inscribed in Aramaic letters, in particular a seal of an officer of Sargon known from an imprint found at Khorsabad, and other objects bearing Assyrian names in Aramaic script, show the same thing.

Mostly, Aramaic was written on perishable materials, papyrus or leather or wax-covered wooden boards, which have not survived. In the Levant local kings set up inscribed stone stelae commemorating their achievements in Aramaic and there are a few other Aramaic inscriptions on stone, but there were no such rulers in Iraq to erect monuments there in a script rivalling cuneiform. Some cuneiform tablets of the 7th century B.C. carry notes scratched in Aramaic indicating their contents; obviously some secretaries could not read cuneiform at this time in the heart of Assyria. A few tablets are written wholly in Aramaic. They show Assyrian legal formulae transferred into Aramaic.[9] I believe these texts were written on clay when papyrus or leather was not available.

Fig. 5.3. Aramaic note on the edge of an Assyrian cuneiform legal document (BM 123369, 7th century B.C.)

Sargon and Sennacherib, *State Archives of Assyria* XVII, Helsinki: Helsinki University Press (2003), no 2.

[8] 2 Kings 18: 26.

[9] F. M. Fales, *Aramaic Epigraphs on Clay Tablets of the Neo-Assyrian Period*, *Studi Semitici, Nuova Serie* 2, Rome: La Sapienza, (1986); A. Lemaire, *Nouvelles tablettes araméennes*, Geneva: Droz (2001).

Ephemeral texts were written on potsherds. Broken pottery was the scrap-paper in ancient societies where writing was done with ink, in Egypt, in the Levant of the Iron Age, and in Greece. A few inscribed sherds, ostraca, have been unearthed in Assyria. One, from Nimrud, is a list of people with West Semitic, perhaps Ammonite, names, apparently deportees. Most remarkable is the Ashur Ostracon, a large piece of a vessel, about 42 cm. high and 60 cm. wide. It contains a message from an official at Uruk in Babylonia to his colleague in Ashur and was written about 650 B.C., perhaps taken from dictation in Assur rather than transported from southern Babylonia. Clearly, Aramaic was becoming a widely used language in Iraq in the last century of Assyria's life, but the examples of it are few. The large number of West Semitic, predominantly Aramaic, personal names in cuneiform legal deeds of the 7th century B.C. indicates a high proportion of Aramaic speakers, although, of course, bearing an Aramaic name does not imply the person's native language was Aramaic. Some of these people reached high office in Assyria.

Throughout the first centuries of its existence as a written language, the alphabet used by the Aramaean scribes maintained a fairly static form. The Tell Fekheriyeh statue has an unusually archaic script, but thereafter the letters follow a gradually evolving pattern. Those engraved on hard surfaces tend to be formal, but the notes scratched on clay tablets and the few ostraca reveal more cursive forms. From them descended the standard handwriting of the Persian period (called 'Assyrian writing' in Egyptian) and eventually both the square Hebrew script (also known as 'Assyrian writing' in Hebrew), and through Nabataean, the Arabic alphabet.

Fig. 5.4 Brick of Nebuchadnezzar from Babylon with Aramaic inscription *byt'ldlny*

(c) Under Babylon

The Neo-Babylonian Empire that replaced Assyria is sometimes known by the term Chaldaean. That is taken from the Hebrew Bible where the name is used in parallel with Babylonian, Nebuchadnezzar is called a Chaldaean and the Chaldaeans spoke to him in Aramaic.[10] Again, the assumption can be made that Aramaic was current in daily life, but the physical evidence is slight. There are some summary notes on cuneiform tablets and, rather curiously, a few personal names stamped on bricks of Nebuchadnezzar and Nabonidus. The latter include the Aramaic name Bethel-dilani (*byt'ldlny*) and also the name of Nabonidus (*nbwn'd*). Their significance can only be a matter of speculation.[11]

(d) Under Persia

It was under the Achaemenid Persian rulers that Aramaic came into its own. Having spread across the Fertile Crescent in the previous century, it now became the common administrative language from the Indus to Egypt. Examples of Aramaic from Iraq continue to be rare: several dozen notes scratched or written in ink on cuneiform tablets are preserved,[12] and there are two brief ostraca, one from Larsa and one from Nippur, both bearing lists of personal names, mostly Babylonian. Cylinder and stamp seals continue to carry their owners' names in Aramaic script, some of the names now being Old Persian. One seal, now displayed in the Royal Ontario Museum, is inscribed in Aramaic letters with a Persian owner's name and his father's Persian name, followed by his profession 'scribe' in Aramaic, *ḥtm 'ryrmn spr' br mzdysn*, 'Seal of Ariyaramna, the scribe, son of Mazdayasna'. The style of engraving on the seal allows a date in the late 6th or early 5th century B.C.[13] Dry areas of Egypt have preserved Aramaic texts from this time on papyrus and leather. They indicate the range of writing practised in Aramaic there and which can be assumed to have been equalled in Iraq. Among them are literary compositions, notably the Wisdom of Ahiqar, a story set in the Assyrian court of Sennacherib and Esarhaddon and probably composed in Assyria, although the proverbs it contains may have originated further west - they are written in a slightly different dialect sharing some features with Old

---

[10] 2 Kings 25: 4, 13, 25 etc.; 2 Chronicles 36: 17; Daniel 2; 4.

[11] The Aramaic names on bricks are listed by P.-R. Berger, *Die neubabylonischen Königsinschriften, Alter Orient und Altes Testament* 4/1, Neukirchen-Vluyn: Butzon & Bercker Kevelaer (1973) 22,23; for illustrations see R. Koldewey, *The Excavations of Babylon*, trans. A. S. Johns, London: Macmillan (1914) 80,81. B. Sass and J. Marzahn are preparing a publication of over 300 examples.

[12] For a recent consideration of some Persian period Aramaic notes see E. Cussini, 'A Re-examination of the Berlin Aramaic Dockets' in M. J. Geller, J. C. Greenfield, M. P. Weitzman, eds., *Studia Aramaica: New Sources and New Approaches. Journal of Semitic Studies Supplement* 4, Oxford: Oxford University Press (1995) 19-30.

[13] M.B. Garrison & P.E. Dion, 'The seal of Ariyaramna in the Royal Ontario Museum, Toronto', *Journal of Near Eastern Studies* 58 (1999) 1-17.

Aramaic texts from Syria.[14] This allows us to imagine that there was an Aramaic literature in Assyrian and Achaemenid Iraq which has disappeared. The stories in the first chapters of the biblical book of Daniel may preserve other examples.

One discovery in Egypt gives a unique glimpse of what did exist. A leather bag was found containing a group of letters written on leather. The collection may have been kept in an office, or it may have been lost in the post; since it was acquired through the antiquities' trade, its provenance is unknown. The significance of these letters is that they were sent to Egypt by the Persian governor of Egypt and his staff who were busy either in Babylon itself or in Susa. They exemplify, therefore, the Aramaic of the local chancery. Comparable documents, official letters from the royal court, are preserved in the biblical book of Ezra. There is good ground for accepting them as genuine, although some scholars are very sceptical. They were sent from Persia, but one letter to a Persian king ends, 'let a search be made in the royal treasury in Babylon, to discover if a decree was issued by king Cyrus'. This implies the existence of an archive in Babylon where, presumably, the records were kept in Aramaic. In fact, the narrative continues, the decree was found on a scroll in Ecbatana, the Median capital.[15]

Across the Persian Empire clerks wrote Aramaic in a fairly standard form, although some regional variations can be traced and loanwords were adopted from local languages. This form of the language is called Imperial or Official Aramaic. It contrasts with the Aramaic of the previous centuries, which is termed Old Aramaic. Among the notable differences are a shift in the representation of certain sounds. Where Old Aramaic used the letter *z* for the sound /dh/, the letter *d* is commonly written and where Old Aramaic marked the sound /th/ with the letter *š*, *t* is now written, so *ʾ^{a}ḥaz*, 'to hold', becomes *ʾ^{a}ḥad*, *š^{e}qel*, 'shekel', becomes *t^{e}qel*. Double or lengthened consonants often result in nasalization. The causative forms of the verb tend to have initial ʾ rather than *h*. The jussive form of the verb has a prefixed *l* (as in Akkadian) and the word order is freer, with the verb sometimes standing last, as in Akkadian.

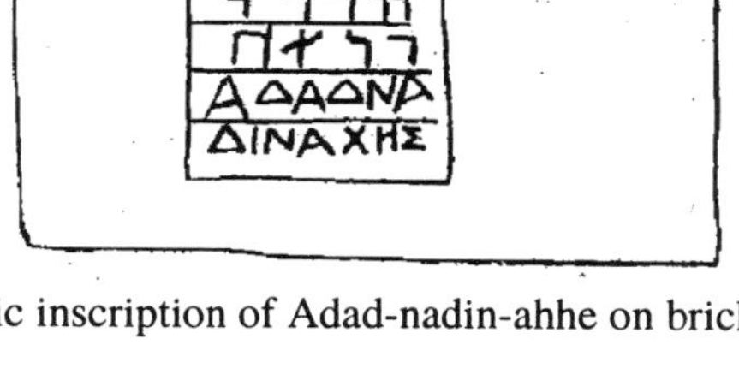

Fig. 5.5 Aramaic inscription of Adad-nadin-ahhe on bricks from Telloh

[14] See J. M. Lindenberger, *The Aramaic Proverbs of Ahiqar*, Baltimore, Johns Hopkins University Press (1983) 280-304.

[15] Ezra 5: 17; 6: 1,2.

(e) Under Greece

With the advent of Alexander, Aramaic lost its dominant position in government, but remained the everyday language for the majority of the populace. Documents remain rare. A unique cuneiform tablet preserves a magic spell written in Aramaic in the 3rd century B.C.,[16] while in the 2nd century bricks at Telloh were stamped in Greek and Aramaic with the Babylonian name Adad-nadin-ahhe and a series of glazed ones at Uruk name another local notable, Anu-uballiṭ, and give his other (Greek) name, Kephalon, in Aramaic letters.

The legacy of Aramaic is seen today not only in the forms of the language which are alive, but also in the alphabets used for writing Arabic and Hebrew, both descended from the Aramaic script of the Persian chancery.

Further reading

For inscriptions mentioned without references, see J. A. Fitzmyer & S. A. Kaufman, *An Aramaic Bibliography, Part 1. Old, Official and Biblical Aramaic*, Baltimore: Johns Hopkins University Press (1992).

Beyer, K. 1986. *The Aramaic Language*, trans. J.F. Healey. Göttingen.

Degen, R. 1969. *Altaramäische Grammatik der Inschriften des 10.-8. Jh. v. Chr.* Wiesbaden.

Dion, P.-E. 1997. *Les araméens a l'âge de fer: histoire, politique et structures sociales.* Paris.

Hoftijzer, J. & Jongeling, K. 1995. *Dictionary of the North-West Semitic Inscriptions.* Leiden.

Huehnergard, J. 1995. 'What is Aramaic?', *Aram* 7.2: 261-82.

Hug, V. 1993. *Altaramäische Grammatik der Texte des 7. und 6. Jh.s v. Chr.* Heidelberg.

Kaufman, S.A. 1997. 'Aramaic', in R. Hetzron (ed.), *The Semitic Languages*. London:114-30.

Kutscher, E. Y. 1970. 'Aramaic', in T. A. Seboek (ed.), *Current Trends in Linguistics*, 6. *Linguistics in South West Asia and North Africa*. The Hague: 347-412.

Segert, S. 1975. *Altaramäische Grammatik mit Bibliographie, Chrestomathie und Glossar.* Leipzig.

[16] See now M. J. Geller, 'The Aramaic Incantation in Cuneiform Script (AO 6489 = TCL 6,58)', *Jaarbericht Ex Oriente Lux* 35-36 (1997-2000) 127-46.

Aramaic in the Medieval and Modern Periods

Geoffrey Khan

University of Cambridge

The intention of this paper is to present a survey of the main types of Aramaic that have been used in Iraq over the period of the last two millennia. First the written sources will be discussed and this will be followed by an examination of the spoken dialects.

Main written records in Aramaic from late antiquity to the present

Various *written* forms of the Aramaic language have been produced in Iraq over the last two millennia. The texts that have come down to us may be classified into the following categories:

1. In the Hellenistic and Roman periods Greek replaced Aramaic as the administrative language of much of the Near East. Aramaic, however, continued as a written form of communication. In the territory controlled by the Parthians, which included Iraq, Aramaic still functioned to some extent as an official language. This has survived in various inscriptions. The language of these is very close to the official Aramaic of the Achaemenid period. The tradition of this official Aramaic had been weakened by this period, however, and several local varieties of Aramaic emerged. Most of the surviving texts of this nature from Iraq have been discovered in the site of the desert city of Hatra in the north-west of the country, which guarded the two main caravan routes connecting Mesopotamia with Syria and Asia Minor (see Figs. 6.1-2). This city was a cultural centre of considerable political importance, reaching its height during the 1st century A.D. A smaller corpus of Aramaic inscriptions from this period has been discovered also in nearby Assur.[1] From Uruk (Warka) we have an extraordinary case of deviation from the Aramaic literary tradition in the form of an

---

[1] The most comprehensive edition of the inscriptions from Hatra and Assur is currently that of Beyer 1998.

Aramaic magical text represented in cuneiform.[2] This is datable to the end of the Seleucid period around 150 B.C.

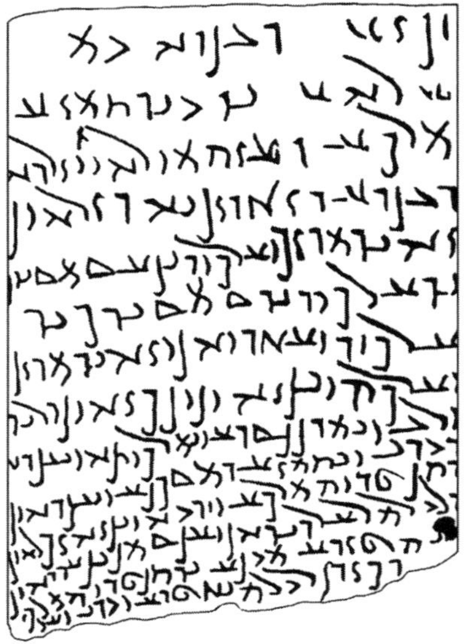

Fig. 6.1 Aramaic inscription from Hatra (after Beyer 1998, p. 10).

2. When Christianity became established in Iraq in the 1st millennium A.D., the Christians used Syriac (*lešana suryaya*) as a written language. Syriac was a literary language that was developed in Edessa, now Urfa in south-eastern Turkey. Christianity reached Edessa around 150 A.D., though a written form of Aramaic that was a precursor of classical Syriac was already in use in the pre-Christian periods, which has come down to us mainly in the form of inscriptions. The Aramaic speaking Christians preferred to designate themselves 'Syrians', a term used by the Greeks to designate the inhabitants of the Fertile Crescent, rather than the term 'Aramaeans', which had come to be used with the sense of 'pagans'. The Aramaic word *suryaya* or *suraya* eventually came to have the sense of 'Christian', as is the case in the modern Aramaic dialects.[3]

Edessa was a cultural centre in the early centuries of the Christian era. The Syriac translation of the Bible was widely adopted by the Eastern Christian communities together with the Syriac language as a means of literary expression. Syriac was written in various types of rounded script, which were distinct from the scripts used by other religious communities. An extensive literature was produced in

[2] Numerous studies have been published on this text. The latest is that of Geller 1997-2000, which contains a full bibliography.

[3] For the semantic development of the word *suraya* see Heinrichs 1993.

Fig. 6.2 Medieval and Modern Aramaic: map to show places mentioned

this language. The most creative period of Syriac literature was from the 4th century up to the time of the Islamic conquests in the 7th century. Many Syriac literary works in this period were produced by Christian scholars in Iraq, although the main schools were in what is now southern Turkey. Most of the Christians of Iraq followed Nestorian Christianity after the theological conflicts over the nature of Christ in the 5th century split the Syrian Church into two. A large number of Syriac literary works

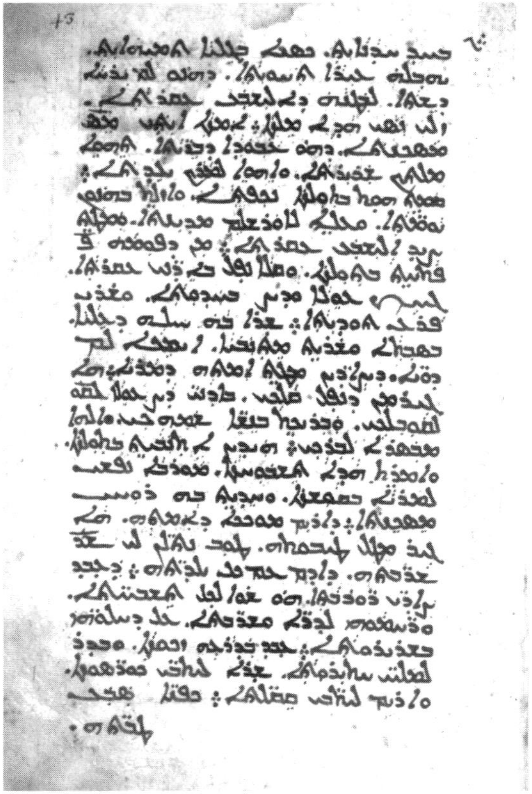

Fig. 6.3 Syriac with Eastern (Nestorian) vocalization.
© Biblioteca Apostolica Vaticana. VatSyr 83 Folio 43.

continued to be produced during the period of Arab rule until the period of the Mongols in the 13th and 14th centuries, when the creativity was considerably reduced. The Syriac language, however, was not totally abandoned but has been used by Christian writers in subsequent centuries down to modern times (Brock 1989, 1997).

In the 17th century a Christian literature emerged written in a form of Aramaic that was based on the spoken dialect of the town of Alqosh near Mosul. By this period the Nestorian Patriarchate had been split. The Christians of the northern Iraqi plain adhered to a patriarch based in Alqosh whereas those in the mountains further north had their own patriarch. Subsequently the patriarchate of Alqosh entered into communion with the Roman Catholic church and came known as 'Chaldean', and the term 'Church of the East' came to be restricted to the Nestorian Christians of the mountains. The aforementioned neo-Syriac literary language has been used by

Chaldean Christians in the region of Mosul down to modern times (Macuch 1976, Mengozzi 2000).

Another type of Neo-Syriac literary language emerged in the 19th century in Urmia, in Azerbaijan. This was originally developed by Western missionaries to that region in order to propagate Bible translations in the vernacular, but subsequently gave rise to a very variegated literature (Murre-van den Berg, 1999). This form of written Neo-Syriac, which is known as *swadaya* ('colloquial language'), was based on the spoken Christian dialect of the Urmia region, but came to be used widely by Christians in Iraq. Within the last few decades there has been an increase in the production of literature written in this form of neo-Syriac. This has been stimulated by two developments. Firstly, in 1972 in Iraq cultural rights were granted to 'speakers of the Syriac language', which allowed them to publish literature in their own language. These cultural rights, however, were rather short-lived. Secondly, since the end of the Gulf War in 1991, Christians in northern Iraq under Kurdish control have been free to publish in the Neo-Syriac language.

Fig. 6.4 Yemenite Rabbinic Babylonian Talmud

3. In the 1st millennium A.D. Aramaic was used as a literary language by Jews in Iraq. Various types of Jewish Aramaic can be distinguished, all written in the Hebrew script. These fall into three broad categories
(i) The language of the Babylonian Talmud, which was composed between the 3rd and 6th centuries, known as Babylonian Talmudic Aramaic.
(ii) The language used in the writings of Jewish scholars in the early Arab period from the 7th to the 11th centuries. This is known as the Geonic period, i.e. the period of Jewish leaders known as Geonim, and the literary form of Aramaic they used is known as Geonic Aramaic.
(iii) The language of translations of the Bible known as Targums. It is generally thought that these Targums were not composed in Iraq but in Palestine at the beginning of the 1st millennium A.D. In the course of the 1st millennium, however, they were used and transmitted in Iraq rather than in Palestine.

In the 17th century, in the same period as a literary form of Neo-Syriac emerged in the Mosul region, a type of written vernacular Jewish Aramaic began to be used in Northern Iraq. This was used mainly for recording Bible translations in the Jewish vernacular, though the extant manuscripts include some other types of texts, such as homilies. This type of written Jewish Neo-Aramaic was used down to the 20th century.

4. A literary form of Aramaic written in a distinctive script was also employed by the gnostic sect of the Mandaeans in southern Iraq known as Mandaic. This was used by them in the 1st and 2nd millennia A.D. mainly to record their sacred texts and traditions. The earliest Mandaic texts seem to have their roots in the first half of the 1st millennium, though all extant manuscripts are relatively late.

5. Finally we should mention the Aramaic that has been preserved on a corpus of magic bowls datable to the 1st millennium A.D. These were written in Syriac, Hebrew and Mandaic script, but it is often problematic to identify the type of Aramaic language represented by the scripts with other attested forms of Syriac, Jewish Aramaic and Mandaic. One reason for this may have been that the texts of the bowls were sometimes copied from one script to another. In general, however, the language of this corpus exhibits a blend of features characteristic of the other written types of Aramaic of that period.

Fig. 6.5 Aramaic incantation bowl from Babylon

Spoken vernacular Aramaic

The foregoing survey presents the main types of written Aramaic that have been produced in Iraq over the last two millennia. The question I should like to address now is to what extent these written texts reflect the vernacular language that was spoken by the people who wrote them.

It is not possible to determine with any certainty the precise distribution of vernacular languages in Iraq of earlier periods, it appears, however, that a large proportion of the population of Iraq at the end of the 1st millennium B.C. and in the first half of the 1st millennium A.D. were Aramaic speaking. Most of the territory was under the control of Iranian rulers during this period, first the Parthians (2nd century B.C.-3rd century A.D.) then the Sassanians (3rd-7th centuries A.D.). There was an aristocratic Iranian administrative upper class, who would have spoken an Iranian language. This applied also to a certain proportion of the general population who were Iranian Zoroastrians. On the fringes of the desert in the west of the country at this period Arabic would have been spoken by certain elements of the population. Most of the remainder of the population were Aramaic speaking. It is unlikely, however, that these were monolingual language communities, but rather there must have been a considerable degree of bilingualism or multilingualism.

The language of the ruling administration was Iranian, though they represented this in a writing system that was a legacy from the Official Aramaic of the Achaemenid period. This involved the use of many Aramaic words used as logograms for Iranian words. It is not possible to establish how widely the Iranian language of the ruling administration was spoken throughout Iraq, though it is likely that a considerable proportion of people were bilingual in Aramaic and Iranian. This is reflected by the existence of lexical and grammatical elements in the Aramaic of this period that were borrowed from Iranian.

We cannot be certain exactly what vernacular Aramaic was like in the 1st millennium A.D., but it is probable that none of the aforementioned types of written Aramaic corresponded exactly to the form of Aramaic that was spoken by the writer. These were all literary languages that followed traditions from earlier periods and transcended much of the local diversity that would be expected to have existed in the spoken vernaculars. It should be pointed out, however, that some of these written languages appear to have diverged from the spoken Aramaic dialects more than others. Also one should distinguish between the orthographic written form of the language and the way this language was read aloud. We have evidence for such oral reading of a number of the aforementioned types of literary Aramaic.

The pre-Christian epigraphic materials from the Seleucid and Parthian periods still exhibit the influence of the literary tradition of Achaemenid Official Aramaic, though a few local features surface in the texts. This appears to be the result of the weakening of the literary tradition of Aramaic rather than an attempt to represent the vernacular. It should be noted that many of the inscriptions were produced in an environment where Aramaic was not the only vernacular language that was spoken. Indeed in the city of Hatra, from where most of the inscriptions emanate, various languages are likely to have been spoken, including Arabic, since the city was ruled at a certain period by the chieftains of Arab tribes, and Aramaic may not have been the first language of the scribe.

A special case is the Uruk text from the end of the Seleucid period, which contains Aramaic in cuneiform transcription. There has been no complete scholarly consensus concerning the interpretation of the Aramaic in this text, but it clearly exhibits some features that are characteristic of the eastern Aramaic dialects of the 1st millennium A.D. rather than the official Aramaic of the Achaemenid period. It appears to be relatively unconstrained by the conventions of an Aramaic literary tradition and is likely to reflect quite closely the vernacular Aramaic of the scribe. No doubt the fact that the text was not written with the Aramaic alphabet weakened its connection with the literary tradition of Aramaic.

Syriac, as remarked, was a literary language that was developed in Edessa. In this region the continuity of the Aramaic literary tradition had been interrupted by Greek in the Hellenistic period, so the new literary language of Syriac seems to have risen largely from the local vernacular. This presumably was closest to the spoken language of the region of Edessa. Syriac was used as a literary language of Aramaic speaking Eastern Christians over a vast area throughout Syria, Iraq and beyond. Although it was of a largely fixed uniform structure, the writers who used this literary language must have spoken a wide variety of vernacular dialects. The spoken form of Aramaic that has survived to the present day exhibits considerable dialectal diversity, especially among the eastern dialects of Iraq and the adjacent regions and it is likely that a similar dialectal diversity would have existed at an earlier period.

The traditional pronunciation of Syriac reflects linguistic developments that are not represented in the written orthographic tradition of the language, such as the elision of final vowels in certain contexts. This is likely to be due to the fact that the reading tradition is a closer representation of the vernacular than the orthographic tradition. The elision of these short vowels can be traced to an early date. Moreover, the reading tradition of Syriac exhibits regional differences in that the western tradition of the Jacobite church is distinct from that of the eastern tradition of the Nestorian church. These pronunciation traditions exhibit features that are distinctive of the modern western and eastern dialects respectively, so they are likely to have had their origin in the regional vernaculars of the 1st millennium. One of the distinctive features, for example, is the pronunciation of an original long *ā* vowel. In the Western Jacobite tradition this was pronounced as a mid rounded vowel *o* whereas the Eastern Nestorian tradition preserved the unrounded quality *a*. Likewise the western form of modern Aramaic spoken in Syria has the rounded vowel *o* whereas the modern eastern dialects have the unrounded vowel *a*. These differences in pronunciation traditions of Syriac, although apparently having their roots in the regional spoken dialects, came to be associated with the denomination of the church that a community belonged to, irrespective of the local vernacular. Examples of this can be found in the way that Syriac is pronounced in the Christian communities of modern Iraq. All surviving vernacular dialects of Aramaic in Iraq have the unrounded *a* vowel as a reflex of an original long *ā*. Some villages on the Mosul plain changed their allegiance from the Nestorian church to the Jacobite church around the 7th century, such as Qaraqosh. In Qaraqosh today the Syriac that is used in the liturgy is recited with the western type of pronunciation with *o* for original long *ā*, whereas the reflex of this vowel is unrounded *a* in the local spoken Aramaic dialect.

The grammatical structure of Syriac is considerably different from that of the surviving spoken Aramaic dialects in Iraq and, crucially, it appears that they are not direct descendants of Syriac. Although the modern dialects have undergone far-reaching linguistic changes, some of the spoken Christian dialects in Iraq exhibit features that are typologically more archaic than Syriac. It is likely, therefore, that already in the first half of the 1st millennium A.D. the literary language of Syriac would have differed from the vernacular of the writers. This must have been *a fortiori* the case in later periods. Indeed, in medieval Syriac literature one can find allusions to the 'corrupt' form of the language that was spoken by the common people. Moreover, after the Arab conquests in the 7th century, many Christian communities became Arabic speaking. The details of the Arabicization of the Christians are not completely clear, but it is known that some Arabic speaking Christians continued to use Syriac as a literary language.

The literary form of neo-Syriac that developed in Alqosh in the 17th century was clearly much closer to the spoken vernacular than classical Syriac. One should be cautious, however, of assuming that this was identical to the spoken language of the writers. Although based on the vernacular, it contains numerous classical Syriac features, at least in the orthography. Furthermore, the scribes who used this language did not come exclusively from Alqosh, but from a variety of villages where different dialects were spoken. The language, therefore, functioned to some extent as a supra-dialectal literary language. The same remarks apply to the literary neo-Syriac known as *swadaya*, which was based on the Urmia dialect.

The Jewish Aramaic of the Babylonian Talmud at first sight appears to be much closer to vernacular Aramaic than is the case with Syriac. The language exhibits a high degree of diversity in its phonology and morphology, which is a phenomenon that one often meets in a spoken vernacular but which is generally avoided in a standardized literary language. This is one of the reasons why classical Syriac is easier to learn and describe than Babylonian Talmudic Aramaic. Syriac is a literary language with standardized rules, whereas Babylonian Talmudic Aramaic is more of a transcription of oral traditions of debates between scholars that were conducted in a language closer to the vernacular. Various features of the language anticipate developments that are found in the modern Aramaic vernaculars of Iraq but that are absent in classical Syriac. One case in point is the particle *qā*, which in Babylonian Talmudic Aramaic is prefixed to active participles that are used as present tense verbs. This is the forerunner of the preverbal particle *k-* of the modern dialects. Such a particle is not used in Syriac, but it is interesting to note that the Syriac scholar Barhebraeus, writing in the 13th century, reports the occurrence of this particle (with the form *kā*) in the Aramaic speech of Eastern Christians (Moberg 1922: 205; 1907: 30; Heinrichs 2002 :249).

Even Babylonian Talmudic Aramaic, however, is unlikely to correspond completely to the spoken language of the period. We have various sources for reconstructing the pronunciation of this form of Aramaic. One of these is a corpus of medieval manuscripts with vocalization signs. A particularly interesting source is the reading tradition of the Babylonian Talmud that was transmitted among the Jews of Yemen until the 20th century. It has been demonstrated (Morag 1981, 1988) that this Yemenite reading tradition has its roots in early medieval Iraq, when Yemenite scholars used to travel to study with Talmudic scholars in the Iraqi Rabbinic schools. The reading tradition used by Iraqi Jews in modern times, by contrast, is a later type of pronunciation. The Yemenite reading tradition seems to preserve a rather more vernacular form of the language than is reflected in the traditional written text of the Talmud. As remarked already, the oral reading tradition of a literary language often reflects a more vernacular form of the language than is represented by the orthography of the written tradition.

Texts written in so-called Jewish Geonic Aramaic between the 7th and 11th centuries follow more closely literary traditions of Aramaic than is the case with the language of the Babylonian Talmud. In these chronologically later texts one finds typologically earlier grammatical features. These are grammatical features that can be traced to literary forms of Aramaic that were in use at the beginning of the 1st millennium A.D. The Jewish Aramaic Targums that were transmitted in Iraq were composed in such a literary language in Palestine and so do not in principle reflect the vernacular of the Iraqi Jewish communities. It should be noted, however, that the reading tradition of the Targums reflected by the vocalization of the medieval manuscripts, which originates in Iraq rather than in Palestine, may reflect some features of the vernacular, as is the case with the reading traditions of Syriac. To give one example, there is a tendency in the Iraqi reading tradition of the Targums to use one set of pronominal suffixes on both singular and plural nouns, which is a feature of the modern Aramaic dialects. Finally, it should be pointed out that some sections of the Babylonian Talmud contain types of Aramaic that are more literary in form than others and resemble Geonic Aramaic.

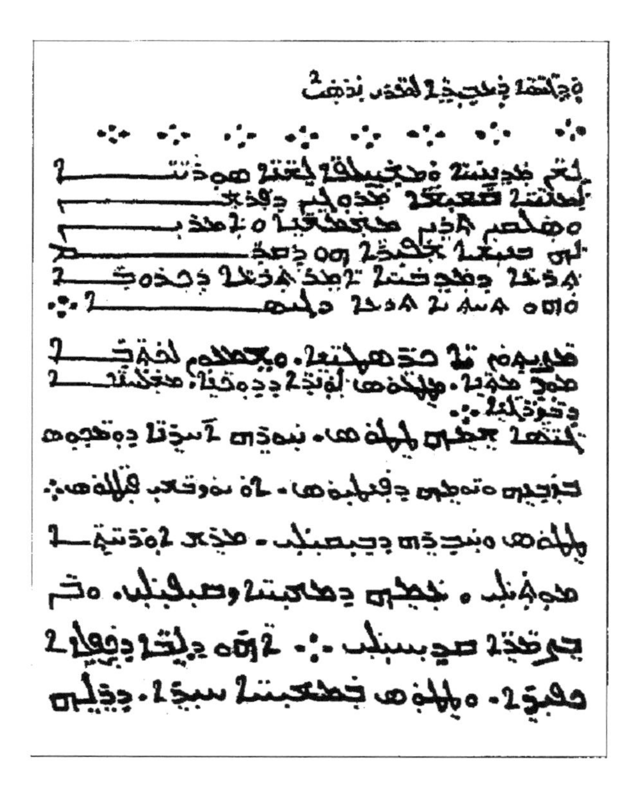

Fig. 6.6 Christian literary neo-Aramaic manuscript of 'The thief and the angel' (after Pennacchietti 1993, p. 124).

The literary form of Jewish Neo-Aramaic that emerged in the 17th century in Northern Iraq was clearly very close to the spoken vernacular. It also came to be used in several regional varieties that reflected the local dialects. It is not possible to establish how closely this written language corresponded to the spoken dialect before the 20th century. We can, however, compare it with the spoken dialects in the 20th century and we see that the written language is not an exact reflection of the contemporary spoken language. The written language, which was still being used in the 20th century, exhibits various archaic features that are not found in the vernacular.

Mandaic is closely related to Babylonian Talmudic Aramaic and exhibits many of the developments in phonology and morphology that appear to be characteristic of the vernacular of the 1st millennium A.D. As with Babylonian Talmudic Aramaic, however, it is likely that the written language never corresponded to the vernacular completely. Some features of the orthography are archaic and continue conventions of the official Aramaic used during the Parthian period (Beyer 1986: 30). There exists today a modern spoken dialect of Mandaic, which has survived in the region of Ahvāz in south-west Iran. At an earlier period this was spoken also in southern Iraq, though now the Mandaeans of Iraq are all Arabic speaking (with the exception of a few families who are migrants from Iran). This modern spoken dialect of Mandaic seems to be more or less a direct descendant of the classical Mandaic language (Macuch 1976, introduction), but in order to undergo the linguistic developments that it exhibits, it must have started to evolve many centuries ago. By the time the earliest surviving manuscripts of classical Mandaic were written in the 2nd millennium A.D., the forebear of the modern spoken vernacular must have been noticeably distinct from the classical written language. Indeed in most written Mandaic texts that have survived in the manuscripts there are traces of the modern vernacular form of the language.

The Aramaic of the magic bowls is not at all uniform. Numerous linguistic differences are found across the corpus. In general, however, most bowls exhibit a combination of features characteristic of the early literary traditions of Aramaic together with more advanced features that appear to be closer to the vernacular and often have parallels with Babylonian Talmudic Aramaic or Mandaic. Although many of these texts seem to have been written by poorly educated scribes, on balance they exhibit more literary and less typologically developed features than the two aforementioned written languages.

After the Arab conquests in the 7th century A.D. the Aramaic speaking population of Iraq began to adopt Arabic as their vernacular. Converts to Islam, as a matter of course, adopted the Arabic language, though the speech also of the inhabitants of the region who did not convert was gradually Arabicized. This shift from Aramaic to Arabic in the non-Muslim population was quite slow in some areas. Indeed it can be said that it is still on-going today. Arabic became established in the urban centres of central and southern Iraq before the rural communities. The Jews in Iraq ceased using Aramaic as a written language by the 11th century and adopted

Arabic as a written language. The survival of written Jewish Aramaic for four centuries after the Arabic conquests may be due in part to the fact that the Jewish academic centres of Sura, Nehardea and Pumbeditha were situated in rural areas rather than in the large cities. It appears that still in the 10th century there were Jews throughout Iraq who were Aramaic speaking, since the Jewish Karaite scholar al-Qirqisānī complained that at that period the Hebrew recited by the Jews of Iraq had been influenced by the Aramaic vernacular, which he, like many medieval Arabic authors, refers to as the language of the *nabaṭ* ('Nabataeans').[4] The majority of the Jewish population of central and southern Iraq, however, were based in the urban centres, as was the case down to the 20th century, and they appear to have adopted Arabic as a vernacular reasonably quickly. It should be pointed out that the process of Arabicization would have begun with a period of bilingualism, which has, indeed, left the imprint of Aramaic on some of the Jewish dialects of Arabic that survived into the 20th century.

The Christians were found more in rural communities and it is difficult to establish how quickly they were Arabicized. It should be noted that some Christians in the western region of the country, on the margins of the desert, appear to have been Arabic speaking even before the rise of Islam. This is likely to be the case, for example, with the Christians of al-Ḥīra. Syriac was familiar to such Arabic-speaking Christians as a literary language. This is demonstrated, for example, by the famous translator of Syriac texts Ḥunayn ibn 'Isḥāq who was a Nestorian Christian from al-Ḥīra. As Arabicization progressed many Christians in Iraq began to write in Arabic, with a burgeoning of Nestorian Arabic literature in the 11th century. Syriac, nevertheless, continued to be used for many centuries by Arabic speaking Christians. As with the Jews, Arabicization would have begun with a period of bilingualism. In the course of the Middle Ages many of the Christians of central Iraq migrated to the North of the country to avoid forced conversion with its consequent Arabicization. We know, for example, that around the 11th century a large proportion of the Christian population of Tikrit, together with the Christian primate known as the *maphryan*, migrated northwards and settled in the Mosul region, many in the town of Qaraqosh. In the Timurid invasions of the 14th century the Christian communities of central and southern Iraq were decimated, which would have hastened the end of any vestiges of Aramaic in this region. However, the Christian communities in the mountains in the North of the country and in villages on the nearby plain who fled to the mountains were largely spared the ravages of these invaders.

In modern times spoken Aramaic has indeed survived in the North of the country, and it is to these modern spoken dialects that we shall now turn our attention. A spoken form of Mandaic survived in southern Iraq down to at least the 19th century, but by the 20th century it had virtually fallen from use. It has remained

---

[4]Khan 1990: 66.

alive, nevertheless, in the Mandaean community in south-western Iran. In what follows we shall restrict ourselves to a consideration of the northern dialects.

Since there have been major changes in the linguistic situation over the last few decades, we shall first look at the situation that existed in the middle of the 20th century. At that period Aramaic was spoken by Christian and Jewish communities in an area that can be defined roughly as the region lying to the North of a line drawn diagonally across a map connecting Mosul and Kirkuk. The southern boundary of the Aramaic speaking area, therefore, was far further down on the east side than on the west side. Indeed it was spoken by Jews as far south as Khānaqīn. Aramaic was never spoken as a vernacular by Muslims in this area. The Muslims speak Kurdish, Arabic or Turkman. Within this area also some Jewish and Christian communities were primarily Arabic speaking, especially in the larger towns. One should take into account, furthermore, that the Aramaic speaking Jews and Christians were at least bilingual in Aramaic and Kurdish or Aramaic and Arabic and frequently multilingual. Some of the Muslim Kurdish speakers were able to communicate with Christians and Jews in Aramaic. Numerous Aramaic speaking Christians and Jews have converted to Islam in this area over the centuries and have married into Kurdish families. This probably explains why today several Aramaic loanwords can be identified in Kurdish.

The vernacular Aramaic dialect area of northern Iraq continued into north-west Iran and, at least at the beginning of the 20th century, into south-eastern Turkey.

This dialect group, which is nowadays referred to as North-Eastern Neo-Aramaic, exhibits a very great diversity. Differences were found in the dialects from village to village. Of particular interest is the fact that dialectal cleavage occurred not only according to geographical area but also according to religious community. The Jewish dialects were considerably different from the Christian dialects even when the two communities were in close geographical contact. In several cases Jewish and Christian communities inhabited the same town but spoke totally different Aramaic dialects. This applied, for example, to the communities of northern Iraqi towns such as Zakho, Koy Sanjaq and Sulemaniyya. Some examples from the dialects of Sulemaniyya:

Jewish Sulemaniyya	Christian Sulemaniyya	
bela	*besa*	'house'
'ila	*'ida*	'hand'
'at	*'ayit*	'you (ms.)'
'at	*'ayat*	'you (fs.)'
qiṭlale	*tam-qaṭilla*	'He killed her'
-ye	*-ile*	3ms copula
-ya	*-ila*	3fs copula
-yen	*-ilu*	3pl. copula
ya-y	*k-ase-le*	'He is coming'
(infinitive + copula)	(present verb + copula)	

As can be seen, there are substantial differences between these two dialects in phonology and morphology. There are also important syntactic differences. The Jewish dialect of Sulemaniyya was, in fact, much more closely related in structure to other Jewish dialects spoken in towns situated at considerable geographical distances from Sulemaniyya, such as Arbil to the West and Urmia in Iran, than to the Christian dialect spoken in the same town. This communal dialectal cleavage has apparently been brought about by different migration histories of the two religious communities and also by the fact that social proximity has been a more powerful force in the formation of the dialects than geographical proximity.

The Jewish dialects can be divided into two main subgroups, which, in broad terms, are divided by the Great Zab river (see map, p. 97). Dialects that were spoken to the South and East of the Great Zab river, which may be termed the 'south-eastern dialects', exhibit a variety of shared innovative features that are not found in the dialects spoken to the North of the river, which may be termed the 'north-western dialects'. The main Aramaic speaking Jewish communities in Iraq belonging to the south-eastern group were found in Sulemaniyya, Ḥalabja, Rustaqa, Qaladeze, Koy Sanjaq, Ruwanduz and villages on the Arbil plain (though not in the town of Arbil, where the Jews were Arabic speaking). The main Jewish communities speaking Aramaic dialects in the north-western group were found in Zakho, Amedia and Dohok. One of the most conspicuous features of the south-eastern group of Jewish dialects that distinguishes it from the north-western group, and indeed from all of the Christian dialects, is the shift of interdental consonants to the lateral consonant /l/, e.g.

Jewish Dohok	Jewish Sulemaniyya	
beṯa	*bela*	'house'

Such a clear-cut subgrouping cannot be identified in the Christian dialects of Iraq, though in general the dialects spoken in the villages on the plain of Mosul tend to be more archaic in structure than the other dialects. The dialect of the village of Qaraqosh lying on the Mosul plain at the southern periphery of the Aramaic speaking area is one of the most archaizing of the spoken Aramaic dialects in Iraq. The Christian dialects are spoken in a greater number of settlements than the Jewish dialects. Whereas the Jews tended to be urban residents and worked as craftsmen or merchants a large proportion of the Christians were agriculturalists residing in scores of small villages across the Aramaic speaking region. As already remarked, however, some Christians resided in towns side-by-side with Jewish communities.

Neither the Jewish nor the Christian spoken dialects appear to be direct descendants of the earlier literary forms of Aramaic such as Babylonian Talmudic Aramaic and Syriac, which emerged in the 1st millennium A.D. The historical phonology of the Jewish dialects is different from that of Babylonian Talmudic Aramaic. To give one example, in Babylonian Talmudic Aramaic, and also in closely related Mandaic, the unvoiced pharyngal *ḥ* was weakened to a laryngal *h* whereas in the modern Jewish spoken dialects a historical **ḥ* has generally shifted to a velar fricative *x* or has been retained. The weakening of this pharyngal does not occur in the eastern reading tradition of Syriac. In this respect, therefore, it appears to be closer to that of the modern dialects, which suggests that the reading tradition originated in the north in the region where the North Eastern Neo-Aramaic dialects were spoken in modern times. The eastern reading tradition of Syriac conforms to the historical phonology of the modern dialects in another respect, namely the pronunciation of the fricative alternant of *b* as a bilabial *w* (cf. Bar Hebraeus, in Moberg 1922: 205; 1907: 30). It is interesting to note that some of the Syriac magic bowls from the 1st millennium exhibit a weakening of the unvoiced pharyngal *ḥ* as in Babylonian Jewish Aramaic and Mandaic (Juusola 1999: 40), which may reflect the southern provenance of such bowls. In other respects, nonetheless, modern dialects differ from Syriac. What is particularly significant is that some of the modern Christian dialects exhibit features that are more archaic than the corresponding features in classical Syriac. In the dialect of Qaraqosh, for example, the infinitives of all verbal stems lack an initial *m-*, by contrast with Syriac infinitives, which have acquired this prefix by analogy with the participles.

The lexicon of the modern dialects, moreover, has preserved some words from antiquity that are not found in the earlier literary languages. These include several words from Akkadian. They are usually connected with agriculture. Several such cases can be found in the dialect of Qaraqosh. In that dialect, for example, the word *baxšimə* denotes a storeroom (for grain) in the roof of a house. It is reasonably certain that this is a descendant of the Akkkadian term *bēt ḫašīmi* 'barn, storehouse'.[5] Another possible example in the dialect is *raxiṣa* 'pile of straw (usually barley)', which could well be related to Akkadian *raḫīṣu* 'pile of harvest produce (especially straw).'[6]

Despite such archaisms, however, the dialects in general exhibit radical linguistic developments from what is found in the earlier literary dialects. This is seen particularly in the verbal system. The two finite verb forms of earlier Aramaic, known as the suffix conjugation (*qṭal*) and the prefix conjugation (*yiqṭol, liqṭol, niqṭol*) have been completely replaced by participles, which have acquired verbal properties and verbal inflection. One of the most fascinating aspects of the verbal system is the use of ergative inflection in the past tense forms, i.e. past actions are expressed by a passive construction with the patient being presented as the grammatical subject rather than an active construction with the agent as the grammatical subject, e.g.

kalba ngiz-le gora

'The dog — was bitten by him the man' = 'The dog bit the man'

[5] CAD vol. 6, p.141; AHw, vol. 1, p.334.

[6] Salonen 1968: 274; AHw, vol. 2, p.943.

The dialects have been extensively influenced by the Iranian languages of the region, especially Kurdish. This is evident in the high proportion of lexical borrowing from Kurdish. In some of the Jewish dialects up to 65% of the nouns are loans from Kurdish. It seems that contact with Kurdish has induced the development of the ergative inflection in the Aramaic dialects, since Kurdish dialects have similar ergative constructions, which are a heritage from earlier Iranian dialects. We are not, however, dealing here with a straightforward transfer of linguistic structure from modern Kurdish into modern Aramaic. Most spoken Aramaic dialects in Iraq exhibit an analogical extension of the ergative inflection from transitive verbs to intransitive verbs. This has not happened in Kurdish. It seems, rather, to be a development internal to Aramaic that must have a considerable time depth. In fact, traces of ergative inflection of past tense verbs is found in Aramaic as early as the 5th century B.C. and also in the main literary languages, Syriac, Babylonian Talmudic Aramaic and Mandaic, in the 1st millennium A.D. This must have arisen by contact with earlier forms of Iranian, such as Old Persian and Middle Persian, where ergative constructions are found. What is particularly interesting is the fact that in classical Syriac texts a number of cases are found where the ergative inflection is used with intransitive verbs. This is presumably the result of interference from the vernacular and shows that the analogical extension of the ergative inflection to intransitives had taken place many centuries ago in the vernacular.

Furthermore, the Aramaic dialects often exhibit contact-induced features that do not correspond to what is found in the Kurdish dialect with which it has been in contact in modern times but can, nevertheless, be identified with features in Kurdish dialects, or indeed in other languages, in a more remote location. This presumably indicates that the ancestors of the Aramaic speakers of such a dialect must have migrated from other regions at some historical period. It appears from the investigation of the background of such contact-induced features, for example, that many of the ancestors of the Jewish dialects in the south-eastern Iraqi group migrated from North-West Iran and Azerbaijan.

Conclusion

In sum, the spoken Aramaic dialects offer a fascinating field of linguistic research. They exhibit a remarkable diversity, which includes some features that are more archaic than what is found in the earlier literary languages and some features that are more typologically advanced. They also show how the social boundaries of religious communities can be important linguistic boundaries. The dialects are unlikely to be direct descendants of the literary languages, but rather existed side-by-side with them at an earlier period. Some of the innovations seen in the modern dialects appear to have emerged at a much earlier period and these occasionally surface through the cracks in the literary languages.

Much of the foregoing description of the modern dialects has been presented in the past tense. This is because I have been describing the linguistic situation up to the middle of the last century. Since that date much of this situation has changed. In the early 1950s all the Jewish communities left Iraq and settled, for the most part, in Israel. Now, good speakers of these dialects are becoming increasingly difficult to find and they are all of an advanced age. Over the last few decades many of the Christian Aramaic dialects in Iraq have become endangered. One way this has come about is through the enforced Arabicization of the Aramaic speaking communities by the Ba'thist regime. Another cause is the displacement of the communities due to the destruction of their villages. In the late 1970s and early 1980s, for example, hundreds of Kurdish and Christian villages were destroyed along the border with Turkey. This included the Aramaic speaking villages of the Barwar valley, whose dialect exhibits fascinating developments in the verbal system. The inhabitants of these villages fled to the big towns or, like many thousands of Iraqi Christians over the last few decades, to a new life outside Iraq. In previous decades many other Aramaic Christian communities in the region were destroyed, the most horrific incident in the 20th century being the destruction of the Nestorian Christian villages in south-eastern Turkey during the First World War.

For these reasons the spoken Aramaic dialects of Iraq and the surrounding region, which are the last vestiges of a language with a history of almost 3,000 years, are now in serious danger of extinction. Many of them still remain undescribed. I believe the description of these dialects is one of the most important and urgent tasks for Semitic philology in the next two decades.

Further reading, references and abbreviations

AHw = W. Von Soden, *Akkadisches Handwörterbuch.*

Beyer, K., 1998. *Die aramäischen Inschriften aus Assur, Hatra und dem übrigen Ostmesopotamien (datiert 44 v. Chr. bis 238 n. Chr.).* Göttingen: Vandenhoeck & Ruprecht.

Brock, S., 1989. Some observations on the use of Classical Syriac in the late twentieth century, *Journal of Semitic Studies* 34, 363-75.

Brock, S., 1997. *A Brief Outline of Syriac Literature.* Kottayam: St. Ephraim Ecumenical Research Institute.

CAD = *The Assyrian Dictionary of the Oriental Institute of Chicago.*

Geller, M.J. 1997-2000. The Aramaic Incantation in Cuneiform Script (AO 6489 = TCL 6, 58), *Jaarbericht ex Oriente Lux* 35-36, 127-46.

Heinrichs, W. 2002. Peculiarities of the verbal system of Senāya within the framework of North Eastern Neo-Aramaic (NENA), in W. Arnold & H. Bobzin (eds.), *"Sprich doch mit deinen Knechten aramäisch, wir verstehen es!" 60 Beiträge zur Semitistik. Festschrift für Otto Jastrow zum 60. Geburtsag*, Wiesbaden: Harrassowitz, 238-68.

Heinrichs, W. 1993. The modern Assyrians - Name and Nation, in R. Contini, F.A. Pennachietti, M. Tosco (eds.), *Semitica. Serta Philologica C. Tsereteli dicata.* Turin: Silvio Zamorani, 99-114.

Juusola, H. 1999. *Linguistic Peculiarities in the Aramaic Magic Bowl Texts.* Helsinki: Finnish Oriental Society..

Khan, G. 1990. The opinions of al-Qirqisānī concerning the text of the Bible and parallel Muslim attitudes towards the text of the Qur'ān, *Jewish Quarterly Review* 81, 59-73.

Macuch, R. 1976. *Geschichte der spät- und neusyrischen Literatur.* Berlin: de Gruyter.

Mengozzi, A. 2000. *A Story in a Truthful Language: Neo-Syriac Poems by Israel of Alqosh and Joseph of Telkepe (North Iraq, 17th century).* Leuven: Peters.

Moberg, A. 1907, 1913. *Buch der Strahlen. Die grössere Grammatik des Barhebräus.* Erster Teil, 1913, Zweiter Teil, 1907. Leipzig: Harrassowitz.

Moberg, A. (ed.) 1922. *Le Livre des Splendeurs. La Grande Grammaire de Grégoire Barhebraeus.* Lund: Gleerup.

Morag, S. 1981. On the background of the tradition of Babylonian Aramaic in the Yemenite community [in Hebrew], in S. Morag & I. Ben-Ami (eds.), *Studies in Geniza and Sephardi Heritage presented to Shelomo Dov Goitein.* Jerusalem: Magnes, 137-171.

- 1988. *Babylonian Aramaic: The Yemenite Tradition* [in Hebrew]. Jerusalem: Ben Zvi Institute.

Murre-van den Berg, H.L. 1999. *From a Spoken to a Written Language : the Introduction and Development of Literary Urmia Aramaic in the Nineteenth Century.* Leiden: Nederlands Instituut voor het Nabije Oosten.

Pennacchietti, F.A. 1993. *Il ladrone e il cherubino. Dramma liturgico cristiano orientale in siriaco e neoaramaico.* Turin.

Salonen, A. 1968. *Agricultura Mesopotamica nach sumerisch-akkadischen Quellen. Eine lexikalische und kultutrgeschichtliche Untersuchung.* Annales Academiae Scientiarum Fennicae B/149. Helsinki: Finnish Academy of Sciences.

Fig. 7.1 The author with an Alqoshi informant at his home in Damascus

Fieldwork in Neo-Aramaic

Eleanor Coghill

University of Cambridge

Fieldwork is a term that is used in many disciplines, among them anthropology, biology and sociology, and describes the activity of gathering raw data. In the context of language it entails finding speakers of the language (termed 'informants'), recording samples of their speech and asking them questions about the language. Later the fieldworker transcribes these sessions and analyses the data to build up a picture of the language, in particular its grammar and lexicon.

Fieldwork is not always a part of the work of linguists. When the language studied is dead, then of course it is not possible to find speakers of the dialect and one must depend on written sources. But in research on Neo-Aramaic fieldwork is essential, as the vast majority of dialects have no written form. What is more, there is a great deal of variation among the dialects, even from one village to the next, as Prof. Khan outlines in his paper. This may seem surprising, as languages are often viewed as monolithic entities with a single grammar and lexicon, laid down in books. This impression is encouraged by the spread of standard forms of languages, which are taught to children as the only correct form. In fact across the world, variation is the norm, in some places from region to region, elsewhere from village to village. The rise of literacy as well as improved communications and more centralised government tend to erode these differences, yet in many parts of the world they are still very marked. For instance a Syrian friend told me that he could tell whether people in his village came from the centre of the village or from the edge, only judging by their accent. My grandmother reported something similar for the small crofting area in Shetland where she grew up.

So the rich variety we find in Neo-Aramaic is nothing strange. Unfortunately dialectal variation is sometimes neglected in Linguistics. One might ask why it is so important to document all the different dialects of Neo-Aramaic. Surely it is enough to document one or two to get an idea of how the language works? But in fact it is often in the details that the most interesting facts emerge. In every dialect there are features that are new and features that are very ancient and each dialect that we look at casts some new light on the history of Neo-Aramaic. If we do not try to uncover the full diversity that exists, then we may overlook some very interesting linguistic features, sometimes very old ones that can cast light even on the ancient Semitic languages.

The ideal, therefore, would be to record all the dialects of the villages and towns where Neo-Aramaic is spoken, or was spoken till recently, and this is what Neo-Aramaicists try to do. But there are constraints on such research. In an ideal world linguists would go to each of the villages in turn, recording the speech of the villagers in their community, making sure they had a cross-section of the generations. Due to the political situation, however, fieldwork in Iraq has not been an easy undertaking. This has not made research impossible however, as there are large communities living abroad, many of whom have only left their villages or towns in the last ten years. Therefore most fieldwork has been done outside Iraq in these exile communities: in London, Germany, Detroit, Chicago, Jerusalem and many other places. In the case of the Jewish dialects, fieldwork in situ is no longer even theoretically possible as there are no communities left in their original towns and villages, the Iraqi Jewish community having emigrated in the 1950s.

So fieldwork in Neo-Aramaic, unlike in other endangered languages, does not usually entail trips to very exotic places. Many linguists studying endangered languages go to the Amazon rainforest or Papua New Guinea, living with tribes in remote areas. My experience was rather more mundane: most of my fieldwork on the Christian dialect of Alqosh has been conducted on day-trips to Hampton Wick and Golders Green.

Of course, the disadvantage of doing fieldwork in exile communities is that the language is heard outside its native environment. The linguist misses out on an understanding of the cultural and material environment that comes naturally when one lives in a place. So it takes a greater effort to understand distinctions between, for example, one type of pot and another. I often have to rely on the speaker's descriptions of things I've never seen, and try to find an accurate English translation. Another problem is that the variety of language use that we are able to record is limited. We hear natural, spontaneous conversation less, especially when the informant does not live with people from his own village. We also hear the language in a restricted variety of contexts. We may never hear what people say when they go into a shop, or when they greet each other on the street. Instead, we have to ask the speaker to describe these things and hope that their description and our interpretation are both accurate.

In addition to these problems, the language of exiles is often changed by their residence abroad; it is influenced by the new languages that they speak and hear. So in Baghdad you would find many more Arabic loanwords, while in London or Detroit you may find English influence. In Detroit I found that they were not only borrowing English nouns, which are relatively easy to borrow, but even English verbs, despite the fact that the Semitic verbal system is very alien to English: lexical meaning is primarily expressed by a three-consonant 'root' while vowels primarily express grammatical distinctions. One example I heard was 'they charged it up', which came out as *kemčarjila*, where English 'charge' has been completely adapted to the Semitic Neo-Aramaic verbal system, with prefixes and suffixes. Another example quoted to me was *kemkaneṣluxla* 'we cancelled it':

kem-čarj-i-la (root *črj*)	*kem-kaneṣl-ux-la* (root *knṣl*)[1]
PAST-charge-they-it	PAST-cancel-we-it

In addition to influence from other languages, there may also be influence from other Neo-Aramaic dialects. Even when people live among their community, they may not necessarily use their own dialect on a regular basis. If their village dialect is not familiar to most of their community, they may modify it or switch dialect in order to be understood. This can also happen if they marry someone from a different village. So when we collect data from people living in this situation we have to understand that it may differ in certain aspects from the data we would collect in the village itself, were we able to go there.

While taking these difficulties into consideration, we have to work with the situation that we have. Fortunately, with a good informant, especially one who has only recently left the village and perhaps lives with family members who speak the same dialect, these difficulties are not too serious. They are further minimized if one can find a reasonable number of informants from the same village and confirm the findings with different people.

Wherever fieldwork is conducted, the basic methodology is the same. There are two main methods. One is to record samples of speech. The speaker is asked to talk about topics and is recorded as he or she talks. These samples, which we call texts, are later transcribed and the grammar and lexicon contained within them is analysed. It may be most useful to ask about aspects of village life, such as festivals, people's professions, the food they eat, traditional clothing etc. Such topics tend to yield more Aramaic vocabulary, rather than, for example, Arabic loanwords, and they are also of ethnological interest. We also gather stories, which are useful for getting examples of the past tenses and can be of interest in themselves. I have gathered some traditional tales and also some true stories. For example, one such story tells how a traditional doctor healed a broken back; another recounts the story of the disappearance and death of the informant's grandmother.

The other main method of research is to ask questions about the grammar or lexicon. We may ask straightforward questions like, 'How would you say "I want to go"' or 'What does such and such mean?' Or we may present them with two words or two sentences and ask what the difference is. If I wish to get the precise meaning of a

[1] 'Cancel' is interpreted as a four-consonant root, which is rarer than the standard three-consonant root.

word, I may ask the informant to think up typical situations or contexts in which it might be used.

Both these methods are indispensable for a good description. Texts provide samples of relatively natural speech where words and idioms can be heard in context, but even very large and varied corpuses will not provide the researcher with complete paradigms or exhaustive lexical lists. Questioning allows the linguist to fill in the inevitable gaps that arise and also to benefit from the informant's native intuitions about his language. Problems can arise when the informant has preconceived ideas about what is correct, based on a prestige language or dialect, which may not reflect the actual way in which he uses his language. There is also the danger that he may translate too literally from English to his own language. But if the two methods are used in conjunction with each other, they complement each other and the fieldworker becomes aware of what data is suspect and must be checked.

If there are several informants, it often happens that they have talents for different tasks. Some people can be very shy when a microphone is put in front of them and they are asked to talk. The result may be that they are very hesitant and or that they may dry up altogether after a few sentences. I have found that older people are often better for this task. Over a lifetime they have gathered many anecdotes and polished them through much retelling. They enjoy having an audience and so talk enthusiastically and without too much hesitation. I visited one elderly lady with a long list of questions, expecting her to be a little shy, but I never reached the second question, as after the first she didn't stop talking for an hour.

But people who are good at speaking are not necessarily good at answering grammatical questions, however simply they are put. With some people, hypothetical questions about language are very confusing. If you ask, 'How would you say, "It is cold"', they will go and put the heating on. And when you ask, 'How do you say "You are coming"', then they say 'I am coming', because they think you are *addressing* them. But there are some who can look at the language from a distance, quite objectively. They can grasp hypothetical questions and can think consciously about distinctions in meaning. This does not always require a good grammatical education. Some people are just natural linguists.

If several informants are available, it is not a problem if some can only help in one of the above ways. The fieldworker simply uses some for recording texts and others for answering questions, according to their talents.

All the things that I have discussed above depend on one crucial thing: co-operation. The fieldworker cannot get very far if there are no speakers of the language willing to help. Fortunately most people are proud that you are showing interest in their language and culture and the Neo-Aramaic-speaking communities are no exception. I have found people of the Chaldean and Assyrian communities to be exceptionally generous in giving up their time to sit and work with me, for no ecompense. My main informant, Ghazwan Khundy, has given hours and hours of his ime over several years. Everywhere I have undertaken fieldwork, I have found eople to be welcoming and enthusiastic.

Of course, it is first necessary to make connections in the community and it elps if one is introduced to new people by people they trust. Religious or community eaders are invaluable in helping with this, as they know many people and are enerally trusted. When a colleague and I travelled to Detroit, the most useful onnection we made was a Chaldean priest, Father Emanuel Shaleta, who, with pparently limitless energy, organised a busy social schedule for us and put us in ontact with many people from his congregation. After giving a service, he gathered ogether some of the older members of his flock and lined them up outside his office, ummoning them one by one and asking them to tell a short story or anecdote in their wn dialect. They all seemed to be quite happy to oblige and we collected some nteresting stories. One woman entertainingly described her rather accident-prone ttempts to learn to drive in America.

Fieldwork in any discipline never goes entirely smoothly. It is important to e aware of cultural sensitivities. For instance it may be difficult for a male ieldworker to have access to female speakers. It can also happen that people suspect he fieldworker's motives, especially in Iraqi exile communities who had some reason o be paranoid about people who came asking questions.

Problems can also arise when there is a difference in understood aims etween the researcher and the speaker. In the case of Neo-Aramaic, informants ometimes assume a linguist wants the *proper* language, i.e. Syriac or the modern iterary form of Neo-Aramaic. Many people have prejudices about the colloquial lialects, similar to the attitudes that Arabs have towards Arabic dialects: that they are ust slang, with no grammar or subtlety of expression. It is therefore important for the ieldworker to make it very clear exactly what is wanted.

I have described the problems of gaining material for research. But of course he greatest problems lie in dealing with the raw material - the processes of ranscribing and analysing recordings. One of the problems that causes the most eadaches for Neo-Aramaicists is how to devise a suitable transcription method. This nay seem quite simple. But the sound systems of Neo-Aramaic dialects are actually ery complex and it is impossible to have a system with a simple one-to-one orrespondence of sound with letter.

I mentioned above the oral texts that fieldworkers gather for their research. I ow include one to show one kind of text that is collected, and also to show the anguage as it is transcribed by the fieldworker. I recorded this text in Baghdad in 2001 from Sa'id Shamaya, who is a member of the Alqoshi community there. The tory hinges on the ambiguity of the word *nāša* 'person', which can mean somebody', as in 'somebody important', but can also mean 'human being', with the mplication of 'humane'.

THE STORY OF THE BAD SON
RECOUNTED IN THE CHRISTIAN DIALECT OF ALQOSH

(1) *ġðа-ḥukkεθa men 'alquš 'iba ḥaxemθa mmaḥkēla ṭaloxu 'axonoxu sa'id šāmāya.*
A story from Alqosh which has a moral, which will be told to you by Sa'īd Šāmāya.

(2) *'eθwa xa-bāba 'u 'eθwāle xa-brona 'aziza. māqad mjureble de-mdābēṛe b-dubāṛe ṭāwe!*
There was a father and he had an only son. How hard he tried to bring him up in good discipline!

(3) *brona ... la-wēwa dex de-b'ēle bābeḥ. rxešle b-'urxāθa plime.*
But his son was not as his father wished. He followed crooked ways.

(4) *mā-qad kemnāṣeḥle. 'u kem'āmēre. la-šmēle qāled-bābeḥ.*
How often he advised him and spoke to him! But he did not heed his father.

(5) *'u p-xarθa, npeqle m-bεθeḥ, 'reqle, 'u bābeḥ bimāra ṭāleḥ: broni, la-kpεšet nāša.*
Finally he left his home, ran away, his father telling him, 'Son, you will never be a human being {somebody}!'

(6) *'u zelle ... l-*[2]*'aθṛa raḥūqa, 'u fetle zona, 'u yemma bimāra ta bāba: xzi mā brēle me-bronux!*
He went to a far-away place. Time passed and his mother was saying to the father 'Find out what became of your son!'

(7) *'u bāba ḥenne lebbeḥ, 'u qemle bejyāla l-broneḥ wel de-mṭēle le-ġða-mðita 'u šmēle d-ile broneḥ b-ε-mðita.*
The father relented and he started to search for his son, until he reached a town and heard that his son was in that town. ...

[2] Originally *b-* but corrected by another informant to *l-*.

(8) *'an de-wēwa ... [A]hurrās[A][3] b-'ɛ-mðita kem'ārɛle. man-iwet 'āyet? kud-ile nexrāya.*
Those who were [A]guards[A] in that town apprehended him (asking him), 'Who are you?'- as he was a stranger.

(9) *'u zellɛ mērɛ ta ... wazira. 'u 'o-wazira broneḥ-wēwa.*
And they went and told the mayor. Now, that mayor was his son!

(10) *mērɛ ṭāleḥ: 'iθ xā' nexrāya; hādax-ile, hādax-ile šemmeḥ w-ādax-ile šekleḥ.*
They said to him, 'There is someone, a stranger. He's like this and such and such is his name and he looks like this.[4]

(11) *'āmerwa: so moθole p-qešyūθa, 'u p-qapoxe, 'u bgo ... ṛpāsa, ... 'u b-'ɛna maṛetta.*
He said, 'Go and bring him with cruelty and blows and kicking, and without mercy.'[5]

(12) *zellɛ, kemqārɛle bāba-u kemmɛθɛle qam broneḥ-u*[6] *'āw mri'a 'u jehya 'u m'aðba.*
They went, they called the father and brought him before his son, in pain, tired and tortured.

(13) *kud qemle, kemxāzēle broneḥ, kemyāðēle.*
When he rose, he saw his son and recognized him.

(14) *mēre: hā kem'ēðetti! mēre 'ē, kem'ēðennux.*
(The son) said, 'Well, do you recognize me?' He said, 'Yes, I recognize you'.

(15) *mēre: hā bābi! la-'amretwa ṭāli: la-kpɛšet nāša? xzi m-iwen daha! daha wazira ṛābɛ-wen.*
He said, 'Well, father! Didn't you used to say to me, 'You will never be somebody {a human being}'. 'See what I am now. Now I am a great mayor'.

---

[3] [A]...... [A] means that the enclosed words are in Arabic.

[4] Literally: Thus is his appearance.

[5] Literally: with a bitter eye.

[6] Originally *bābeḥ* 'his father' but corrected by another informant.

(16) *mēre: broni 'āna la-mēri la-kpɛšet wazira. mēri: la-kpɛšet nāša.*
He said, 'Son, I did not say you would not be a mayor. I said you would never be a human being {somebody}.'

(17) *w-en hāwetwa nāša, la-kmɛθetwāli b-aθ-ḥāl de-kemmɛθɛli p-qapoxe-u j'āfa 'u p-ṣurta maṛetta. šukran.*
'If you had been a human being {somebody}, you would not have brought me in this way that you brought me, with blows and pushing and scowling'. [A]Thank you[A].

Further reading

The following books give informative and entertaining accounts of linguists' experiences of fieldwork:

Dixon, R.M.W. 1984. *Searching For Aboriginal Languages: Memoirs of a Field Worker.* University of Queensland Press.

Newman, P. & Ratliff, M. 2001. *Linguistic Fieldwork.* Cambridge: Cambridge University Press.

Colloquial Iraqi Arabic

Clive Holes

University of Oxford

The Arabicization of Iraq took many centuries to complete. Before the Arab conquest of the mid-7th century AD, there was already a population of Christian, Arabic-speaking semi-settled tribesmen on the western edge of the *sawād*, the alluvial plain that has always been the hub of Iraqi civilisation. At that time, the bulk of its population must have spoken various dialects of Aramaic and been confessionally Christian or Jewish, the descendants of Iraq's ancient Semitic and non-Semitic populations. No doubt there would also have been a sprinkling of Persian-speaking land-owning nobility in the countryside and a Persian-speaking class of civil servants in the towns, administering what was then a province of the Sasanian Empire.

Initially, the pattern of post-conquest Arab settlement involved the setting up of military cantonments: a major one at Kufa in central Iraq, and a smaller one at Basra in the south. Eventually, as elsewhere in the conquered territories, these military bases developed into towns. But in contrast to what happened in neighbouring Syria, there was a large and early migration of Arabs from the peninsula, and it is likely that Arabic would have quickly become the dominant language in the erstwhile Sasanian capital of Iraq at Madā'in, and in other urban areas, as the language of government and administration and as a lingua franca between the incomers and the local people. However, for probably a century or more, there was no drive to mass religious conversion: this would have eroded the taxation base, non-Muslim *ḏimmis* ('protected persons'), unlike Muslims, having to pay the *ǧizya* or 'poll-tax' in return for protection by the state. We know precious little of the detail of Arab settlement in Iraq over the succeeding centuries, and virtually nothing about how Arabic replaced Aramaic as the language of daily life. The Arab historians maintain complete silence on this topic, but the fact that, thirteen centuries later, there are still pockets of neo-Aramaic speakers in northern Iraq suggest that in some areas it must have been a slow process. Topographical and ethnic factors would certainly have had an influence. Southern and central Iraq, apart from the marshes, were easily accessible from the deserts of northern Arabia, had plentiful water and were very fertile; the rural population which was already there spoke a language cognate with Arabic.

Much of the north, by contrast, was more difficult, mountainous country, and in part populated by Kurds and other non-Semites. It was never fully Arabized or Arabicized.

Iraq, as is well known, produced the great grammarians of the Arabic language. In the 8th century, Khalīl ibn Aḥmad and his Persian pupil Sībawayh laid the foundations of Classical Arabic grammar, and were followed by generations of schoolmen who refined and amplified their descriptions, and established schools of grammatical theory, though Sībawayh's great *Kitāb* ('Book') has never been superseded and remains the cornerstone of all subsequent indigenous treatments of Arabic grammar. Like Sībawayh himself, many of these were Persians or the offspring of mixed Persian and Arab marriages. Iraq also produced, for its population, a disproportionate number of the great figures of Arabic literature: al-Mutanabbī, considered by many the greatest Classical Arabic poet, was born and died in Iraq (murdered by Bedouin), even if he made his name in the Hamdānid court of Syria; Abu Nuwās, born of Golban, a Persian mother, gay libertine and doyen of Arab wine poets, was an Iraqi and the court-poet of Hārūn al-Rashīd in Baghdad; al-Jāḥiẓ ('the Goggle-Eyed'), the 8th/9th century polymath who wrote on everything from the principles of rhetoric to the psychology of misers to the superiority of heterosexual over homosexual relations, was a native of Basra. It is surely no accident that the unparalleled intellectual, artistic and scientific efflorescence which took place in Iraq between the 8th and 13th centuries occurred in a stable, prosperous urban society, in which Muslims, Christians and Jews, Arabs and Persians lived side by side and all made their distinctive contributions. The Baghdad of the Abbasids was a multicultural melting pot, but its language, Arabic, was spoken by Arabs, Christians and Jews alike.

Fig. 8.1 Illustration from the *dīwān* of Mullā 'Abbūd al-Karkhī (taken from his poem "The Cat and the Rats", a satire on the British in Iraq).[1]

[1] The opening line reads: *unḍur ila l-hirr il‿dirağ sayyidiyya / bi rāsah w‿iftaras ğumla ğrēdiyya* "Look at the cat that put on its head / the Sayyid's fez, and on rats fed".

	All/ almost all Iraqi dialects	Damascus/ Jerusalem/ Beirut
ṯ, ḏ, ḍ	e.g. *ṯalāṯa, hāḏa, ḍuhr* (an exception is the Christian dialect of Baghdad)	*talāta, hāda, ḍuhr* (or *salāsa, hāza, ẓuhr*)
q	e.g. *qāl* or *gāl* (never *'āl*)	*'āl*
Imperfect suffix -*n*	e.g. *tketbīn, tketbūn, yketbūn* (always with final -*n*)	*(b)tketbi, (b)tketbu, (b)yketbu (b)yketbu*
Object marker *l-*	e.g. Muslim Baghdadi *šeft-a, l-axūya* 'You saw my brother' (lit 'you saw-him, *l*-my- brother')	*šuft axūyi*
'There is/ is not ...'	*āku / māku*	*fīh / mā fīh*
'a ...'	*fadd kitāb* 'a book'	*kitāb* 'a book'
'of, belonging to'	*il-bēt mālak* 'your house'	*il-bēt taba'ak / btā'ak*

Table 1: Some features shared by all (or almost all) Iraqi dialects

But for a dialectologist like me, the attractions of Iraq lie in a different sphere, though they too are a consequence of its remarkable social and confessional diversity – its spoken Arabic dialects. Whilst it is true that the modern Arabic dialects of Iraq have many features in which they all or almost all agree, and in which they differ as a group from neighbouring areas (a few of the ways they differ from the city dialects of the Levant are in Table 1), Iraq nonetheless presents one with a fascinating linguistic mosaic, virtually unique in the Arab World.

In Baghdad, at least up until the early 1950s, three distinct Arabic dialects were spoken, such that one only had to hear a few words in order to identify the speaker as a Muslim, a Christian or a Jewish Baghdadi.[2] A few years after the establishment of the state of Israel in 1948, most of the Jewish population of Baghdad left and took with it its dialect, which can now only be heard in the mouths of a few 80 year-olds in Israel, but the Christian dialect still survives alongside the majority Muslim one. Alongside this confessionally-based dialect cleavage in the capital, there is also a north-south dialect split which could be termed religio-ecological (that is, appertaining to life-style) and which divides the country in two, the dividing line

[2] The standard descriptive works for the three dialects, listed in the bibliography, are Erwin 1963 (Muslim B), Abu-Haidar 1991 (Christian B), and Mansour 1991 (Jewish B); Woodhead & Beene 1967 is a useful dictionary of Muslim B.

running roughly from Fallūja on the Euphrates to Samarra on the Tigris. Baghdad is about 50 miles to the south of the line; Tikrit, 'Āna, and Mosul are to the north of it. In both the Baghdad case, and the national north-south split, two *dialect types* are involved, which are referred to for short as *qəltu*-dialects on the one hand and *gelet*-dialects on the other, on account of the way their speakers say the word for 'I said' - *qəltu* or *gelet*. This is not of course to say that *qəltu* and *gelet*-dialects do not themselves contain significant subdivisions, but they each contain a sufficient number of shared features differentiating one group from the other, for the division to be justified.

In Table 2, I summarise the geographical, confessional and ecological distribution of these dialect types within Iraq. M stands for Muslim, J for Jewish, C for Christian. The term 'sedentary' refers to those communities that live in towns and cities, and includes all the Jews and Christians but not all Muslims. 'Non-sedentary' refers exclusively to certain communities of Muslims in both southern and northern Iraq that continue to lead a life-style that involves animal husbandry and a semi-nomadic life-style.

	Muslim (M)		Non-Muslim (C, J)
	non-sedentary	sedentary	(all sedentary)
Baghdad	-----------	*gelet*	*qəltu*
Southern Iraq	*gelet*	*gelet*	*qəltu*
Northern Iraq	*gelet*	*qəltu*	*qəltu*

Table 2: Geographical distribution of gelet- and qəltu-dialect types in Iraq

There are a number of striking facts about the distribution of dialect types in this Table.

(a) The non-Muslim dialects, which are by definition those of sedentaries, are all of the *qəltu*-type, wherever they are located. Thus Christians in Mosul, Baghdad and Basra, cities separated by hundreds of miles in which there are no intervening Christian populations, all speak this kind of dialect, as do (or rather did), the Iraqi Jews.

(b) The non-sedentary Muslims, on the other hand, wherever in Iraq they live, all speak a *gelet*-type dialect, typologically similar to the dialects of other non-sedentary populations in neighbouring Jordan, Syria and Kuwait.

(c) The sedentary Muslims are split, dialectologically speaking: south of the imaginary line which runs from Fallūja to Samarra, including Baghdad, they speak a dialect, which while not identical with the *gelet*-type dialect of their fellow Muslim non-sedentaries is sufficiently similar to be classifiable in the same group. But in the cities of northern Iraq, the Muslims speak a dialect that to all intents and purposes is identical or nearly so with that of the Christians who live in the same cities - a *qəltu* dialect.

Tables 3 to 5 illustrate some typical differences between these various dialects. My choice of variables is neither comprehensive nor systematic, but is rather on the basis of phonology, morphology and frequency of occurrence. Table 3 contrasts the dialect of Mosul, a typical northern *qəltu* dialect, with that of Muslim Baghdad, a typical *gelet* dialect:

	Mosul		Muslim Baghdadi
q	*qāl*	'he said'	*gāl*
k (front vowels)	*kān*	'he was'	*čān*
(back vowels)	*ykūn*	'he will be'	*ykūn*
r	*ġāḥ*	'he went'	*rāḥ*
'imale' (vowel raising):			
ā before short *i*	*ğēme'*	'mosque'	*ğāme'*
ā before long *ī*	*bazīzīn*	'cats'	*bzāzīn*
Final short *-a*	*badli*	'suit of clothes'	*badla*
3rd msg pron suffix	*abūnu*	'his father'	*abū*
1st sg suffix stem	*katabtu*	'I wrote'	*ktabet*
3rd msg suffix stem	*katab*	'he wrote'	*ketab*
3rd fsg suffix stem	*katabet*	'she wrote'	*ketbat*
3rd pl suffix stem	*katabu*	'they wrote'	*ketbaw*
Common adverbs:	*hōni*	'here'	*hnā*
	hnūka, hōnek	'there'	*hnāka*
	hāked̠	'thus'	*hīči*

Table 3: Some phonological and morphological features that differentiate qəltu and gelet dialects

Table 4 illustrates some of the most salient ways in which Jewish and Christian Baghdadi on the one hand, both *qəltu*-dialects, and Muslim Baghdadi on the other, a *gelet* dialect, contrast with each other:

	Christian B	Jewish B	Muslim B
q	*qāl*	*qāl*	*gāl*
k	*k*	*k*	*k* and *č*
r	*ġās*	*ġās*	*rās*
'imale'			
wāḥid 'one'	*wēḥed*	*wēḥed*	*wāḥid*
šitā' 'winter'	*šeti*	*šeti*	*šeta*
1st sg ending of perfect	*qəltu*	*qəltu*	*gelet*
2nd pl ending of perfect	*qəltəm*	*qəltəm*	*geltu*
3rd pl ending of perfect	*qālu*	*qālu*	*gālaw*

Table 4: Some Baghdadi J & C versus M differences

Table 5 illustrates a few differences between the *qəltu*-dialects of Baghdad, that is, between Jewish and Christian:[3]

	Christian B	Jewish B	(Muslim B)
ṯ, ḏ, ḏ̣	*tnēn, hāda, ḍuhr*	*ṯnēn, hāḏa, ḏ̣uhr*	(*ṯnēn, hāḏa, ḏ̣uhr*)
2nd fsg pron suffix	*abūki, emki*	*abūki, emmek*	(*abūč, ummeč*)
3rd fsg pron suffix	*abūha, emma*	*abūwa, emma*	(*abūha, ummha*)
3rd pl pron suffix	*abūwem, emmem*	*abūhem, emmem*	(*abūhum, ummhum*)
Theme I verbs	*katab, lebes*	*katab, labas*	(*ketab, lebas*)

Table 5: Some Baghdadi J versus C differences

Five sample sentences in the Christian and Muslim Baghdadi dialects, produced by bi-dialectal Christians, show how the same propositions would be expressed in them, and illustrate the dialects 'in action', as it were: [4]

[3] All the data in these tables are taken from Blanc 1964.

[4] Examples based on Abu-Haidar 1991: 144-5.

(i) Phonology (*č/k, r/ġ*); the post-posed copula, found only in C:

C: *l-kaləb əkbīġ yānu*
M: *l-čaləb čəbīr*
'The dog is big'

(ii) Syllabic structure in perfect verbs; vocabulary; phonology (*q/ġ*, r/*ġ*):

C: *ġasalet əḥwēsa qabəl ma tmaṭṭəġ*
M: *xislat əhdūmha gabəl ma tumṭur*
'She washed her clothes before it rained'

(iii) Vocabulary; morphology; phonology (*r/ġ*):

C: *axūyi ġāḥ yətkallal ġada*
M: *axūya rāḥ yitzawwağ bāčər*
'My brother's getting married tomorrow'

(iv) Different clitics, *qa-* and *da-* to mark continuous action:

C: *hay-yōm qayəğōn 'indna xəṭṭāġ*
M: *hal-yōm dayəğūn 'ədna xəṭṭār*
'Today guests are coming to visit us'

(v) Phonology (*č / k*); vocabulary:

C: *kān qayəl'ab čəqqi w qās*
M: *čān dayəl'ab du'bul əw xəsar*
'He was playing marbles and lost'

Finally, here is a list of some common vocabulary items which M, J and C all share (with appropriate modifications in pronunciation), selected to illustrate the degree of foreign linguistic influence even in everyday matters:

bazzūna 'cat'
temman 'rice'
*ğām** 'glass (as a material)'
*čāra** 'remedy, solution'
čarpāya 'bedstead'
čārak 'a quarter'
*čingāl**'hook, fork'
ḥunṭa 'wheat'
*xōš** 'good'

*dazz** 'to send'
*glāṣ** 'glass (for drinking')
*mēz** 'table'
*mēwa** 'fruit'
*nēšan** 'to betroth'
hīč 'nothing'
yēzi 'that's enough'

(Several of these items are from Persian, Turkish or English. Some of them (asterisked) are also found in the Gulf (though not always with the same meanings), which was exposed to the same foreign influences.)

Broadly speaking, there is a sufficiently close correspondence between the dialect of Mosul (as spoken by all its inhabitants, of whatever faith) and Christian Baghdadi for a common historical origin to be supposed. Christian dialects in other Iraqi cities, such as Basra, are also very similar. The Jewish dialect of Baghdad, on the other hand, has maintained itself apart, and contains much vocabulary of Hebrew provenance that the Christian dialects lack. Nonetheless, it is also sufficiently similar to them typologically for a common historical and geographical origin to be supposed.

How are we to explain these at first sight puzzling patterns of dialect difference? How did they arise and how have they maintained themselves? A look at Iraq's political and social history will give us some clues.

The siege and sack of Baghdad by the Mongols in 1258 was probably the most catastrophic event in the history of Iraq. One of its many long-term effects was a complete reshaping of the demography of the country. The Caliph al-Mustaʿṣim billah and his entire family were murdered, and the population of what was then one of the largest cities in the Arabic-speaking world was slaughtered en masse, the Muslims being singled out for especially cruel treatment. It has been estimated, though this is no more than informed guesswork, that a hundred thousand people were killed in pillaging that lasted over a month. The Christians, however, appear to have been spared Hulagu's worst excesses - he is known to have been favourably disposed towards Christianity and among his wives there was even a Nestorian Christian. Hulagu passed on to attack Aleppo and Damascus, apparently by-passing the north of Iraq. However, Baghdad's water distribution system and irrigation canals had been completely destroyed, causing long-term ruin not just to the city itself but also to agriculture in the surrounding countryside; most of the city's public buildings were razed to the ground. All central political control disappeared, anarchy ruled, and the southern half of the country was effectively de-urbanised and re-tribalised. In the words of Stephen Longrigg, Iraq became "from the Lurish hills to the Sinjar a country of few and small towns, while around and between them lay tracts grazed and dominated by the tribes alone".[5] Over subsequent centuries, Baghdad and lower Iraq were gradually re-populated and re-urbanised, but it was a slow process. Many of the major towns of southern Iraq are in fact relatively recent settlements, dating from the late Ottoman period when Midhat Pasha tamed the tribes: Amara was built only in 1862, al-Nasiriyya in about 1870, and Ramadi about 1880; Kut, as late as the mid-19th century, was a small village. The population of Baghdad itself was probably no more than 100,000 at the beginning of the 19th century - probably less than it had been 600 years before.

The sources of this new urban population were various, but the major one was the Bedouin tribes who wandered the ruined *sawād* and its desert fringes. In linguistic terms these were all speakers of *gelet*-dialects. Although we can never know for certain, it seems likely that the original pre-invasion Muslim population of Baghdad and the towns of southern Iraq spoke *qəltu*-dialects similar to those still spoken by the Christians and Jews of the 20th century city, and like those which have continued to be spoken by the urbanites of all religions in northern Iraq. The north, in other words, which escaped the attentions of the Mongols, continued the pre-1258 position, in which town-dwellers spoke *qəltu*-dialects and the nomads *gelet*-dialects. Whatever was left of the original Muslim population in Baghdad was augmented by a continuous flow of Muslim *gelet*-speaking settlers into Baghdad after the 13th century. This eventually resulted in a situation where, by the mid-19th, the ratio of the communities in the city was about 7 Muslims for every 2 Jews, for every 1 Christian. By 1920, the population of the city was estimated at 200,000, comprising about 135,000 Muslims, 50,000 Jews and 15,000 Christians.[6] By no means all the members of each of these communities were Arabic-speakers, of course, but there is no doubt that the Muslims, the *gelet*-speakers, spoke the majority dialect. The long-term effect of the continuous influx of rural *gelet*-speakers from outside the capital settling and marrying in the city over many centuries was to 'Bedouinize' the Muslim dialect but not that of the non-Muslims of the city, whose dialects continued to reflect the pre-Mongol situation. Language differences maintain themselves where there are social barriers, and the fact that these communal dialects have survived so long intact says much about the 'compartmentalised' demographic and social structure of Baghdad. A 17th century map of the city[7] shows a distinct Christian quarter on the East bank of the Tigris opposite Karkh on the West, simply labelled *naṣāra* 'Christians', and a separate Jewish quarter, *ḥārat al-yahūd* to the north. There was of course no intermarriage between members of the three religions, even if there was some social mixing. In the 20th century, Christian communities have tended to

[5] Longrigg 1925: 13.

[6] Blanc 1964: 8.

[7] Longrigg 1925: 83.

Fig. 8.2 Abboud al-Karkhi, whose *Diwan* is the most famous literary work in the Muslim Iraqi dialect

coalesce around the various churches in the city, and some of the original Christian areas have changed their confessional colour. According to Farida Abu-Haidar, who was brought up in Baghdad in the 1950s, the originally Christian *'agd an-naṣāra* in the Batawiyyin quarter of Baghdad was found to contain only two or three Christian families when it was demolished in the 1960s.[8]

Migration from the impoverished towns and villages of southern and central Iraq into Baghdad has massively accelerated since independence and especially over the last 40-50 years. It has far outpaced migration from the north. The point was reached in the 1990s where the population of the Baghdad metropolitan area accounted for perhaps 25% of the population of the whole country. In linguistic terms, this migration has brought ever more *gelet*-dialect speakers to the city. The result is that Baghdad is the only ancient city in the Arab World in which the dominant dialect is Bedouin in character. This dialect is what we are normally thinking of when we refer to 'Iraqi' Arabic, and within Iraq it has all the hallmarks of what we might term the 'national' dialect, exactly as Cairene has that status within Egypt, or Damascene within Syria. Non-Baghdadis who come to Baghdad feel constrained to accommodate to it. Haim Blanc, in his masterly study of the dialects of Baghdad, quotes the example of a student from Musayyab, a southern town between Baghdad and Kerbela, who was ridiculed on returning home from his studies in the city because he had unconsciously adopted the Baghdadi Muslim pronunciation *gā'id* 'sitting' instead of the southern Iraqi *ğā'id*,[9] *ğ* in this word being a rather more 'rustic' *gelet*-feature than Baghdadi *g*. Christian Baghdadis who speak their own *qəltu*-dialect at home feel constrained to use the majority Muslim dialect, which they call *baddāwi*, when they have to speak in public, multi-confessional contexts. These points applied even to erstwhile political leaders like Saddam Hussein, a Muslim born and raised in Tikrit, a *qəltu*-dialect area. Yet, during his speeches, Saddam spoke the Muslim dialect of Baghdad, a *gelet* dialect, whenever he departed from his Modern Standard Arabic script and spoke dialect to his audience, as he occasionally did when trying to project a 'man of the people' image. The point has now been reached in Baghdad where dialects other than that of the Muslim majority are becoming invisible in public contexts, and according to recent research even receding in domestic ones.[10] Depending on how the current situation develops, it may not be long before the Christian dialect of Baghdad, like the Jewish one, disappears, although there have recently been literary attempts to keep the communal dialects, or at least the memory of how they were spoken 50 years ago, alive. Samir Naqqash, an Iraqi Jew living in Israel, has written a novel *nuzūla wa xēṭ aš-šēṭān* 'Tenants and

---

[8] Abu Haidar 1991: 3

[9] Blanc 1964: 28.

[10] Abu-Haidar 1990: 51-3.

Cobwebs', set in Baghdad sometime in the mid 1940s, and entirely in colloquial Arabic, in which the characters, the multi-confessional tenants or *nuzūla* of an old-fashioned multi-storey Baghadi house arranged around a courtyard in a popular quarter of the old city, tell their stories to the reader, each using his own vividly idiomatic communal dialect, M, J or C. There is no central character - the focal points are the house itself, the coffee shop and the street where these emblematic characters play out their lives. The house gradually empties of its cast of colourful characters as the political events of the late 40s and early 50s that are the novel's backdrop, unfold. By the end the house is an empty ruin, inhabited only by a senile old woman and her mad son. In order to make it even comprehensible to the ordinary reader, the author has to resort to frequent footnotes to explicate points of communal dialect usage. The story harks back to a time when that kind of social mix in Baghdad, and indeed Middle Eastern cities in general was possible - indeed was the norm. It is hard to see it ever being so again - the more's the pity, for those of us who value variety not just in our flora and fauna, but in our languages too.

Further reading

Abu-Haidar F., 1990. Maintenance and shift in the Christian Arabic of Baghdad, *Zeitschrift für arabische Linguistik* 21: 51-3.

- 1991. *Christian Arabic of Baghdad.* Wiesbaden.

Blanc H., 1964. *Communal Dialects in Baghdad.* Harvard.

Erwin W.M., 1963. *A Short Reference Grammar of Iraqi Arabic.* Georgetown.

Longrigg S.H., 1925. *Four Centuries of Modern Iraq.* Oxford.

Mansour J., 1991. *The Jewish Baghdadi Dialect.* Or-Yehuda, Israel.

Woodhead D.R. & Beene, W., 1967. *A Dictionary of Iraqi Arabic, Arabic-English.* Georgetown.

'The Kurds are Alive': Kurdish in Iraq

Christine Allison

Inalco, Paris.

'Let no-one say the Kurds are dead, the Kurds are alive' runs the refrain of Dildar's poem, which later became an unofficial Kurdish national anthem. By comparison with some other national anthems, these sentiments are somewhat modest. No wishes are expressed to conquer others, bring in a rolling international revolution, or even rule the waves (the latter being a somewhat impractical proposition for the Kurds). However, the existence of the Kurds, as a group with their own distinctive identity and desires, and even as individual human beings, has been under such concerted attack during the last century that perhaps Dildar was not wrong in his implication that survival itself was something of an achievement for the Kurdish people.

Not that Kurdish is a 'small' language - in terms of number of speakers, it is the largest minority language of the Middle East, after Arabic, Turkish and Persian. Although precise statistics are unavailable, there are probably about twenty million speakers in total. Kurdish is spoken by large groups in Iran, Iraq, Syria and the former Soviet Union, and by long-established communities in Khorasan and Afghanistan, as well as a more recent global diaspora. However, it lacks official status and acceptance in most of the 'home' states. Despite recent developments in Turkey, Iraq remains the only one of the 'home' states where Kurdish has a full official status, a status which it has theoretically had since the foundation of the state. Its role is becoming ever more important in the new structures of Iraq. However, the realisation in practical terms of this official status has been highly problematic; Kurdish in Iraq has passed through many vicissitudes, and Kurdish civilian populations have undergone deportations and massacres. In this chapter I will give a brief description of the language itself and some of its most remarkable features, followed by an account of the situation of Kurdish in Iraq and the other 'home' states. Finally I include a short section on Kurdish literature, which cannot hope to do justice to its vigour and variety, but which aims to give a small taste of the ideas and emotions which characterise the writings of Kurds in Iraq.

The Kurdish Language

Kurdish is a Western Iranian language, with two major dialects and some minor ones. It is thus related to Persian (though not a dialect of Persian, as some popular sources have claimed) and unrelated to Turkish or Arabic. Attempts to prove that it is a debased 'mountain' dialect of Turkish, various examples of which appeared during the twentieth century, were undertaken for the purposes of Turkish propaganda, and should not be taken seriously.[1] However, the nature of the debate on Kurdish in Turkey, which is heavily influenced by Kemalist ideas about the uniformity of language and culture in the Republic, has had a wider impact in Kurdish sociolinguistics and even in Kurdish politics. For instance, one of the lines of argument sometimes advanced by those coming from a Kemalist point of view is that a language must be standardised and uniform to be 'real' and that Kurdish does not exist as a language because it has many mutually incomprehensible dialects. This idea does not hold water in linguistic terms - one would hardly think of saying, for instance, that either Arabic or English does not exist because it contains mutually incomprehensible dialects - but it is surprisingly widespread. Although Iran and Iraq did not possess a fundamental principle of indivisibility of the state and consequent uniformity of race, language and culture, as Turkey did, it is certainly true that dominant languages and cultures, Persian and Arabic respectively, were favoured in the media, in the public sphere and at all levels of State education. Indeed, in Iran under the Shah, publication in Kurdish was forbidden. Moreover, Persian, and later, Kurdish, have both been through several initiatives to 'purge' the language of foreign words, though these measures were in neither case as fundamental and far-reaching as the language reforms undertaken in the Turkish republic (Hassanpour 1992: 393-400). Thus, in a climate where linguistic purity and cultural uniformity were seen as positive, and where the Kurds felt their language to be at risk, it is hardly surprising that not only in Turkey but also in Iraq and Iran, they should view their diversity (both linguistic and cultural) as a weakness which undermines their claim to nationhood; there is a tendency amongst some Kurdish commentators to minimise differences between dialects.

Linguistic studies were carried out in various parts of Kurdistan by 19th and early 20th century Orientalists, such as Alexandre Jaba, Oskar Mann and Piyotr Lerch. In Iraq before the Second World War, some grammars were produced by British political and military specialists such as Soane and Jardine. However, the founder of modern Kurdish linguistic studies was the Iranist D.N. MacKenzie, who worked at the School of Oriental and African Studies, London, and ended his career in Göttingen. His *Kurdish Dialect Studies* analysed a number of dialects, both Sorani

---

[1] These arguments were set out in M.S. Firat's *Doğu İlleri Varto Tarihi*, first written in 1945, published in Ankara in 1961. For an account of Turkish nationalist theories of language and their relation to language policy on Kurdish, see Haig 2004: 133-136.

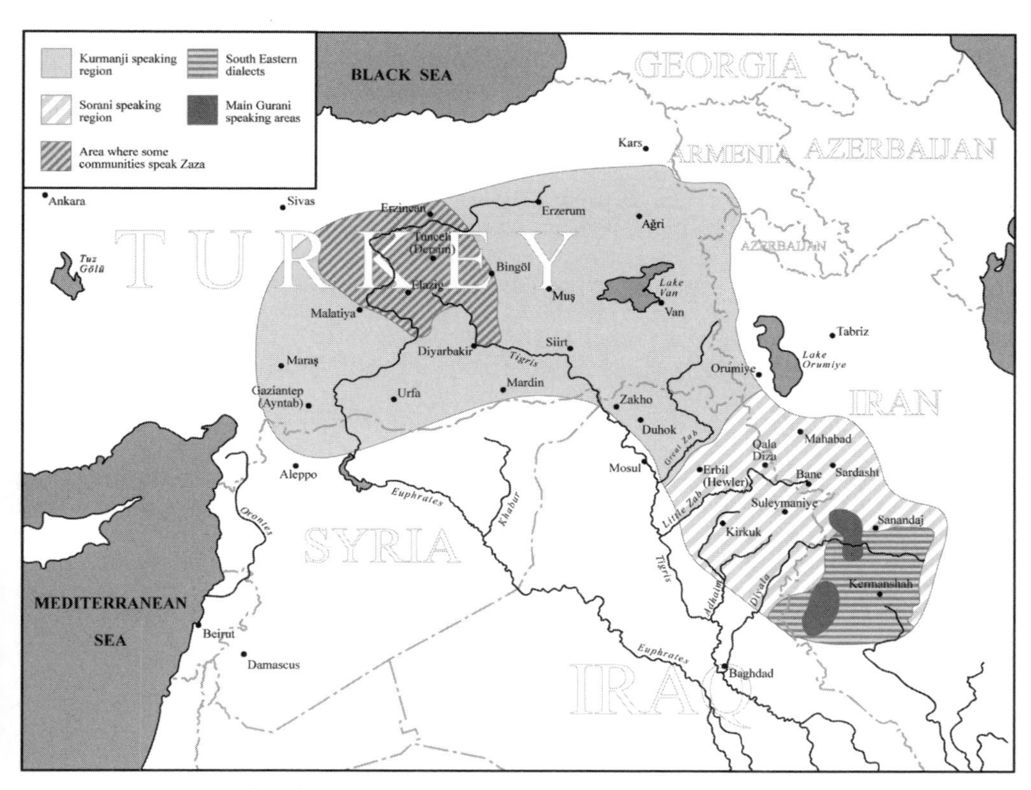

Fig. 9.1 Map to show distribution of Kurdish dialects

and Kurmanji, collected in Iraq in the 1950s (he was refused permission to work in Turkey). He was able to show the (very few) characteristics which set the two major dialects of Kurdish apart from other Western Iranian languages, and also suggested reasons for the differences between these dialects. Thus, though his motives were by his own lights scientific and apolitical, he provided a genuine linguistic answer to political accusations of Kurdish not being 'a real language' in its own right.[2]

Kurmanji is spoken by communities in Turkey, Syria, Lebanon, and some of the former Soviet republics, especially Georgia, Armenia and Azerbaijan, and also

[2] He has been criticised for Orientalist methodology in his analysis of the Hewrami dialects by the contemporary Kurdish specialist Amir Hassanpour; however, given the political climate of his time and its differences from current sensibilities, I find it difficult to single out strong indications of undue political or cultural bias on MacKenzie's part.

the northernmost part of Iranian Kurdistan. It is also spoken in the northernmost part of Northern Iraq, in the province called Badinan, and in Jebel Sinjar. Many Iraqi Kurds therefore refer to it as Badini or Badinani. Within Kurmanji there are various subdialects, which are mutually comprehensible, except where highly localised vocabulary is concerned, but in terms of grammar one can distinguish between the norms of the Southern and Eastern subgroups, that is Badini, which has much in common with the dialects of Hakkari in the far east of Turkey, and the Former Soviet Union group subdialect, and the subgroups of the North-West, further into Turkey.[3]

The second major dialect is called Sorani, after the former principality of Soran where it is spoken. Some authors call it Middle Kurmanji or Central Kurdish. This is the part of Iraqi Kurdistan south of the Great Zab river (that is, most of it); thus, Sorani is the majority dialect in Iraqi Kurdistan. The dialect is also spoken in most of Iranian Kurdistan, where it is often called Mukri. The subdialect of Mahabad in Iran, home of the celebrated though doomed Kurdish Republic of 1946, has in the past challenged the subdialect of Suleymani (the dominant form of Sorani in Iraq) in terms of prestige (Hassanpour 1992: 385-391).

There is also a rather heterogeneous group of Southern (sometimes called south-eastern) dialects, such as Kermanshahi and Kalhori, veering towards Lakki and Luri. Most speakers of these dialects live in Iran, though some dialects found in the areas around Khanaqin in Iraq also belong to this group, as does the dialect of the Fayli Kurds, who lived in urban centres of Iraq.[4]

Zaza and Gorani are two closely related north-western Iranian languages, which are, in purely linguistic terms, distinct from Sorani and Kurmanji. However, the vast majority of their speakers claim Kurdish identity, so the issue of their definition is sensitive. One might perhaps say that Zaza and Gorani are politically and socially, if not linguistically, Kurdish. Zaza, which is often called Dimlî, Kurmanjkî, Kurdkî, by its speakers, is spoken, roughly speaking, to the north-west of the main Kurmanji-speaking areas. Very little Zaza literature has been published, though there are now some enthusiastic writers developing the language, mostly based in Sweden.[5]

Gorani, by contrast, is relatively high-status in Kurdistan. It is often called Hewrami by Kurds, after one of the areas in which it is spoken, the mountainous Hewraman, just to the W of Sanandaj in Iran. Some of its speakers belong to heterodox religious groups, and it is the language of the sacred texts or *kelams* of the Ahl-e-Haqq, ‘People of the Truth’ who in Iraq are more often called Kakaî. It has been a literary language in the past, much used at the courts of the Ardalan chieftains in Sanandaj, who dominated the area in the 18th century, but the literary language

[3] These are very broad generalisations, severely hampered by the lack of comparative research on the range of subdialects spoken in Turkey.

[4] A recent landmark study, Fattah 2000, has brought together much new information on these dialects.

[5] For example Malmisanij and the late Ebubekir Pamukcu.

called Gorani is in many respects somewhat different from the local language called Hewrami; the relationship between the two has not yet been exhaustively studied.

The major dialects of Kurdish, Sorani and Kurmanji, are of course both spoken in Iraq. Although there have been some well-meaning attempts to produce a unified Kurdish, such as Nebez 1976, there are some crucial differences between Kurmanji and Sorani - Kurmanji, for instance has gender differences between nouns, whilst Sorani does not; Kurmanji has a case system, with a direct case, a vocative case, and an oblique case which fulfils other functions, such as accusative and dative; Sorani does not. Sorani has a definite noun suffix *-eke* and a set of pronominal suffixes, neither of which Kurmanji has. Linguists have commented on the differences between the dialects in terms of ergativity. The type of ergativity found in a number of Iranian languages, whereby the agent of transitive verbs occurs in the oblique case in the past tenses, is clearly identifiable in Kurmanji,[6] but less clear in Sorani, which has led linguists to argue that Sorani has become 'accusative' (Bynon 1979, 1980; Matras 1993). These are all major differences and would be difficult to reconcile in any unified language.

Linguists have sought the reasons behind these differences between the dialects. MacKenzie suggested that Sorani was influenced by a Gorani substratum, which means that Gorani speakers who began speaking Sorani Kurdish would have imported Gorani patterns into Sorani. The Gorani influence seems undeniable, but a Dutch scholar, Michiel Leezenberg suggests that the influence is rather the result of prestige borrowing, i.e. borrowing of Gorani vocabulary rather than underlying grammatical structures. This would be done for reasons of status, Gorani being a language of culture in S. Kurdistan. At the moment there is simply not enough data collected or analysis done to prove or disprove either of the theories; MacKenzie is still more generally favoured by linguists, but it remains a 'live' question.

The issue of the differences between Sorani and Kurmanji has important political ramifications. MacKenzie's successor in Goettingen, Philip Kreyenbroek, wrote in an article in 1992 that the two were as different as German and English (1992:71). This was received with fury by Kurdish nationalists who feared it would be seized upon by those who espoused a Turkish propagandist point of view, namely that Kurdish was not a 'real language' but a cluster of mutually unintelligible dialects.

Within Iraq, it is safe to say that the degree of mutual intelligibility is quite high, especially for people living near the dividing line between the dialects, and especially in this era of Kurdish-language education. However it is important to note that as Sorani dominates, it is *more* likely that Kurmanji/Badini speakers will understand Sorani than vice-versa. On a wider scale, the uncomfortable fact remains that the average Diyarbakir Kurmanji speaker will not find it easy to communicate with the inhabitants of Suleymaniya or Halabja.

---

[6] Though it is often unstable and subject to change in Kurmanji. See Dorleijn 1996 for a study in Diyarbakir.

Kurdish in the Modern Nation-States

Kurdish has fared differently in different States, and though considerations of space rule out a detailed account of the situation in each, it is worth sketching the salient points very briefly, as the differences are qualitative as well as quantitative. In Turkey, Kurmanji was effectively a proscribed language for most of the twentieth century, though never deliberately cited by name. Rigorous assimilation policies accompanied language reform in the Republic, with large-scale education campaigns to promote literacy in Turkish. In 1991 a law which had been in the 1982 constitution prohibiting 'all languages that are not the first official languages of states recognized by the Turkish state' was abolished. Since then publications have emerged, but publication, education and broadcasting in Kurdish are still often perceived as acts of separatism. However, the impact of Kurdish satellite broadcasting has been such that Turkey has now instituted a small amount of State broadcasting in Kurdish. The teaching of Kurdish in Turkey is also permitted, but tellingly, not to young children. This makes the creation of a reading public for Kurmanji much more difficult, as people who have learned to read during childhood are much more likely to read easily and fluently; acquiring literacy in a language in adulthood requires a sustained effort. Many of the Kurdish language schools which have recently opened in Turkey teach Zaza and Sorani in addition to Kurmanji.[7]

Kurmanji also encountered difficulties in other countries. In Syria, the French mandatory authorities permitted publication in Kurdish, but not education. Since independence Kurdish has never been recognised as an official language, and its use is not tolerated in public or official contexts. Several decrees have been issued, some highly localised, forbidding the use of non-Arabic languages in various contexts, such as weddings and the workplace. Since neo-Aramaic and Armenian are tolerated in Christian schools, it seems that only Kurdish is the target of these policies.[8]

The use of Kurdish dialects was not permitted in Iran for most of the Pahlavi period and at some points was suppressed by force. Despite the presence of notable Kurdish poets and scholars such as Hejar and Hêmin in Iran, by the time of the short-lived Republic of Mahabad (1946), the language had failed to develop for use in official contexts and the Republic's officials had difficulty producing paperwork in Kurdish. The situation under the Islamic republic is, in terms of linguistic freedom, more tolerant, with publications produced in Sorani and Kurmanji, though the State forbids use of the Latin script as un-Islamic. However, Kurdish still has no part in State education, and the content of broadcast and publications is monitored. Several commentators, both Kurdish and Western, see this more relaxed policy as an attempt to win Kurdish hearts and minds over to the régime's Shi'ism.[9]

---

[7] See Haig 2004 for a succinct account of the situation in Turkey, and Skuttnabb-Kangas and Bucak 1995 for a human rights perspective.

[8] For more details see McDowall 1998.

[9] See Hassanpour (1992: 125-132) for an account of the situation in Iran.

In the Soviet Union, Kurdish was used as a medium of teaching in Transcaucasia, and broadcasting and publication were encouraged, until a wave of repression in the late 1930s and early 1940s, when forced deportations of Kurdish populations to Central Asia took place. In the early 1950s cultural activities resumed, and have continued. Publishing in, and on, Kurmanji has been relatively plentiful, if subject to predictable political sensitivities - in particular, Kurds were not encouraged to communicate with their compatriots in the Kurdish homeland. Soviet universities kept the study of Kurmanji folklore alive whilst scholars were unable to collect material in Turkey, and the Kurdish broadcasting of Radio Yerevan had a considerable impact in Turkey.

Kurdish in Iraq

The situation of Kurdish in Iraq is different from the other countries. It is an official State language, with rights of education, broadcasting and cultural life enshrined in various laws and decrees since the time of the British Mandate. Implementation of these laws on the part of governments, however, has often been lax, and has often coincided with persecution of Kurds and so-called 'Arabization' policies. A full account of political events relating to language policy is given in Hassanpour (1992: 102-125).

British policy on Kurdish language changed over the period of the Great War and the subsequent Mandate. Indeed, Hassanpour distinguishes a period of encouragement (1918-26) and discouragement (1926-32). During the War, it was in the British interest to encourage nationalism amongst the Kurds, as a subject people of the Turks. As the political officer C.J. Edmonds commented in 1925: 'One of the devices adopted by the British Officers in Kurdish territory for consolidating Kurdish national sentiment was the introduction of Kurdish as the official written language in place of the Turkish of government offices and the Persian of private correspondence.' (1925: 85, cited by Hassanpour).

The British found themselves in the uncomfortable situation of promoting Kurdish nationalism for propaganda purposes and at the same time trying to restrain it, in order to encourage perceptions of Iraq as a viable entity.

After the war protracted peace negotiations followed, and the need for resolution of the thorny question of the *vilayet* of Mosul. The treaty of Sèvres, with its provision for possible independent Armenian and Kurdish states, complicated matters further. However this was nullified by the Treaty of Lausanne in 1923, though negotiations on Mosul, mediated by the League of Nations, continued until the Treaty of Ankara in 1926, when Turkey renounced her claim and Mosul became part of Iraq. However the needs of the Kurds of the area were taken into account by the League; the commission which recommended that Mosul be part of Iraq also included the following: 'Regard must be paid to the desire expressed by the Kurds that officials of Kurdish race should be appointed for the administration of their country, the dispensation of justice, and teaching in the schools, and that Kurdish should be the official language of all these services' (League of Nations 1925: 89, cited by Hassanpour).

These three demands proved to be points of contention in the years that followed. In 1929, for instance, six Kurdish deputies petitioned the Prime Minister, demanding Kurdish-born administrative officials, the creation of a Kurdish *liwa* and more expenditure on Kurdish education. Their demands were rejected as 'separatist', which caused Edmonds to make a complaint to the High Commissioner that the authorities were failing to keep their promises. Various individual British officers were unsatisfied with the state of provision for the Kurds, but it was in the wider British interest to use Arabic as a means of unifying the state, and to play down Kurdish tensions in preparation for Iraq's entry into the League of Nations.

Iraq was duly admitted into the League in 1932, subject to certain official undertakings, including: 'Iraq undertakes that, in the *liwas* of Mosul, Arbil, Kirkuk and Suleimaniya, the official language, side by side with Arabic, shall be Kurdish in the *qadhas* in which the population is predominantly of Kurdish race.[10] In the *qadhas* of Kifri and Kirkuk, however, in the *liwa* of Kirkuk, where a considerable part of the population is of Turkman race, the official language, side by side with Arabic, shall be either Kurdish or Turkish.' (League of Nations: July 1932: 1347-1350).

However, these conditions were not fulfilled - notably (and very pertinently for Kurmanji speakers) Kurdish never became official in Mosul *liwa*, or in Kirkuk.

The Local Languages Law of 1931 specified the *qadhas* and *liwas* in which Kurdish was to be official, and where it was to be used in the courts and in government departments. It did not answer the concerns of the Kurds. Some areas of Kurdish majority were not covered, and the decision to recruit non-native speakers to local administration on condition that they had knowledge of Kurdish was particularly strongly criticised. There was also anger among Kurds at the lack of provision of Kurdish schooling at higher levels. Arabisation of schools remained a concern until autonomy in 1991.

The overthrow of the monarchy in 1958 changed the political landscape of Iraq entirely, and Article 3 of the provisional Constitution described the Kurds as 'co-partners with the Arabs'. However, there was no concrete progress from the Kurds' point of view on the issues of language officialisation and Kurdish language education. The rebellions of Mulla Mustafa Barzani during the 1960s were in part demands for the implementation of Article 3. The Constitution of 1970 recognised the official status of Kurdish, but the Treaty of Algiers in 1975, which reconciled the Iraqi and Iranian governments, resulted in the exile of Kurdish leaders, who were no longer able to exert direct military pressure on the government. In the late 1970s and 1980s Arabisation of Kurdish areas, and movement and concentration of Kurdish populations, became an important feature of government policy, with many notorious episodes such as the Anfal. However, Kurdish remained taught in schools, in the

[10] My own italics.

Sulaimaniya area at least, and studied at University level in a Kurdish faculty in Baghdad and at the Salahaddin University, which was moved from Sulaimaniya to Erbil. Kurdish cultural production in Iraq has been very lively, especially in times of greater autonomy, with the production of prose, poetry, journalism and theatrical plays.

After 1991, effective (though unofficial) autonomy posed a number of challenges, not the least of which was the restoration of some kind of State education system which would be congenial to the Kurds. Limited resources dictated that changes in the curriculum and the books used were minimal at first, though as the years passed and Kurdish revenues accumulated, new Kurdish textbooks were printed and new centres of education established, most notably the University of Dihok. These achievements rest largely on the goodwill of many ordinary people, such as schoolteachers, who were prepared to work for very little in the early days of the autonomous zone.[11] At the time of the first Kurdish elections in 1992, plans for Kurdish education were in place, though a lack of Kurdish-language learning materials prevented their immediate implementation. The official language of the government of Erbil (which at that time controlled the entire Kurdish zone) was of course Sorani, and some Kurmanji speakers in Badinan expressed discontent at having Sorani as the medium of instruction in their schools, since as far as they were concerned it was as difficult to learn as a foreign language, and, they said, far less useful than Arabic, which they had had before. By the early years of the new millennium, Kurdish was the medium of instruction in schools in the autonomous zone in general, at primary and secondary levels, with Kurmanji (Badini) as well as Sorani taught in the schools of Badinan. A great change during the period of Kurdish autonomy has been the difference in the status of Arabic; it has been reduced to the status of 'foreign language' rather than a major medium of instruction, and a young generation has grown up without great fluency in Arabic. In fact, amongst foreign languages, English is more favoured. Another element of this outlook is the tendency in some quarters to favour the writing of Kurdish in Latin script, though in Iraq it has always been written in a modified Arabic script, which continues to be the norm. My question to a Kurdish politician, Sami Shoresh, Minister of Culture of the Kurdistan Regional Government in Erbil, about this lack of knowledge of Arabic amongst young Kurds, met with a robust response, to the effect that the Kurds wish to distance themselves from Arabic culture and should not have the language forced upon them. There is no doubt that the Kurdish language as spoken in Iraq has become even more self-sufficient and adapted to all high-status purposes over the past fifteen years, but

[11] In a personal account posted on the Kurdistan Regional Government website, a former schoolteacher, attests that many teachers were not paid for months on end in the early days of autonomy. This is consistent with my own observations in 1992. (Tahir Taeb Ahmed 'Education in Kurdistan, Past, Present and Future' on www.krg.org, dated 18 February 2005, consulted 16 May 2005).

consequences of this great change in linguistic balance for the social and economic mobility of young Kurds remain to be seen.

In Iraq under the new order, Kurdish moves from strength to strength. The status of Kurdish was set out in the law of administration for the state of Iraq for the transitional period, published on 8 March 2004:

'The Arabic language and the Kurdish language are the two official languages of Iraq. The right of Iraqis to educate their children in their mother tongue, such as Turcoman, Syriac, or Armenian, in government educational institutions in accordance with educational guidelines, or in any other language in private educational institutions, shall be guaranteed. The scope of the term "official language" and the means of applying the provisions of this Article shall be defined by law and shall include:

(1) Publication of the official gazette, in the two languages;

(2) Speech and expression in official settings, such as the National Assembly, the Council of Ministers, courts, and official conferences, in either of the two languages;

(3) Recognition and publication of official documents and correspondence in the two languages;

(4) Opening schools that teach in the two languages, in accordance with educational guidelines;

(5) Use of both languages in any other settings enjoined by the principle of equality (such as bank notes, passports, and stamps);

(6) Use of both languages in the federal institutions and agencies in the Kurdistan region.'

The role of the Kurds in the government of Iraq has recently been consolidated by the inauguration of Jalal Talabani as President, and by the appointment of Kurdish politicians, such as Hoshyar Zebari, to key Cabinet posts. The process of implementation of the new laws is moving slowly, but if stability can prevail in Iraq, there is every reason to suppose that the official status of Kurdish, so often promised in the past, will at last be realised.

زیادکردنی مووچەی فەرمانبەران و کارمەندان و خانەنشینا

لیستی هاوپەیمانی کوردستا

لیستی نیشتمانی دیموکراتی کوردستان

بەکارهێنانی زمانی کوردی لەعیراق
فیدرالدا دەکرێتە یاسایی

کوردستانی نوێ
KURDISTANÎ NWÊ

A Kurdish Daily Newspaper Published by The PUK - Iraqi Kurdistan Mon. 10/1/2005 No. 3568

مام جەلال بۆ کەسایەتیی و نوێنەرانی دەڤەری گەرمیان:
ئەگەر هاتوو دەستووری ئایندەمان بەدڵ نەبوو، بەپێی یاسا دەتوانین هەڵیبوەشێنینەوە

Fig. 9.2 The daily *Kurdistani Nwe*, published by the PUK, 10 January 2005

Kurdish Literature: Writers' Choices

Given the cultural milieu of Kurdistan and the high status of the literary languages, especially Persian, writing in Kurdish necessitated a conscious choice. The Kurdish writers of the past, most of whom had at least one other literary language at their disposal, often had something to say about why they were choosing to write in Kurdish and how it ought to be done. Although the focus of this paper is Sorani in Iraq, even a sketch of the history of the literature would not be complete without a brief consideration of writing done in other dialects in other parts of Kurdistan, material which has often inspired Sorani writers.

During the period of the Ottoman and Persian empires, before the 1st World War and the creation of Iraq, there are two crucial parts of the cultural background to Kurdish literary composition, which were always present though rarely discussed by writers. The first of these was the vast multitude of works of oral literature - epics, romances, lyrical songs about battles and losses of the past, songs about love that could be passionate, sad, angry, crude and touching - sometimes all at once! This was an environment where even those who could not read could compose songs for their loved one, where bards competed against each other in village guest-houses and noblemen's courts alike. These popular traditions were always there - their characters, their storylines, sometimes their metre and structure, provided the literary poets with inspiration, and could often lend a truly 'Kurdish' authenticity to the literature they produced.

The other important and constant factor is the absolute cultural dominance of Persian as a language of letters. Arabic was of course learned in religious schools, but many of the literary and religious texts studied were Persian, and Persian was used as a common language in many parts of Southern Kurdistan. For those living in such places as Halabja or Sulaymaniya, who were used to Persian as the language of literature and Ottoman Turkish as the language of administration, the institution of the state of Iraq and subsequent Arabisation of all official systems must have been felt as a 'pull',as it were, from one centre of gravity towards another.

The first flowering of Kurdish literature took place in Kurmanji during the 16th and 17th centuries in the area of Jazire Botan (around the modern Cizre in Turkey). A school of poets grew up surrounding Shaikh Ahmad Nishani, also known as 'Melayê Cezîrî' 'the mollah of Jezireh' (1570-1640). His *Dîwan* of mystico-religious poetry was very much in the Persian tradition and is still read today. However, he was outshone by Ahmad Khani (1650-1707) who has become an icon not only of Kurdishness but also of Kurdish nationalist aspirations. Khani's *magnum opus* was *Mem û Zîn*, a poem in *masnavi* form of some 2500 verses, loosely based on a folkloric tradition called *Memê Alan.* Khani explains his motives for writing in Kurdish at some length, and clearly aimed to found a new Kurdish literary tradition which would rival Persian in beauty and accomplishment. The story on which it hangs is purely Kurdish, but the work is stuffed full of allusions to Persian literature, to Sa'di, Hafez, Nizami, Firdowsi, to science via Avicenna and Aristotle, to current Sufi ideas and to Kurdish poets. It would be impossible for a public which was not highly educated to appreciate all of this; it is clear that Khani is trying to elevate Kurdish to the heights of Persian, rather than bring literature to Kurdish masses.

In the introductory sections where Khani declares his reasons for writing the work, he devotes a considerable space to bewailing the lack of unity of the Kurds, extolling their sterling national qualities, and stating that if they had strong leadership (a king, in fact) they could dominate their neighbours instead of being dominated by them. This has given rise to a debate. Some cite the passage as an outright call for a Kurdish state (Shakely 1992; Hassanpour 2003); others dismiss such concepts as anachronistic, given that the poem was written long before the French Revolution, usually seen as a point of departure in the development of the modern nation state

(Vali 2003). What is clear is that Khani ascribed certain values and qualities to the Kurds[12], and that, if not a nationalist in the modern sense, he was certainly a patriot.

Khani is esteemed all over Kurdistan, and his tomb in Doğubayazit is still visited. After his time, however, the literary centre of gravity shifted southwards, and during the 18th and 19th century it was Gorani, used at the court of the Ardalan princes in Sanandaj, which dominated. Of this literature it is probably the *ghazal*s and elegies of Mewlewî (Sayyed Abdolrahim Tawgozi, 1806-1882) which are most fondly remembered. He used metres which recalled those of oral tradition, and, perhaps because he suffered a great deal in his personal life, much of his work is very sad in tone. The Gorani language, in both its literary and oral forms, enjoys a special status in Iraqi and Iranian Kurdistan, though it is currently spoken by very few people. It remains strongly associated with the spectacular Hewraman region, seen as the cradle of many ancient cultural elements, such as the religion of the Ahl-e-Haqq.[13]

Sorani became important as a literary language after the rise of the Baban dynasty of Sulaimaniya in the 19th century and was used by various classical poets, including Nali (1800-1855) who is described by some as the greatest Kurdish classical poet, Kurdi (1809-1849) and Haji Qadiri Koyi (1817-1897). By Koyi's time, the age of the quasi-independent Kurdish principalities was over, and he embraced a modern nationalist position, for which he is much respected today. Although he qualified as a mollah, he came to see men of religion in general, including mollahs and shaikhs, as a force impeding the progress of the Kurdish people, a position shared by many of the early Kurdish nationalists. Koyi was born in Iraqi Kurdistan and travelled throughout Iranian Kurdistan. From the 1870s onwards he lived in Constantinople, and was a tutor to the Bedir Khan family, whose members were a focal point of early Kurdish nationalism; the brothers Kamuran and Celadet Bedir Khan later pioneered the system of writing Kurmanji in Roman script which is used today.

Despite Koyi's fame today, he was probably something of a voice in the wilderness in his own time. Most of the Kurdish people remained very influenced by the views of mollahs and shaikhs, and the revolts of the late 19th and early 20th century were centred around those with religious influence (such as Shaikh Obeydullah, Shaikh Mahmud Barzinji, Shaikh Said) rather than secular intellectuals such as the Bedir Khans. Koyi's *diwan* was not published until long after his death.

Koyi linked questions of nationalism explicitly to questions of language in his poetry. All translations of Koyi in this chapter are quoted from Hassanpour's very able translations into English (Hassanpour 1992: 90-94). Koyi asserted the value of Kurdish by comparison with Persian:

---

[12] However, it remains a debatable point who exactly Khani had in mind when he used the term 'Kurd'. In past sources it is often used to mean tribal or nomadic groups, rather than the modern sense of an *ethnie*.

[13] For the Ahl-e-Haqq religion, also known as Yaresan, and Kaka'i in Iraq, see Hamzeh'ee 1990.

Meḷên fesaḥetî Kurdî be Farsî naga
Belaxetêkî heye hîç zimanê naygatê
Le bête 'esubî Kurdane bêṛewac û beha.
(Hîwa vol 3 no. 4, May 1960: 22).

Do not say that Kurdish is not as eloquent as Persian
It possesses such eloquences unmatched by any language,
It is due to indifference of the Kurds that it is not fashionable.

He reproached mollahs and sheikhs in particular for their uses of Arabic and Persian rather than Kurdish:

Kurdî axir bḷê çiye 'eybî?
Her kelamî heqqe niye 'eybî
Ya legeḷ Farsî çi ferqî heye
Boçî ew raste, boçî em kemiye?
(Mala Kerim 1960: 19)

Tell (us), what is wrong with Kurdish?
It is only the word of God that is faultless.
why is it (Kd.) different from Persian,
Why is one fine, the other debased?

For Koyi, the Kurds were disadvantaged as a nation by a lack of literature and literacy in Kurdish:

Her Kurde le beynî kullî millet
Bê behre le xöndin û kitabet
Bêgane le tercumey zubanî
Esrarî kitêbî xeḷkî zanî
Yekser 'ulema dirişt û wirdî
Ney xönduwe hîç dû herfî Kurdî
(*ibid.*: 15-16).

Only the Kurds, among all nations, are
Deprived of reading and writing.
By translating into their own languages, the foreigners
Became familiar with the secrets of other peoples' books,
None of our scholars, great or small,
Has ever read two letters in Kurdish.

His trenchant remarks on the duty of Kurds to speak Kurdish have become proverbial (Hassanpour 1992: 92)

Eger Kurdê zubanî xoy nezanî
Muḥaqqeq daykî hîze û babî zanî.
(*ibid.*: 17)

If a Kurd does not know his own language
Undoubtedly his mother is infidel and his father adulterous.

and, more brusquely:

Le Kurdî ḥez neka Kurdê, meḷên 'boçî?' we ya 'çone?'
Le dayki pirsiyarê ken ew bêçuwey le kö hêna!
(*ibid.*: 18)

If a Kurd does not like his language, do not ask 'Why?' or 'How?'
Ask his mother where she got this bastard!

During the twentieth century, Kurdish literature in Iraq developed enormously, though considerations of space limit this discussion to a few famous names; I shall single out three poets in particular who exemplify some of the most important features of the literature. Nationalist sentiment, and Kurdish struggle and sufferings, became an ever-present dimension of Kurdish literature, though writers also drew on the great themes of the literary heritage of previous centuries, such as love and devotion. Let us turn first to Dildar (Yunis Rauf, 1917-1948) and his poem 'Ey reqib', which was set to music and has become the Kurdish national anthem. Translated into Kurmanji and sung by Shivan Perwer, it is also known among the Kurds of Turkey. The following version is often sung in Northern Iraq:[14]

Ey reqîb her mawe qewmî kurd ziman,
Nay şikênî danerî topî zeman.

(Refrain) Kes neḷê kurd mirduwe; kurd zînduwe,
Zînduwe qet nanewê alakeman.

Lawî kurd hestaye ser pê wek dilêr,
Ta be xwên nexsîn bike tacî jiyan.

[14] I am grateful to Zubeida Abdulkhaliq for this version.

Fig. 9.3 The poet Dildar, from an edition of his verses and poems

Eme roley Midya u Keyxosrewîn,
Dînman, ayînman her niştiman

Eme roley rengî sor u şorişîn,
Seyrî ke xwênawî ye rabirdûman.

Lawî kurd her hazir u amadeye,
Giyan fîdane, giyan fîda, her giyanfîda.

O enemy, the Kurdish people and their tongue still survive,
They cannot be broken by the weapons of time,

(Refrain) Let no one say Kurds are dead, the Kurds are alive!
The Kurds are alive, their flag will never fall!

The young Kurds have risen up like lions
To adorn the crown of life with blood,
(Refrain)

We are the children of Medya and Kay Khusrow
Kurdistan is all - our faith, our creed,
(Refrain)

We, the young ones, are the colour red, we are the revolution
See our blood, which we shed along the way,
(Refrain)

The young Kurds are ready and waiting,
Always ready to sacrifice, to sacrifice their lives,
(Refrain)

At the very beginning of this poem, language is singled out as a marker of Kurdish presence and identity. The socialist imagery, of the colour red, revolutions and self-sacrifice, particularly that of the young, is also present in many twentieth-century Kurdish authors. Koyi's rejection of traditional religion is continued in this discourse - it is Kurdistan which is the object of veneration. A continuity with the distant Iranian past is also evoked, along with an allusion to the belief, very prevalent amongst nationalist intellectuals, that the Kurds are the descendants of the Medes. These elements are all constants in Kurdish literature of the first half of the twentieth century, and are equally visible in the work of writers from other parts of Kurdistan, such as Cigerxwîn, a Kurd from Turkey who wrote in Kurmanji and continued to treat these themes until his death in Sweden in 1984.

No consideration, however brief, of Kurdish modern literature can be complete without a mention of 'Goran' (Abdullah Sulaiman, 1904-1962) who is much beloved among Sorani speakers in particular. As his early work shows, he was well educated in the traditional literary and metrical forms bequeathed to Kurdish by Persian, but as time moved on he began to use more and more forms and motifs associated with folkloric poetry, especially that of Gorani, and more and more Kurdish vocabulary rather than Persian or Arabic.[15] His romanticism, which often explicitly linked the beauty of woman and the beauty of nature, spoke to Kurdish sensibilities at a deep and evocative level. An example is the opening of *Ey şewqî gelawêj*:

---

[15] These developments, particularly their metrical aspects, are well chronicled in Ahmed 2004, a work whose excellent translations into French were the basis for my version of these couplets from *Ey şewqî gelawêj*.

Ey şewqî gelawêjî beyan nûrî nîgahit!
Ey 'etrî seba boy nefesî zuḷfî siyahit!

Ey husnî tulû' wêneyekî feyzî huzûrit
Ey huznî xurûb ṛojî reşî dûrî tebahit!

You whose glance shines like the morning star,
Your breath, your dark hair perfumes the breeze,

The grace of your presence is painted by the beauty of the dawn,
The dark day of your leaving is the sadness of the sunset.

Images and descriptions of the landscape, geographical features, flora and fauna of Kurdistan play an enormous role in the culture of the Kurds, who, despite their rural idyll, are predominantly city-dwellers.

Geşt le Hewraman[16]
Komele şaxêk sext û gerdenkeş,
Asmanî şînî girtote baweş ;

Serpoşî lûtkey befrî zor sipî
Bi daristan reş naw dolî kipî ...

Cogey awekan tîyaya qetîs maw:
Her eron naken pêçî şax tewaw.

Hawar û hajey kefçerênî çem
Bo tenyayî şew laye layey xem!

Tûlerêy barîk, tûnawtûn pişkin
Rêbwar exate endêşey bê bin ...

Naw rêga teqteq, larêy berdî zil
Ke hêşta gerdûn pêy nedawe til!

Ga serew jûre, ga serew xware
Taliw şîrînî dinyay rêbware! ...

(Goran 1980: 127-8)

[16] I am grateful to Amr Ahmed for corrections to this text.

A Tour in Hawraman
A mountain mass, wild and defiant,
Has gathered blue heaven in its embrace;
The mantle of its peak is brilliant white snow,
Dark with forest are its silent dales.
Waters imprisoned in their tunnels
Flow on, nor cease their windings round the hills;
The roar and hiss of foam, the shrill song of the brook:
Lullabies for grief in the solitude of night.
The narrow footpath, feeling its way from tunnel to tunnel,
Throws the wayfarer into anxiety without end;
On the track rocky stairways, on the side great boulders,
That heaven has not yet sent rolling down.
Now up hill, now down hill,
The bitter and sweet of the wayfarer's world.[17]

Even by local standards, the Kurds are remarkably attached to their land. The geographer Maria O'Shea (2004: *passim*) diagnosed an acute case of topophilia, and indeed the territory is constantly evoked in songs, stories, paintings and films, and children are often named after rivers, ancient principalities and mountains. Allusions to features of landscape, which may sometimes also be allusions to generally known events which happened there, can evoke complex emotional responses for Kurds. These are only enhanced by the migrations, forced or otherwise, which many Kurdish families have undergone over the past few generations. Goran was a master of such allusions, and enjoys a special place in the Kurdish canon.

Finally, in any discussion of distinguished Kurdish poets, Sherko Bêkes (b. 1940) cannot possibly be omitted. Born in Sulaimaniya, he is the son of poet Faîq Bêkes, and has spent time in the mountains with Kurdish guerrilla fighters, a period in prison, and some years in exile, before returning to Kurdistan to play a prominent political and cultural role. In his poetry he evokes classic Kurdish subjects - love, the land, the sufferings of the people. For instance, like Goran, he has written about Nowruz, the story of the Iranian New Year which the Kurds retell as a liberation myth. He mentions the Kurdish poets who came before him, and the national heroes, such as the film-maker Yilmaz Güney. He also refers to personalities and issues associated with international liberation struggles - Chile, Palestine, Algeria. However, his work is perhaps easier for international readers to appreciate as he manages to combine the particularity of the Kurdish experience with general aspects of the human condition - suffering, love, and humour, often with great deftness of imagery and a lightness of touch. It is easy to imagine his neighbour Umm Saad, with her face

---

[17] This translation was posted anonymously on the 'Kerkuk Kurdistan' website, with source cited as Kurdish Democratic Party, Ankara. http://www.kerkuk-kurdistan.com, 27 June 2005.

like burnt bread, her past of unimaginable suffering, her tales of the desert, her indomitable energy. Some of his ideas are whimsical - the rebellion of the lightbulbs which refuse to shine any longer because, though they have faithfully illuminated countless statues, nobody has ever erected a statue to Thomas Edison. He has produced long poems, including an integrated autobiographical one entitled 'The Cross, the Snake and the Diary of a Poet' where all the eponymous elements have their own symbolism. However, the images of the short poems tend to stay in the mind and lend themselves well to translation.

Yadaşt
Gul yadaştî xoy nûsîwe
Nîwey yadaşt
le ser nîgay ciwanî aw bû
Aw yadaştî xoy nûsîwe
Nîwey yadaşt
le ser bejnî şûxuşengî daristan bû
Daristanîş ke yadaştî xoy nûsîwe
Nîwey yadaşt
le ser xakî desgîran bû
Ke xakîşman yadaştekanî nûsîwe
Hemû yadaşt
Hemû yadaşt
Le ser daykî mîhrebanî azadî bû

Memoirs
The rose wrote her memoirs.
Half the memoirs
Were devoted to the delightful landscape by the water.

The water wrote her memoirs.
Half the memoirs
Were devoted to the lovely outline of the orchard.

When the orchard also wrote her memoirs
Half the memoirs
Were devoted to the earth of her beloved.

And when the earth
Wrote her memoirs
All the memoirs
- All her memoirs -
Were devoted to sweet mother Freedom.

2005 پیروزبێت

بارزانی نامەیەك بۆ تارق عەزیز دەنێرێت

هەواڵ

Hawal

No. (113) 4th Year 1 January 2004

www.hewal.org

هەڵبژاردنی پارێزگای کەرکوک بەتەوافق دەکرێت

٤١ کورسیەکە بەو ڕێژەیەی ئێستا دەمێنێتەوە تەنها دەمو چاوەکان دەگۆڕدرێن

بەرامبەر بەرەخنەیەك لەسەر وەزارەت

وەزیری پەروەردەی سلێمانی ئەندامێکی سکرتاریتی

١٥٠ پاسەپۆرتی

Fig. 9.4 The independent weekly newspaper *Hewal* ("News")

Conclusion

The Kurds, then, *are* alive, and so is their language, and whatever may be said about the political success of the Kurdish experiment in autonomy, in the light of the civil war of 1996 and the subsequent partition of the zone, by all accounts the education system and cultural life in general have seen great improvements since 1991. There are now universities in all three of the governorates of the former autonomous region (Dihok, Erbil, Sulaimaniya). These universities remain in need of outside help and sponsorship but they are functioning. Educational and other books are being published in Kurdish, and foreign works translated into Kurdish. Hundreds of newspapers and magazine titles, with many interest groups amongst the various sectors of the population, have been published, though the number of these which are able to stay in existence with an assured readership and income remains small. Broadcasting is well established, in Kurdish and the minority languages (especially neo-Aramaic and Turcoman), and the Erbil government has plans for the development of Kurdish cinema, following the great success of Kurdish-interest films in Iranian cinema. The lively Kurdish-language theatre of resistance which existed during the Ba'ath regime continues to develop.

At the time of writing it seems almost inconceivable that Kurdish language should die in Iraq in the foreseeable future. The future of Iraq as a whole is unclear, but even if the country were to disintegrate, the Kurdish region now has an extremely strong cultural identity, well consolidated in Kurdish language broadcasting, education and written literature. It seems unlikely that Arabic could dominate again, unless this were to be done by force; it is unlikely that other Iraqis would be able to exert such pressure on the Kurds without outside help, even if they wished to. There seem to be few question marks over the survival of Sorani. For Kurmanji in the form of Badini, the situation is less clear. There is talk at Kurdish government level of 'language union', though it is highly unclear what form this would take beyond a sharing of common vocabulary, and how far a Kurdish government would go in imposing language change. Given the tension between, on the one hand, the considerable differences between the dialects, and on the other hand their growing tendency to develop vocabulary and discourses in common, it remains to be seen how far Badini will go down the road towards union with Sorani, or assimilation into it, and how far it will diverge from the Kurmanji spoken by the Kurds of Turkey, whose standard language is developing in other directions. It is possible that Iraqi Kurdistan, small as it is, might have a viable future as an area of two standard Kurdish languages (after all, efforts are made to protect minority languages such as neo-Aramaic and Turcoman, so the area is already multilingual); another possibility is that in the future the dividing line between the Kurdish major dialects of Kurmanji and Sorani might no longer be the Great Zab, but the international frontier between Iraq and Turkey.

Further reading and references

Ahmed, A. 2004. *Nimā Yušij et 'Abdollah Goran : aspects formels du renouvellement politique*, DEA thesis, Université Paris III, Sorbonne Nouvelle. Paris.

Ardalan, S. 2004. *Les Kurdes Ardalân entre la Perse et l'Empire ottoman*. Paris.

Blau, J. 1975. *Le Kurde de 'Amādiya et de Djabal Sindjār ; Analyse linguistique, textes folkloriques, glossaires*. Paris.

- 1989. 'Le kurde' et 'Gurânî et Zaza', in *Compendium Linguarum Iranicarum*. Wiesbaden: 327-335; 336-341.
- 1984. *Mémoire du Kurdistan*. Paris.
- 1996. 'Kurdish Written Literature', in Kreyenbroek P.G. and Allison, C. *Kurdish Culture and Identity*. London: 20-28.

Bêkes, S. 1995. tr. Maarof, K., *Les petits miroirs*. Paris.

- 1997. tr. Mirza, R. and S., *The secret diary of a rose : a journey through poetic Kurdistan*. Greystone, NSW.

Bynon, T. 1979. 'The Ergative Construction in Kurdish', *Bulletin of the School of Oriental and African Studies* 42: 211-224.

- 1980. 'From Passive to Active in Kurdish via the Ergative Construction', in *Papers from the 4th International Conference on Historical Linguistics*. Amsterdam:151-163.

Dorleijn, M. 1996. *The Decay of Ergativity in Kurmanci*. Tilburg.

Edmonds, C.J. 1925. 'A Kurdish newspaper: "Rozh-i Kurdistan", *Journal of the Royal Central Asian Society of Great Britain and Ireland* Vol XII: 83-90.

Fattah, I.K. 2000. *Les Dialectes kurdes méridionaux*, Acta Iranica 37. Louvain.

'Goran' 1980. *Dîwan*, edited by Mihemed Mela Kerîm. Baghdad: Union of Kuridsh Writers.

Hamzeh'ee, M.R. 1990. *The Yaresan: a sociological, historical and Religio-Historical Study of a Kurdish Community*. Berlin.

Haig, G, et Matras, Y. 2002. 'Kurdish linguistics: a brief overview,' Sprachtypologie und Universialienforschung (Berlin) 55/i: 3-14.

- 2004. 'The Invisibilisation of Kurdish: the Other Side of Language Planning in Turkey', in Conermann, S. & Haig, G. (eds.), *Die Kurden: Studien zu ihrer Sprache, Geschichte und Kultur*, Asien und Afrika: Beiträge des Zentrums für Asiatische und Afrikanische Studien (ZAAS) der Christian-Albrechts-Universität zu Kiel, Band 8. Schenefeld: 121-150.

Hassanpour, A. 1992. *Nationalism and Language in Kurdistan 1918-1985*. San Francisco.

- 1998. 'The Identity of Hewrami Speakers: Reflections on the Theory and Ideology of Comparative Philology', published on Internet http://www.cogsci.ed.ac.uk/~siamakr/Kurdish/Papers.

- 2003. 'The Making of Kurdish Identity: Pre-20th Century Historical and Literary Discourses', in Vali, A. (ed.), *Essays on the Origins of Kurdish Nationalism*. Costa Mesa.

Jaba, A. 1860. *Recueil de notices et de récits kurdes servant à la connaissance de la langue*. St. Petersburg.

Jardine, R.F. 1922. *Bahdinan Kurmancî, a Grammar of the Kurmanji of the Kurds of Mosul Division and Surrounding Districts of Kurdistan*. Baghdad.

Kerîm, M.M. 1998. 'Mewlewî: A Great Poet and 'Âlim of Southern Kurdistan' in van Bruinessen, M. & Blau, J. (eds.), *Islam des Kurdes*, Les Annales de l'Autre Islam no. 5. Paris: 59-82.

Kreyenbroek, P.G. 1992. 'On the Kurdish Language', in Kreyenbroek, P.G. & Sperl, S., *The Kurds: an Overview*. London:. 68-83.

- and Allison, F.C. (eds.) 1996. *Kurdish Culture and Identity*, London.

League of Nations 1925. *Question of the Frontier between Turkey and Iraq*.

- 1932. *Official Journal*, July 1932, 13th year, no.7.

Leezenberg, M. 1993. 'Gorani Influence on Central Kurdish: Substratum or Prestige Borrowing?', http://www.cogsci.ed.ac.uk/~siamakr/Kurdish/Papers/

Lerch, P. 1857-8. *Forschungen über die Kurden und die iranischen Nordchaldäer I-II*. St. Petersburg, repr. Amsterdam 1979.

MacKenzie, D. N. 1961. 'The Origins of Kurdish', in *Transactions of the Philological Society*, 1961, 68-86.

- 2nd. ed. 1990. *Kurdish Dialect Studies*. London.

Mann, O. 1906, 1909. *Die Mundart der Mukri-Kurden*, 2 vols. Berlin.

Matras, Y. 1993. 'Ergativity in Kurmanji (Kurdish): Notes on Its Use and Distribution', *Orientalia Suecana* XLI-XLII: 139-154.

Nebez, J. 1976. *Zimanî Yekgirtûy Kurdî* (Towards a Unified Kurdish Language). Bamberg: National-Union Kurdischer Studenten in Europa.

O'Shea, M.T. 2004. *Trapped between the Map and Reality: Geography and Perceptions of Kurdistan*. London and New York.

Shakely, F. 1992. *Nationalism in 'Mem û Zîn' of Ahmedê Khanî*. Uppsala.

Skuttnabb-Kangas, T. & Bucak, S. 1994. 'Killing a mother tongue - how the Kurds are deprived of linguistic human rights', in T. Skuttnabb-Kangas and R. Phillipson (eds.), *Linguistic Human Rights: Overcoming Linguistic Discrimination*. Berlin and New York.

Soane, E.B. 1913. *A Grammar of the Kurmanji or Kurdish Language*. London.

- 1919. *Elementary Kurmanji Grammar, Suleimania District*. Baghdad.

Vali, A. 2003. 'Genealogies of the Kurds: Constructions of Nation and National Identity in Kurdish Historical Writing', in Vali, A. (ed.), *Essays on the Origins of Kurdish Nationalism*. Costa Mesa.

Iraqi Turkman

Christiane Bulut

University of Mainz

Present-day Turkey, Iran and Iraq form a region in which the three major Oriental languages meet. For more than a millennium, the people of Iraq have performed in various languages or dialects of the Iranian, Semitic and Turkic language families. While the existence of Arabic and Kurdish dialects of Iraq is known to a broader public, Turkic varieties have remained *terra incognita* even to specialists. Thus far, turcologists have hardly taken notice of the Turkic minority of Iraq, its language and its historical affiliations.

Until recently, Iraqi Turkmans themselves displayed little awareness of ethnicity or national identity. Moreover, there has been no central political organization representing the Turkic minority.[1] Accordingly, estimates of the actual Turkic population of Iraq vary a great deal. Recent publications from Turkey maintain that there are up to 3 million Turks in Iraq, while sources from Iraq arrive at a more moderate figure of roughly 600,000.[2] The correct ethnonym is still a matter of debate. Writers from Turkey prefer the expression *Irak Türkleri* 'the Turks of Iraq',

---

On the 24th of April 1995, the Iraqi Turkman Front was founded. The First Turkman Congress held in Erbil on the 5th of February 1997 elected the president and the members of the Executive Board of the Iraqi Turkman Front. They represent four Turkman organizations: the Iraqi National Turkman Party, the Turkmeneli Party, the Turkman Independents' Movement and the Turkman Brotherhood Organization.

Fischer (1993) compares various statistics from pre-colonial data and an Iraqi census conducted in 1957. According to Fischer, Benderoğlu reported a number of 600,000 for the year 1989. That is 3.3% of the total population of Iraq (18.27 million in 1989). Buluç (1980) mentions a figure of 750,000.

which stresses the close relationship with their former Ottoman compatriots. The Turks of Iraq, on the other hand, call themselves *Turkman* [tʊrʒmæn], and their language *Turkmanja.*

The Turkic area of settlement in Iraq is by no means homogeneous. Traditionally, the Turkman live in a number of separate areas, villages and towns situated within a belt stretching from Tel'afer in the northwest to Bedre in the southeast. Thus, they are sandwiched between the Kurdish regions to the north and east and Arabic-speaking areas to the south. Most larger cities, such as Kerkuk and Erbil, have a mixed, mainly Turkic-Kurdish population. An important group of Turkman is also found in Baghdad. The migration in recent years, which was caused by the Arabization policy of the Baath-Party and subsequent wars and civil wars, has considerably changed the ethnic map of Iraq. Moreover, many villages and traditional environments of the Turkman, such as the old quarters within the citadel of Kerkuk, have been destroyed in recent years.

It is obvious that Iraq is far off from the Turkic heartland, and the Turkic minority does not represent an autochthonous or very old population of the region. One may thus ask who these Turkic speakers are, where they came from, and when they settled in Iraq.

1. *Historical background*

The history of Turkic settlement in Iraq dates back to the first century of Islam. It is well documented in Islamic historiography that the first Turks came to southern Iraq as military slaves (*ġilmân*) of the Omayyads. In 673/674 AD (54 d.H.),[3] the governor of Khorasan, 'Ubaydallâh b. Ziyâd, conquered Bukhara. Part of his booty were 2000 Turkic *ġilmân*, whom he took along to Basra the following year. During the Omayyad Caliphate, the governor of Khorasan used to send a yearly contingent of 2000 soldiers levied in various regions of Turkestan to Baghdad. With the shift of power to the Abbasid clan, the need for Turkic troops must have been quite considerable. Within a single year, 755 AD, 20,000 Turkic *ġilmân* came to Iraq.[4]

Under the Abbasids, especially the caliphs al-Ma'mun and al-Mu'tasim, Turkic military slaves played an important role in the army. The famous Arabic author al-Ǧâḥiẓ of Basra praises the military qualities of the Turkic soldiery.[5] The Turkic troops in the services of the caliphs were garrisoned at Samarrah; they were strictly forbidden to mix or marry with the local population. Al-Mu'tasim took further measures to keep the pagan Turks separated from his Muslim subjects. Thus, he ordered a contingent of Turkic slave girls and married them to the *ġilmân*.[6] These

---

[3] I.e. under the reign of the Omayyad caliph Mu'âwiyya.

[4] aḍ-Ḍâbiṭ, Šâkir Ṣâbir. Mu'ğaz ta'rîḫ at-Turkmân fî'l-'Irâq. Baghdad 1984; see: Saatçi 1996: 39 ff.

[5] See his *Risâla fî manâqib at-Turk wa 'âmmat ğund al-ḫilâfa*, extracts in Pellat 1969: 91-97.

[6] For an extensive description of the Turkic garrisons in Iraq see Töllner (1971).

Chronological chart

ꞏeriod of time	dynasty or ruler	location	languages
ı/8th century	Omayyad caliphate	Turkic *ġilmân*/military slaves in southern Iraq	Ancient Eastern Turkic varieties (?), Arabic
0-1258	Abbasid caliphate	since the decline of the central power during the 10th century semi-dependent Turkic governors in Iran/Iraq	Arabic; Persian as administrative language
th-13th ntury	Saljuqids	Iran, Iraq, Anatolia	mainly Oghuz ('South-western') Turkic varieties/ Persian as administrative language
th century	raids of Jengiz Khan	Iran, Iraq, Anatolia, Central Asia, China	Turco-Mongolian varieties
th-14th ntury	Atabegs, Ilkhanids, Jalayirids	Iran/Azerbaijan, Iraq, Anatolia	under the Ilkhanids Uigur is the official language in Iran; formation of Ajam Turkic in Iran/Iraq and of Old Anatolian Turkish in the West
e 14th/15th ntury	raids of Timur	Iran, Iraq, Anatolia, central Asia	(emergence of the eastern written language Chaghatay)
th-16th ıtury	tribal confederations of the Qaraqoyunlu, Aqqoyunlu, Qızılbaş	eastern Anatolia , Iran, Iraq	Ajam Turkic/Oghuz Turkic varieties with few eastern (Chaghatay) elements
th-18th ıtury	simultaneous rise of Ottomans and Safawids	series of wars in the border regions/Iraq	Persian as official language in Iran, while the court at Isfahan speaks Turki; Ottoman Turkish in the West
th-19th ıtury	Qajar dynasty in Iran; tribal confederation of the Shahseven	increasing Ottoman influence since Tanzimat in 2nd half of 19th century	Ottoman Turkish is the official language and lingua franca in Iraq; varieties of Kurdish, Turkic, Arabic

ladies received a fixed salary from the caliphal purse, and their names were registered in the *divân*.[7]

As a result of the weakening of the central power of the Abbasid Caliphate in the 10th century, a number of *de facto* independent principalities arose. As in the case of the Samanids, many of them again favoured the services of Turkic troops. Some Turkic commanders succeeded in seizing power; they founded various local dynasties, such as the Ghaznawids of Afghanistan. A century before the Saljuq conquest of Iran, Turkic commanders of the Buyid Dynasty (capital: Ray), who had reached high positions in the army, were in control of the province of Hamadan in western Iran (Spuler 1952: 252).

In 1055, the Saljuq prince Ṭoġril Beg conquered Baghdad. While in former times most of the Turks sent to Iraq were pagan military slaves, in the wake of the Saljuq conquest Islamicised Turkic clans and tribes became settled in the area.

In the early 13th century, during the Mongol raids under Hülegü, the Turkic community in Iraq must have increased considerably. In addition to refugees who had fled from Central Asia, Turks formed an important part of the Mongol troops.

In the following centuries, the region was part of the Turco-Mongolian empires of the Ilkhanids and the Jalayirids (1335).[8] During this period many Turkic tribes, as e.g. the Bayat who today are living west of Kerkuk, must have entered Iraq.[9] Timur's raids in the late 14th century brought other Turco-Mongolian elements into the region; some were refugees from the East who had escaped the approaching invaders, others formed part of the mixed Turco-Mongolian troops themselves. The importance of the Turkic population may have consolidated under the so-called *Turkoman* confederations of the Aqqoyunlu and Qaraqoyunlu, who ruled over eastern Anatolia, Iraq, Azerbaijan (Tabriz) and parts of Iran. The Aqqoyunlu reign over Iraq came to an end in 1508, when Shah Ismail conquered Baghdad.

In 1534, after the raids of Qanûnî Sultan Süleyman, Iraq became part of the Ottoman Empire. From 1623 (Shah 'Abbâs) to 1638 (Sultan Murat IV), Iraq again was part of the Safawid Empire, where Iranian culture had begun to dominate over Turkic elements. In 1704, Georgian *Mamluks* reigned in Baghdad, while in 1726 Mosul was in the hands of the clan of the *Jalîlî*. These local dynasties lasted till 1831 when the Ottoman sultans again seized power over Iraq; Ottoman influence increased considerably during the reform period of the *Tanzimat* (1839-1876), when the Sultans tried to re-establish the central power in the provinces.

---

[7] Töllner (1971: 43).

[8] Sümer (1952:383) mentions that the genealogy of the Sarulu-clan goes back to one of the ministers of the Jalayrids.

[9] Sümer (1952:383).

1.1 *History of settlement and language*
What does the foregoing historical development imply with regard to the Turkic languages spoken in the region? Turkic migration into Iraq comprises several waves over a period of at least five to six centuries. Each wave has certainly left traces in the development of the language or dialects. Yet, it is impossible to reconstruct the oldest strata. From the early times of Islam, different groups of Turkic or Turco-Mongolian origin are known to have settled in Iraq. The earliest Turkic immigrants came from Central Asia in the time of the first Khaghanate (644-744 AD). In all probability, their language was Ancient Eastern Turkic.[10] Yet, it would be highly unusual that the recent dialects preserved archaic traits of such great antiquity. Moreover, we do not know whether these first Turkic speakers have left traces on the linguistic map of Iraq at all, or whether they remained present to pass their linguistic heritage to fellow-Turk newcomers.

A regular Turkic immigration to Iraq begins more than 200 years later, under the reign of the Saljuqs, and it was enforced under the Mongol states of the Ilkhanids and the Jalayirids. After the decline of Mongol power, Iraq became part of the realms of the heterogeneous confederations of the Aq- and Qaraqoyunlu.

Subsequent to the Saljuqid conquest, nomadic tribes played an important role in the historical development of the area comprising today's Iran, Iraq, Anatolia, and parts of Syria. Their old Turkic tribe or clan names appear in early sources such as the *Divân-ı luġat-ı Turk*, which the Khaqanian prince Maḥmûd al-Kâšġarî composed in Baghdad in the year 1070 AD, or Rašîd ad-Dîn's *Ta'rîḫ-ı Ġâzânî,* written for the Ilkhan *Ġâzân* in the early 13th century.

What is so characteristic of these tribes is their high mobility and frequent grouping and re-grouping in different confederations throughout the region. It should be remembered that some of the newly formed tribes or confederations took to old, prestigious names. Thus, the appearance of certain Turkic tribal names alone can not be taken as a sound indicator of historical continuity. Moreover, it is far from certain that the groups behind these names shared the same origins or the same ethnic or linguistic textures. During the 13th and 14th centuries, Turkic tribal names are not mentioned in chronicles. Oberling (1985: 582) supposes that "the historical works of that time generally use the vague term Turkoman instead of more specific names for any and all Turkic tribes". The ethnonym Turkman started to appear in Islamic historiography of the 10th century, denoting "Nomadic Turcs who have embraced Islam". Thus, it was also used as a collective term for the tribes which joined the Saljuqs on their westward migration.

---

[10] Following Doerfer (1976: 83), in the eighth century the formation of the Turkic languages had not gone very far. Accordingly, the predecessors of the present Turkic language groups (Oghuz, Qıpchaq, Uyghur) were still closer to each other, having developed less divergent features.

From the time of the Saljuqs, the Turkic language of the region must have displayed predominantly Oghuz or south-western Turkic traces, with some additional Kipchak or Central Asian elements and strong influences from the official or administrative language, New Persian. The language of communication or *lingua franca*[11] which developed between the tribes of East Anatolia, Iran and Iraq is sometimes called 'Ajam Turkic'.[12] Ajam Turkic was spoken at the courts in Tabriz under the Aqqoyunlu and the early Safawids, and Shah Ismail's poems were written in this idiom. Although Modern Persian was to become the official language of Iran, Ajam Turkic maintained its position as the language of the court during the 16th century, when the Safawids and their entourage of Turkic tribes moved to Qazvîn and later to Isfahan in central Iran, and in the 18th century, when the capital became Shirâz in the southern province of Fars.

In the 16th and 17th centuries the history of Iraq was dominated by border conflicts between two powers which rapidly began to consolidate: the Ottoman Empire in the West, patronizing Sunni Islam, and the Safawid Shahs in the East, who had introduced the Shia as the official religion of Iran. Religious propaganda also affected the movement of the Turkic tribes. For centuries, they had migrated from the East. In the time of the great confederations, a number of tribes began to return to the East. This holds true especially for the Shii or Qızılbaş-tribes, such as the Şam-Bayadî from Syria, or the Bağdâdî from Iraq, parts of which returned to Iran under Shah Ismail (late 15th/early 16th century).[13]

As Iraq was part of a disputed border region, both Ottomans and Safawids had reliable tribes moved into the area. Shah Ismail brought a considerable number of Shii tribesmen from the region of Maraghe into Iraq. Strategic settlement continued during the 18th century, when Nader Shah (1733-1743) had Shii Turkic tribes from Iran settled in Iraq. At the same time, the Ottomans tried to fortify the Turkic stronghold which lay behind the notoriously unreliable Kurdish principalities. Much of the peculiar crescent-shaped form of the Turkman belt coincides with the environment of the Great Trunk Road from Mosul to Baghdad, which implies strategic movements of local populations in Ottoman times. There is also evidence that, in addition to the local Turkman population, Anatolian Turks were settled in this region, as for instance, under Sultan Murad IV (1623-1640).[14] Toponyms such as

---

[11] It should be remembered that the tribal confederations, although predominantly Turkic, contained also different ethnics, such as Kurds and Arabs (like, for instance, the Farsi-Madan of the Khamse).

[12] The original expression *le Turc Agemi* for the Turkic language between Rum/Ottoman Turkish and Eastern Turkic/ Chaghatay was coined by the Capuchin missionary Raphael du Mans in his *Estat de la Perse en 1660*. It also refers to the "historical Azerbaijani literary language" (Bellér-Hann1995: 39) or pre-Azeri.

[13] Sümer (1952).

[14] See Marufoğlu (1998: 57).

Shahseven (i.e. the confederation which formed the military backbone of the Qajar state in the 18th and 19th centuries) indicate that, in later times as well, Turkic tribes adhering to the Shii sect settled in Iraq.

For the Turkic dialects of Iraq these less spectacular movements of minor tribes indicate that there was constant influence both from the West and the East, which continued after the formation of the most important written languages of the greater region, Ottoman Turkish and Azeri Turkic. It also explains the fact that the map of Iraq-Turkic dialects is a patchwork rather than a continuum. (The same is true for Anatolian and Iran-Turkic dialects.)

Moreover, the distribution of the Islamic confessions also reflects the position of the Turkmans of Iraq between Sunni Ottoman and Shii Safawid poles. At present, the majority adheres to the Hanafi school of Sunni Islam, which was the official *mazhab* or confession of the Ottoman Empire. To the north, around Erbil, some also follow the Shafii *mazhab*, which is traditionally wide-spread among Kurds. According to recent sources from Iraq, only 23% of the Turkmans are Shii. In the 19th century, parts of the Shii Turkman population concentrated in settlements along the highroad from Kerkuk to Baghdad.[15]

Of the Turkic tribes of old, some few names, such as the Bayat and the Begdili, have survived in Iraq.[16] Like the Bayat, who have settled in the lowlands stretching west and southwest of Kerkuk, most tribes have long been sedentary. Their language displays characteristics which seem to be regional features rather than inherited traces of old nomadic dialects.

2. Present-day Iraqi Turkman dialects

2.1 *The Turcological model of classification*

The development of the Turkic languages or dialects of Iraq must be seen in a broader regional context, as Iraq was part of political or administrative entities such as the Eastern Caliphate, the Saljuq Empire and the Mongol states, and later belonged to the sphere of influence of the tribal confederations of the Aq- and Qaraqoyunlu and the Qızılbaş, which formed the military backbone of the Safawid state. Most of these political or administrative units and the places of settlement of the tribes which had begun their westward migration under the Saljuqs comprised the historical area of East Anatolia, Iran and Iraq.

It should be remembered that the reconstruction of historical stages of spoken languages or dialects of this area is rather complicated. There are very few historical sources on older stages of the dialects. Some features which hint at the stage of their development may be reflected in older texts in the standard or official languages. Yet,

---

[15] Marufoğlu (1998: 58).

[16] For information on the names of the Turkic tribes of Iraq see the comprehensive list in Saatçi (1996: 294-300).

the relation of dialects and written language is largely a matter of speculation. While linguistic evidence is missing for the most part, the reconstruction of languages without a coherent written tradition is mainly deduced from the history of settlement.

In terms of Turcology, most Turkic dialects of present-day Iran, Iraq and Anatolia belong to the Oghuz or southwestern group of the Turkic languages. This group is divided into a western branch, which comprises mainly the language of Turkey, Gagauz and the Balkan dialects, and a central or Azeri branch. Eastern Oghuz, on the other hand, denotes the Turkman dialects which are found today in the Turkman Republic and in north-eastern Iran/ north-western Afghanistan. It is the language of those Oghuz tribes who did not take part in the Saljuqs' westward migration. In other words: The Turkman dialects of Iraq are not part of the Turkman or Eastern Oghuz language group, and their speakers are far from closely related to the Turkman of the former Soviet-Union and adjoining regions.

Turcologists have thus far done little research on the dialect area which stretches from eastern Anatolia over Iraq into western Iran. Thus, mapping the respective Turkic *Dialektlandschaft* ('dialect-landscape') and establishing a catalogue of criteria of classification for the transitional dialects of the borderlands remains a desideratum.

Traditionally, the varieties of the area were grouped as dialects of the two great Oghuz written languages, Ottoman Turkish in the West and Azeri Turkic in the East. Doerfer (1990: 19) introduced a new model of classification, proposing a third language group called Southern Oghuz for Qašqâ'î and Aynallu and some adjoining dialects in southwest Iran, which are closely related to Iraq-Turkic.

2.2 *Linguistic situation*

Today, most Turkic speakers in Iraq are bi- or trilingual, which is characteristic of speakers of a so-called low-prestige variety. At least the older generations grew up with Turkman as their mother tongue. At a very early age, most learn Kurdish or Arabic as a second language in their neighbourhood.[17] Arabic is also acquired through mass media and at school.

Until 1920, there was a strong influence of Ottoman Turkish. Ottoman Turkish was not only the language of administration of the Empire; it also functioned as a *lingua franca* in Iraq, and throughout the sphere of Ottoman influence. At the same time the official language of the Ottoman Empire, it established a prestigious variety. Presently, a cultural orientation towards Turkey still prevails among the Turkman intellectuals. As a consequence, diglossia (Turkman/ Turkish of Turkey) is very frequent in educated circles, especially in Kerkuk.

---

[17] As marriages between Turks and Kurds seem to be quite frequent, many speakers have a mixed Turkic-Kurdish background and are fluent in both languages.

With regard to phonology, vocabulary, morphology and syntax, the Turkman varieties spoken in Iraq show autochthonous items as well as traces both of Ottoman and of Azeri Turkic. Traditionally, the written Turkman language is dominated by Modern Standard Turkish, while the spoken language differs considerably: it displays additional influence from Arabic, the official language of Iraq, and neighbouring Kurdish dialects such as Kurmanji and Sorani.

2.3 *Sources*

A considerable amount of Iraqi Turkman publications have appeared in Iraq and in Turkey. These books comprise folklore texts, short stories and very rarely even novels, studies on culture, folklore, history, and so on. As their language is Modern Turkish (either in Arabic, Kurdicized Arabic or Latin script), they are quite useless as a source for linguistic investigations.[18] There are only two collections of narrative texts representing the spoken language. Unfortunately, they have never been published.[19] In addition, a small sample text (from the Tel'afer region) was published by Buluç (1973/74), who also wrote some articles on the local varieties of Mandali (1975) and Khanaqin (1973). Different written versions exist of the most famous folklore text, the romantic novel *Arzı ile Qamber*, which the Kerkuk lawyer Ata Terzibaşı recorded in the 1960s.

My collection of spoken data from Iraq consists of broadcasting sequences, narratives, and spontaneous data of native speakers from different regions of Iraq, such as Erbil, Altunköprü, Tuzkhurmatu and Kerkuk. Some of these recordings were made more than 30 years ago; they represent the state of affairs before considerable changes, such as the displacement of the minorities under the regime of the Baath-Party, took place.[20]

2.4 *Language contact*

As we have seen, the linguistic situation in Iraq is rather complex. Accordingly, present-day Iraqi Turkman varieties are by no means uniform or homogeneous. Some of the considerable differences among these dialects go back to the heterogeneous history of settlement, while others may be explained by different constellations of language contact. For more than a millennium, the Turkic varieties of Iraq have been under the influence of structurally different languages, notably, Iranian languages, such as Persian and Kurdish, and Semitic languages, such as Arabic and Neo-Aramaic.

---

[18] For a survey on modern Turkman literature see al-Bayati (1970).

[19] The doctoral theses by Choban Khıdır Haydar (1979) and Hussin Shahbaz Hassan (1979).

[20] I thank Suphi Saatçi, Rabia Kocaman, Mehdi al-Bayati, Ganim Authman, Yalçın Avcı and Bahaddin Kevser for letting me share their own collections of data and helping to establish contacts with speakers of Iraqi Turkman.

Fig. 10.1 Map to show distribution of present day Turkman dialects in Iraq

Thus, in addition to the situation on the intra-Turkic level, which concerns different Turkic dialects of the greater region and their relations, the respective constellations of language contact should be taken into account. Bi- or multilingualism is characteristic for the area; mutual influences have led to a great number of language contact induced phenomena. Moreover, there have been frequent changes in the prestige or official languages in the course of the centuries: under the Saljuqids, who had absorbed Iranian influences both on cultural and linguistic levels, the language of the administration was New Persian. Persian as an official language lasted till it was replaced by Ottoman Turkish in the 17th century.

In 1655, the Ottoman traveller Evliya Çelebi visited Mosul. His description of the city contains a short dialect sample, the only historical specimens of Iraqi Turkman known to me. Evliya Çelebi also comments on the language contact situation in 17th century Mosul (Bağdat Köşkü 305, 403a16-18):

> As the people of Mosul have considerable natural talents and quickness of mind, they know the varieties of the Kurdish language from the time of their forefathers; and they delicately pronounce the Persian language, and speak Arabic as perfectly as the Arabic scholars. And the Armenian language, they know as well as the monk Mighdisi. Yet, their own [Turkic] dialect displays similarities to the Kurdish language, and they say: "Hey g'özüm, varmışıḫ. Birè canım, haradaydıñ?"[21]

2.5 *Criteria for the classification of distinctive features*

In the following, some distinctive items of phonetics, morphology, lexicon and syntax will be discussed.[22] To arrive at a definition of the position Iraqi Turkman dialects occupy on the Turkic linguistic map, three levels of formative influences will be distinguished.

(1) On the intra-Turkic level, the relation of genuine Turkic items and dialect markers to the western (Standard Turkish or Anatolian dialects) or eastern (Azeri or Iran-Turkic) poles has to be defined.

(2) A second group are the so-called areal phenomena, which appear throughout the structurally different varieties or even languages of a certain geographic area.

(3) Third, language contact induced phenomena, or, in other words, items which bear clear traces of different varieties or prestige languages, are an important characteristic of languages in multi-lingual environments.

2.6 *Some characteristics of Iraqi Turkman varieties*

2.6.1 *Phonetics and phonology*

Traditionally, Iraqi Turkman varieties are divided into two groups, using the realization of the velar nasal /ŋ/ in the possessive suffixes of the second person singular and plural as an isophone (cf. Buluç 1975 and Hassan 1979). Thus, the pronunciation of the possessive of the 2nd person singular is *seniy* 'yours' in dialects

---

[21] bu şehr-e Moṣul ḫalqı ġayet tiz-fehm ve pak ṭabi'at olduqlarından ecdadlarından berü cümlè faṣaḥat üzerè Kürd lisanınıñ enva'nı bilirler ve ẓarafet üzerè lisan-ı Farsi tekellüm êderler ve belaġat üzerè meval-i 'arabanî gibi 'Arabi kelimat êderler ve lisan-ı Ermêni r'uhbân-'ı M'iġdisi qadar bilirler amma kendüleriniñ lehcèleri Kürd lisanınà qarib olub hey g'özüm varmışıḫ birè canım haradaydıñ kelimat êderler.

[22] For a more comprehensive discussion of the classificatorial features of Iraqi Turkman see Bulut (1999).

of the y-group, and *senuw* 'yours' in the w-group. In the Bayat dialects, for instance, 'your daughter' is pronounced *qiziy*, which corresponds to *qizuw* in the dialect of Erbil. In larger cities such as Kerkuk, both types of pronunciation are found. This indicates the mixed background of the local population.

On the map (see p. 168), the dialects pertaining to the w-group are indicated by • , those of the y-group by *. It seems that the dialects of the w-group are situated closer to the Iranian border, while the y-dialects are concentrated in the western Turkman belt. As many speakers of the y-group, such as the Bayat tribes, adhere to Shii Islam, the distribution of the dialect groups may go back to the policy of settlement in Ottoman times.[23]

With regard to the intra-Turkic level, the morpho-phonological development {y, w < *ŋ } connects the Iraqi Turkman dialects to other varieties of the historical area of eastern Anatolia, Iraq and Iran. The y-group is also found in Urfa in eastern Anatolia, and in the Bayat dialects of the Hamadan and Saveh provinces in Iran, in the former *'Iraq-ı 'Ajam*. Another representative of the w-group is the small Turkic enclave of Sonqor, north of Kermanshah in western Iran.

Some items with irregular distribution also display a development of old /ŋ/ into [ŋ], [w], [ɣ], and [g]: *soŋra, sora* 'later' <* *soŋıra, gewil* 'heart'<* *göŋül, yalɣuz* 'alone, lonely' <* *yalıŋus, ög* 'front' <* *öŋ* etc.

Other phonetic items which are rather unusual for the inventory of Turkic languages point to the influence of the neighbouring Kurdish and Arabic dialects, such as the tendency to pronounce the retroflex tongue root clusile *'ayn* [ˤ], the pharyngeal fricative [ħ],[24] a bilabial [w], and the uvular clusil [q]. Language contact influence is also responsible for the preservation of an older Turkic item, namely the velar or uvular fricative *ġayn* [ɣ, ʁ]. These fricatives are allophones of the old intervocalic and word-final /g/ in combination with velar vowels. Word-final /-k/ in most instances becomes [-x]: *yemax* 'food', but it also has the voiced allophone [ɣ], in forms such as [jɛmɑɣ].

H-prothesis

Both in Kurdish and Arabic, words do not begin with a vowel. In some instances, Kurdish dialects replace the word-initial *hamza* or *'ayn* of Arabic loans by [h]. This rule of the contact languages coincides with a Turkic tendency to pronounce an

---

[23] At the present stage of research, it is difficult to say how exactly the differences in the dialects coincide with the distribution of the Sunni or Shii population. Yet, it seems that the Ottoman rulers in Iraq had placed contingents of loyal Sunni tribes along the frontier to Iran, west of the Kurdish principalities. The less reliable Shii elements, who might have given in to their sympathy toward the Safawids of Persia, were concentrated behind this borderline.

[24] Kurdish dialects go even farther, replacing /ḥ/ sometimes by [x], cf. *xinne* 'henna'.

additional [h] before word-initial vowels. Yet, Turkic items such as *his* 'soot', which corresponds to the Turkish *is*, and *hörmağ* 'knit' for the Turkish *örmek*, may have preserved an old [h]. In loan-words like *helbet* 'naturally' or *heşye* 'things, belongings' (a plural of the Arabic *šay* 'thing'), on the other hand, the secondary or prothetic nature of [h] is definite.

yı- > i-
Another irregular phonotactic process which occurs also in the dialects of eastern Anatolia and western Iran is the substitution of word-initial [yı-]. In lemmata such as *ilan* 'snake' (for the Turkish < *yılan*), or *il* 'year' (for Turkish *yıl*), the word-initial semi-vowel [y] and the following back unrounded vowel /ı/ are replaced by [i-]. The reason for this substitution may again be language contact influence (?) as *yı-* is alien to the contact languages. On the other hand, some dialects have preserved older forms like *yıɣlamax* 'to weep', which elsewhere became *ağlamak*. Moreover, prothetic [y-] also occurs, in forms such as *yew* 'house' for *ev*.

Palatalization and affrication
Characteristic of all Iraqi Turkman varieties is the strong tendency to palatalize the clusiles [k'] and [g'] and the affricates [dʒ'/tʃ'].

Affrication of [g] and [k] also occurs; in the Erbil or Altunköprü region, for instance, the verb [gɛl-] 'to come' is pronounced [dʒæl-], the short form of the name of the city Altunköprü is [tʃøprʏ]. The original affricates [dʒ] and [tʃ], on the other hand, are fronted to [dz] and [ts/tç], as in [b*a*:dzım] 'my sister' and [tso:x] 'much'.

Palatalization and affrication seem to be a widespread areal phenomenon, which can be found in various eastern Anatolian and Azeri dialects around Tabriz as well as in Zaza, Kurmanji, Sorani and even some Arabic dialects in the region. Yet, in some varieties of Iraq, as in our sample text from Tuzhurmatu, affrication does not occur; nor is it to be found in the nearest Turkic dialects of Iran, in Sonqorî and the Bayat dialects of the Hamadan region.

Vowel system
Compared to other Turkic varieties with strong Iranian or Arabic influences, the vowel system of the Iraqi Turkman dialects has remained relatively stable.

The ideal Turkic vowel system consists of eight (+ 1) vowel phonemes, each of which can appear in the stem of Turkic words. They are symmetrically distributed: Two unrounded front vowels /i/ and /e/, one of which is high, the other being low, and two unrounded back vowels /ı/ and /a/ with the same distribution. Each unrounded vowel phoneme corresponds to a rounded vowel in the same position, namely /ü/, /ö/, /u/ and /o/. The preservation of the ninth vowel, the so-called closed /e/, is characteristic of the greater area.

Phonotactic rules of vowel harmony, which allow for the combination of vowels that share common features such as front vs. back or rounded vs. unrounded, are certainly one of the most important characteristics of Turkic phonology. Unique suffixes such as the infinitive in *-max* break this rule, but they obviously go back to an older stage. Labial harmony also seems to be less developed than in Turkish.

Iraqi Turkman has long vowels; some of them coincide with the Old Turkic length, e.g. *a:d* 'name' vs. *at* ('horse', with an additional fortis-lenis opposition), *yo:x* 'no' and *o:d* 'fire'. Other long vowels seem to be products of contractions or other phonological processes (mostly: a:, e:, o:, ö:).

The levelling of certain labial vowels may point to Iranian or Arabic influence, e.g. /i/ instead of /ü/ or /u/ etc. [*koxi* 'smell'< **koku*, Tel'afer; Mendeli: *vırmâɣ* 'to beat'< **vurmak*, *sîri* 'flock' < **sürü*].[25]

The Turkic vowel phoneme /a/ appears in three different realizations; in some instances, the low central Turkic vowel [a] is kept. It alternates with a labialized variant [ɒ], which is found in Iranian languages.[26] The realization of /a/ as open front [æ] on the other hand, is a typical feature of Iranian contact influence. It appears also with genuine Turkic items, such as in [*qæræ*] for *qara* 'black'. Crossing the line between front and back vowels, [æ] essentially disturbs the rules of Turkic palatal harmony and suffix vocalism.

Phonotactical processes, assimilations

All over the greater area, metathesis and rhotacism appear; the word *topraq* 'ground', for instance, is pronounced [torpax] or [torpaɣ] in most Anatolian, Iranian and Iraq Turkic dialects.

Progressive assimilation is very frequent. After word-final nasal such as [-m] and [-n], the abstracta-suffix {+lIK} takes the form [+nIK]; *ormanlık* 'a wooded place', for instance, appears as [hormannıɣ]. The ablative morpheme changes from {+DAn} to [+nAn]. Accordingly, the ablative of the demonstrative pronoun is pronounced [mʊnnan] < *bundan*. Assimilation after stem-final nasals is even more widespread in the Iran-Turkic Bayat dialects, where it includes the locative suffix {+DA} > [+nA] and is frequently found in Sandhi position.

Throughout the Turkic dialects of Iraq and Iran, nasals trigger assimilation of the labial consonant [b-]. This type of assimilation concerns the pronoun of the first person singular, which is *ben* in Turkish, but in most instances [mæn] or [mɛn] in Iraq and Iran. Accordingly, the dative and the accusative of the demonstrative pronoun *bu* may have alternative forms such as [mʊna] instead of *buna* and [mʊnʊ]

---

[25] See Buluç (1973/74) and (1975).

[26] Yet, a labialized [ɒ] is not unusual for Turkish dialects as far to the West as central Anatolia.

instead of *bunu*.[27] Other examples for this type of assimilation are [mındʒɨɣ] 'bead' for *boncuk* and [mın-] 'to mount (a horse etc.)' for *bin-*.

Regressive assimilation of word-final [-r] to the [l-] of the plural suffix is also characteristic of Turkic dialects of the greater area. Thus, *olurlar* 'they become', is pronounced [olʊllaɹ] in most Iranian and Iraq-Turkic dialects.

2.6.2 *Morphology*

Case morphology

Case morphology displays both similarities with Turkish and Azeri or Iran-Turkic dialects. Genitive, dative and locative show no conspicuous features {+(n)In, +(y)A, +DA}. Like in Iran-Turkic, the possessive accusative is {+n}, in contrast to Turkish {+nI}. Assimilation of the ablative has been described above. The instrumental case, which is {+(I)nAn} in most East Anatolian and Iran-Turkic varieties, has the form {+DAN}. In the equative case {+cA}, the pronominal [n] does not appear, compare forms such as *ardıca* 'following/behind him'.

Verb morphology

The forms of the present tense {-Ir} and the aorist {-Ar} resemble those of Iran-Turkic. As in Iran-Turkic, the perfect displays a mixed paradigm based on the morphemes {-mIş} for 1st and 2nd persons and {-Ip} for 3rd persons (while Altunköprü has {-Ip} in the 1st persons, too). In contrast to the Turkish perfect in {-mIş}, it has no explicitly marked inferential or evidential qualities. As in Iran-Turkic, the potential verbform {-abil-} has the negation {-abilme-}, e.g. [edɛbılmædɣw] 'Were you not able to do so?' In the entire area of eastern Anatolia, western Iran and Iraq, the question particle {mI} does not appear.

Iraqi Turkman has a rich inventory of temporal gerunds; forms derived from the so-called present participle in {-(y)An} are again characteristic for the greater area of East Anatolia, Iran and Iraq. As a result of the growing cultural influence of modern Turkish, non-finite subordinators based on the verbal noun in {-DIK} seem to have been gaining ground recently .

[27] Turcologists have explained this phonological change as word-internal regressive assimilation caused by the nasal /-n/ the pronouns contain. This makes sense with the pronoun of the first person, which in most instances is pronounced [*mɛn*] or [*mn*], while forms with initial /b-/ are less frequent. Yet, with regard to oblique pronominal forms, my material from Iraq and the adjoining Turkic varieties of Iran shows that assimilation of b- > m- is a form of progressive assimilation in Sandhi-position. If the preceding word ends in a nasal, the dative of the demonstrative pronoun will be [mʊna], the accusative [mʊnʊ] etc.; after consonants without nasal qualities and after vowels, the corresponding forms are [bʊna], [bʊnʊ] and so on.

Pronouns: bile

The pronominal system displays an additional paradigm based on the stem *bile*, which always combines with possessive and case markers. Thus, [bılɛsınɛ] < *bile* +POSS+DAT, in a given context, would mean 'to him/her', denoting topic or long distance reference. The appearance of these forms is restricted to western Iran and Iraq-Turkic dialects.[28]

Copied morphemes

The copying[29] of bound morphemes is generally taken as an indicator for deep-reaching processes of language contact. Many varieties have a suffix in {+AkA}, which combines with noun stems and means 'the aforesaid, the one already mentioned in the context'. {+AkA} is a global copy of the Kurdish or, originally, Gorani definite article. The copied element, which also appears in Sonqor-Turkic, is well integrated into Turkic noun morphology. It is attached directly to the stem, precedes the case suffixes and is even subject to palatal harmony:

1	*İpi*	*aç'ar ...*	*di*	*yêr^{i}ş^i*	*mıġar-akâ-ya.*	
	thread:ACC	open:AOR:3SG	till	reach: PRS 3SG	den:SPEC:DAT	(3/90)[30]

'She unrolls the thread till it reaches down to the den'.

In southern dialects of Iraqi Turkman, global copies of the Iranian enclitic personal pronouns appear. These enclitics can be attached to the verb after the personal ending, representing the position of the direct object or a dative.[31]

2a	*almæ*	*âllæm*	***-it***
	apple	buy:AOR 1SG	you:DAT

'I will buy **you** an apple

2b	*yæyipti*	***-şan***
	eat:PF 3SG	them 3PL:ACC

'he has eaten **them**'

As an example **3a** from Dakuk demonstrates, Iranian-style constructions with enclitic pronouns appear throughout the area. The underlying structure of example **3a** resembles the Kurdish periphrasis for 'I need', *garak-im-a* ('necessary/for/me/is') in

---

[28] On *bile* and its distribution see Bulut (2003).

[29] As to the model of code copying cf. Johanson (1992).

[30] Examples marked with (/) are taken from the folklore texts collected by Hassan (1979).

[31] See Buluç (1975: 183), on the dialect of Mandali.

MacKenzie (1961: 105), where the enclitic of the 1st person singular combines with a copy of the Turkic adjective *gerek.*

3a	*Mæm*	*källæsi*	*lâzım-ımdı.*	(10/72)
	My	head:POSS 3SG	necessary:for me:COP 3SG	

I need his head. (literally: 'his head is necessary for me'.)

In the corresponding Turkish benefactive construction **3b**, the dative of the 1st person singular would be expressed by a separate personal pronoun in the dative case.

3b	*Bana*	*kellesi*	*lazım-dır.*
	for me	head:POSS 3SG	necessary:COP 3SG

The suffix {*-iş*} in Buluç (1975: 182) is in all probability a copy of the Kurdish enclitic {*-iş*} 'also, even', which in southern Kurdish [cf. MacKenzie 1961: 128] may be suffixed to either a nominal or a verbal form.

2.6.3 *Syntactic structures*

Copied word-order properties: Postverbal position of the dative/directive case

Iranian languages such as Kurdish and colloquial modern Persian mark the object to which the action expressed in the verb is directed by word order properties. The dative or directive object is in a postverbal position.

Example **1** demonstrates that Iraqi Turkman has obviously copied this structural feature. It should be remembered that in contrast to colloquial Persian, where the indirect object would be in the unmarked case, the syntactic function of *mığar* in the Turkic sentence is sufficiently specified by its dative case.

The copied word order constraint evidently also applies to certain infinitive constructions with the dative, for instance in combinations with the verbs *başla-* ('start to ...') and *çiẖ-* ('set out to ...'):

4a	*Ḥâmsı*	*başladılar*	*gülmäġä.*	(2/33)
	all	begin:PST 3PL	laugh:INF:DAT	

'They all began to laugh'.

4b	*çiẖällär*	*gêzinti*	*êtmäġä*	(18/2)
	set out:AOR 3PL	walk	make:INF:DAT	

'They (usually) set out for a walk'.

Complex sentences/strategies of clause combining

The Turkic strategy of forming subordinated sentences follows a characteristic pattern. Most subordinated clauses are based on a non-finite verb form, which may consist of a verb noun, a participle or a gerund. As a rule, gerunds form adverbial clauses or action phrases, while nominalized verb forms such as verb nouns and participles render so-called actor phrases, such as relative clauses. In this constellation, the non-finite, nominalized verb form or 'subjunctor'[32] is embedded into the matrix clause via case morphology; it can be supplemented by a restricted number of complements ('objects').

On the other hand, most Turkic languages display a second type of clause combining strategy, which resembles or imitates Indo-European models. With regard to structural features, these patterns of clause combining are diametrically opposed to the Turkic ones. The dependent clause contains a finite verb form; it is linked to the main clause by means of a relator or conjunctor. At the same time the conjunctor, which often is rather complex, defines the semantic relation between main clause and dependent clause.

As in Iranian languages, the verb of the dependent clause may additionally be marked by mode. In all probability, Turkic final or purpose clauses have copied this syntactical constraint of Iranian languages. In Iranian-type patterns which appear throughout the Turkic dialects of Iraq, Iran and even eastern Anatolia, the Turkic optative or imperative corresponds to the subjunctive of the Iranian model, cf. the optative *gidäsän* 'that you will/shall go' in the following example **5a**.[33]

5a	*... biz*	*säni*	*näcä*	*qoyaġ*	*ussuya*	*gidäsän?*	(20/48)
	we	you:ACC	how	let:OPT 1 PL	water:DAT	go:OPT 2	

"how can we allow you to go to the water?"

The corresponding Turkic modal clause, on the other hand, would be based on a modal verbal noun such as *gideceğine* 'your having/wanting to go:DAT'.

5b	*suya*	*gideceğine*	*nasıl*	*izin vereceğiz?*
	water:DAT	go:VN:POSS 2SG:DAT	how	allow:MOD 1SG

In some areas of clause combining, Turkic strategies appear alongside the corresponding Iranian patterns. To exemplify the two opposed strategies which occur in Iraqi Turkman relativization, a Turkic-type relative construction **6a** from Hassan (1979) will be transformed into its Iranian-type equivalent **6b**.

The attributive Turkic relative clause *yerinde oturan* 'who was sitting in his [someone else's] place' is based on a nominalized verb form, the so-called present participle in {-(y)An}. It precedes its head, *vekil*, which is in the typical postverbal position of the Turkman directive case.

---

[32] For terminology see Johanson (1990).

[33] On optative constructions in Iraqi Turkman see Bulut (2000).

6a	*bir*	*mektüb*	*yazdı*	*yerinde*	***otur-an***	*vekile*	(18/92)
	a	letter	wrote	place:3POSS:LOC	sit:PART	representative:DIR	

'He wrote a letter to the representative who was sitting in his [the Shah's] place.'

If this Turkic relative construction is transformed according to Iranian-type patterns, a series of essential syntactical changes can be observed. The postpositive relative clause *ki yerinde otururdu* in example **6b** contains a finite verb form. It is connected to the main clause by means of the copied Iranian conjunctor *ki*; to mark the restrictive relative construction, an additional cataphoric pronoun, *o* 'that', introduces the head of the relative clause.

6b	*bir*	*name*	*yazdı*	*o*	*vekile*	*ki*	*yerinde*	*otururdu*
	a	letter	wrote	DEM	representative:DIR	CONJ	place:3POSS:LOC	sit:IMP 3SG

It is characteristic of many Turkic languages of the area that they have restructured their clause combining strategies according to Indo-European or Iranian models. Most recent Iran-Turkic varieties have almost completely abandoned original Turkic patterns, displaying a strongly Iranized sentence syntax.[34]

In the given language contact situation, the syntactical behaviour of the Turkman dialects appears rather unusual. In the field of relativization, Turkic constructions such as in example **6a** dominate, apart from some specialized Iranian patterns following type **6b**. Moreover, Iraqi Turkman has preserved a rich gerundial syntax, whereas gerunds have almost completely disappeared just across the Iranian border. Typical for the whole area of eastern Anatolia, Iran and Iraq, on the other hand, are complex temporal gerunds such as {-(y)AndA} or {-(y)AndAn (son)}. These units are the only representatives of the rich Turkic gerundial syntax that have also survived in Iran-Turkic.

Such obvious difference in the syntactical behaviour of Iran-Turkic and Iraqi Turkman dialects displays the strong influence of the former official or prestige languages, Ottoman Turkish and New Persian. With regard to clause combining strategies, the political border between Iran and Iraq coincides with a syntax border.

---

[34] As Johanson (1992: 259) demonstrates, peripheral Turkic languages in Slavic and Iranian neighbourhoods show a general tendency to use postpositive patterns with a finite verb form instead. It has been maintained that these right-branching clauses imitate the Indo-European type of clause combining. Such copies of combinational patterns may be interpreted as a veritable scale for the degree of non-Turkic influences in the respective variety.

2.6.4 *Lexicon: Foreign items*
With regard to nouns and adverbs, the lexicon of Iraq-Turkic displays a relatively high share of loans or global-copies of the Arabic and Kurdish contact languages; compared to East Anatolian dialects, there is also more Persian vocabulary.

Compound verbs are often copied; I would interpret constructions such as *ḥäz et-* 'to love, like', *xılas elä-* 'to finish' as copies of the corresponding Kurdish compounds *hez kırın* or *xılas kırın*, which contain a global copy of the nominal segment while the auxiliary is being translated into its Turkic equivalent. Another strategy for the formation of secondary verbs is combination with the Turkic denominal verb suffix {*+lA*}. A great number of verbs originating in such formations are characteristic of Iraqi Turkman, as, for instance, *färäḥlä-* 'to be glad', derived from the Arabic noun *faraḥ* 'joy, gladness.

Iraq-Turkic vocabulary reflects the transitional situation between Anatolian and West Iranian dialects: In Iraq-Turkic, isoglosses of both the western and the eastern dialect groups are present.[35] Some may exist simultaneously, such as the eastern *dal* 'back' and the western *arka*. Others have a western flavour, such as *eyi* 'good, nicely' against the eastern *yaxçı*, and the verb *sev-* 'love'. Yet, Iraq-Turkic shares a great portion of its lexicon with eastern or Iran-Turkic varieties: adverbs, such as *bu tay* 'this side', *qanşær* 'opposite side', *harda/harada* 'where', *indi* 'now', *bıtov* 'all, completely', *kimi(n)* 'like, till'; nouns, such as *bulaġ* 'spring, well', *bala* 'child', *toy* 'wedding', *küräkän* 'bridegroom', *nänä* 'mother', *uşaġ* 'child', *ämcäk* 'breast', and verbs, such as *apar-* 'bring away', *axtar-* 'seek', *tap-* 'find', and *işlä-* 'work'. Pronominal forms based on the stem *bilä-* are characteristic of the area of Iraq and West Iran.[36]

In some instances, the same Turkic root appears with different derivation suffixes, such as *suvar-* (as in Iran-Turkic), instead of the western *sula-* 'irrigate'. Exceptional is the formation of 'to speak together'. While western dialects use a reciprocal of *kon-* > *konuş-*, the eastern varieties have a similar construction based on a different stem, *danış-*; in Iraq-Turkic, 'to speak together' is derived by means of same the reciprocal suffix *-Iş* of the verb *sele-/söyle-* 'to speak'; *seleş-* is a typical Iraq-Turkic isogloss.

Due to the influence of Standard Turkish, there is also a number of recent copies of Modern Turkish origin, of which Bayatlı (1996: 407) has presented a survey. In general, such copies are more frequent in the written language.

---

35 The distribution of isoglosses is irregular. Many eastern or Azeri isoglosses also appear in Anatolian dialects.

36 On pronominal systems of the area see Bulut (2003).

3. *Conclusions*

As we have seen, different constellations of language contact have left traces on all levels of the Iraqi Turkman dialects, be it phonetics, morphology, syntax or lexicon.

On the intra-Turkic level, Iraqi Turkman displays a characteristic mixture of eastern and western features, and a number of individual traces. Many developments have parallels with Anatolian or Iran-Turkic varieties, and some dialects seem to be very closely connected to the Bayat dialects of West Iran. As long as the criteria of classification for an independent southern Oghuz language group are still a matter of research, one could characterize the Turkic dialects of Iraq as a transitional dialect group, displaying linguistic features similar to both western and eastern neighbours. Yet, it should be stressed that despite its historical connections to both of the great written languages and dialect groups of the Oghuz branch, Iraqi Turkman is definitely neither Azeri or Iran-Turkic, nor Ottoman or Anatolian Turkish.

Appendix: Language samples

Evliya Çelebi's sample of 17th century Mosul dialect

		translation	*comment*
1	H*ey* g'özüm varm*ı*ş*ı*ḫ hey eye:POSS1SG arrive:PF1SG	Hey, my eyeball, we have arrived!	eastern non-evidential perfect in {*-mIş*}
2	Birè can*ı*m haradayd*ı*ñ Brother soul:POSS1SG where:COP:PST2SG	Brother, dear, where have you been?	eastern isogloss *harada*

Text from Tuzkhurmatu

The following sample in International Phonetic Alphabet script displays a grea number of characteristic features of Iraqi Turkman. The passage transcribed stem from a tale which was recorded in Tuzkhurmatu thirty years ago, with a the mal informant in his seventies. It is the story of a black slave whom a caravan leader ha bought, hoping that he would defend his belongings against robbers. The black mar gets the forty men of the caravan to serve him food to appease his enormous appetite yet, he turns out to be of no use during the first attacks by robbers.

It seems quite natural that a group of transitional varieties displays a grea number of features which, on the intra-Turkic level, have parallels either in th western, that is Anatolian Turkish, or the eastern, Iran-Turkic dialect groups Isoglosses are distributed irregularly, comprising different varieties of the area Iraq East Anatolia and West Iran. The comment classifies such items in the field o phonetics/phonology, morphology and syntax using the attributes western and easter in a rather geographical than strictly Turcological sense.

		Distinctive features
1	bʊ k'ɛrəwɑntʃɪnɪn dʒɑnɪ jɑndɨɣɨnnan this caravan leader soul burn:VN:POSS:ABL	Turkic causal clause based on an infinite verb form; assimilation of the ablative {*+Dan*} > {*+nAn*} after nasals

2	nɪ‿ etsɪn mʊna? gedɪreː ... what do:IMP3SG this:DAT go:PRS3SG	pronominal form displaying b- > m- assimilation (Sandhi); eastern-type present in {*-Ir*}
3	ælɪn‿ajaɣɨn[37] mʊnʊn bʊ qɪrx dænɛˀə hand & foot:POSS his this forty person:DAT ejɪb vɪrdɪ behave badly:PST3SG	assimilated pro-form
4	"gælɪm mʊnʊn..." deːdɪ, "bʊ adamɨ reːʒɪm elɛjɪn!" come on his he said this man stone:IMP2PL	assimilated pro-form; eastern auxiliary *ele-*
5	ɛjə reːʒim ɛtsɪnnɛɹ, n'‿etsɪnnɛɹ, if stone:IMP3PL what do:IMP3PL	assimilation of the plural suffixes; western auxiliary *et-*
6	bʏ gʏnɛ k'ɪmɪn mæsælæ bʊnʊɪdan jɛmax this day to for instance with him food jɪdəlɛːɹ eat: PST3PL	eastern isogloss *kimi(n)*; violation of palatal harmony in [jɛmax]; instrumental {+DAN}
7	duz ɛkmɛg jɛdɪblɛɹ salt bread eat:PF 3PL	initial *d-* in [duz]; eastern perfect in {*-(y)Ip*}
8	vʊrsʊnnæɹ øzinɛ̃ ˤajɪblærənɛ gælɪre beat:IMP3PL him immoral:POSS3 PLcome:PRS3SG	assimilation of the plural; eastern usage of pron. *öz*; eastern present tense in {*-Ir*}; pronunciation of *'ayn*
9	øz jannaɪdɛ bɪr bøjʏg‿ ædam‿də own side3PL:LOC a great person:COP3SG	assimilation of the plural suffixes; eastern [bøjʏg]; eastern copula {*+DE*}
10	bʊndʒa wɒxɪd̥ xɪzmed edɪb̥lɛr øzɪnɛː so much time service make: PF3PL him:DAT	western auxiliary *et-*; eastern usage of pron. *öz* in postverbal (=directive) position
11	jɛmaɣ werɪblɛɹ hɛrkeːʃ food give:PF3PL everyone	inharmonious [jɛmax]; eastern perfect in {*-(y)Ip*}; [hɛrkeːʃ] against western standard [hɛrkɛs]

[37] [ælɪn‿ajaɣɨn] elliptic for *elin ayağın qırılası*! 'may his hand and foot break', that is 'the cursed one'.

12	bɪrə qɪsme ɒɣɑda rɪdʒæ‿ɛtdɪ, one:POSS3SG side leader:LOC beg:PST3SG dɛde: say:PST3SG	western auxiliary *et-*
13	"ɒɣɑ, bɪz bʊ adɑm lord we this man	
14	maxsadɪ‿kɪ bɪzɪm heʒ‿bɪr ʃejɪmɪze considering that our no thing:POSS1PL jɑrɑmɑdɨ be useful:PST3SG	typical Iraq-Turkic conjunctor [maxsadɪ‿kɪ]
15	nɛ jɑpɑrsɑɣ øzɪnɛ, hɛlɛ kɪ mazlım. what do:COND1PL him while innocent:COP3SG	western auxiliary *jap-*; eastern usage of pronominal *öz*
16	bælɪ, bɪz bʊnʊ aɫɫɑħ‿ħawɒlæd‿edɛræx yes, we this:ACC God leave to:AOR1PL	pronunciation of *'ayn*; pharyngeal fricative [ħ]
17	bɪɹ‿ʃej ɛtmɪˀæɣəm" anything do:NEG:AOR1PL	western auxiliary *et-*
18	bæˤaze bɪr‿ɪkɪ tɪfʏr ... tɪpʏrɛg tʃɑɫdɨlæɹ some one or two spittle put:PST3PL tʃærɛsɪnɛ, unto his face	pronunciation of *'ayn*; isogloss [tɪpʏrɛg]; postverbal (=directive) position of [tʃærɛsɪnɛ]
19	bæˤazɪ tʃɑɫmɑdɨ. dɛdɪ: sɪz maxsadɪ‿ke some put:NegPst3Pl he said you considering	pronunciation of 'ayn; typical Iraq-Turkic conjunctor [maxsadɪ‿ke]
20	sɪzdæ bʊŋgænɛ ɪnsɑnɪjɛt wɒr, you:Loc this much humanity exists	[bʊŋgænɛ] variant of the typical Iraqi equative *buncana/muncana*
21	mænɪm ɑlad̥‿ħærbɪmə ħɑːzɪr elɛjɪn, my gear of warfare ready make:IMP2PL	Iranian type izafet-construction; pharyngeal fricative [ħ]; eastern auxiliary *ele-*
22	mɛn ɪndɪ gedɛrɛm bʊ mɑlə I now go:AOR1SG this belongingsACC gæddəm. get: AOR1SG	eastern isogloss *indi* 'now'; eastern contracted form of *getirerem*

23	jɛŋgıdɛn bırdɛ bır qɨlıntʃ pɛjda‿hettəlæɹ again now a sword find:PST3PL øzıjıtʃın for him	eastern pronunciation [jɛŋgı, qɨlıntʃ]; h-prothesis in *hettiler*; eastern usage of pronominal *öz*
24	qɨlındʒi verdəlɛr æləne͂, sword: ACC give: PST3PL hand:3POSS:DAT dæwɒrdɨlɛɹ gereː. turn:PST3PL back	postverbal (=directive) position of [ælənɛ]
25	bʊ qɑxdı‿getdıj bʊlarən ardıdʒæ[a]. this get up go:PST3SG their back:3POSS:EQU	no pronominal /n/ in the equative

Translation

(1) Because the leader of the caravan felt sorry for (that man), (2) what should he do with him? There he goes, [thinking]: (3) The cursed one has given his forty men a hard time. (4) Then he said: "Come on, stone this man!"

(5) No matter whether they stone him or do something else to him, (6) to this very day they shared their food with him, (7) and ate [the sacred] bread and salt with him. (8) Thus, it does not seem right to them to beat him; (9) he has been an important person to them, (10) and all of them have served him for such a long time (11) and given him food.

(12) One of them approached the leader and pleaded for his case: (13) "My lord, whatever we shall do to this man, (14) who has not been of much use to us in any way, (15) (remember that) he is innocent. (17) Maybe we should not do anything [to punish him], (16) but leave his case to the Lord." (18) Some of them spat at him once or twice in the face, (19) others did not. Then he said: (20) "Because you have behaved so humanely, (21) prepare my weapons, (22) and I will set out to get back the goods [which had been stolen]." (23) Thus, they found him a sword again, (24) they put the sword into his hands and turned back. (25) He set out to pursue [the robbers].

Phonetics and phonology

The dialect of Tuzkhurmatu belongs to the y-group. It would lead too far in this context to comment on all supposed intra-Turkic connections of the respective Iraqi Turkman dialects. Yet, it should be mentioned that the variety presented here displays a conspicuous share of similarities to the Bayat-dialects of West Iran: affrication of the clusiles [k] and [g], for instance, which is characteristic of so many Turkic varieties spoken in Iraq, Northwest-Iran and Northeast Anatolia rarely ever appears with this speaker.

The development of initial /t/- > [d]- like in [tuz] > [duz] (see 7) is characteristic of the whole area from Anatolia to Iran.

A number of assimilation processes also have exact parallels in the Iran-Turkic dialects across the border. In many constellations, assimilation is triggered by nasals: Turkic pronominal forms will display an assimilation of initial b- > m- in Sandhi-position, if the preceding word ends in a nasal, (see 2, 3, 4). After nasals, the initial /l/ of the plural-suffix + *lAr* becomes [n] (see 5, 8, 9), while the ablative-suffix {+*Dan*} is pronounced {+*nAn*} (see 1).

Language contact-induced is the pronunciation of *'ayn* (see 8, 18, 19), of the pharyngeal fricative [ħ] (see 16, 21), and of the bilabial [w] (see 10, 11), like in the neighbouring Arabic and Kurdish contact dialects. The frequent occurrence of these copied items is a characteristic feature of Iraq-Turkic varieties.

In Turkic varieties of the whole area of East Anatolia, Iraq and Iran, the voiced velar fricative [ɣ] (see 1, 3, 11, 12, 13 etc.) is kept. The element is also present in Semitic and Iranian contact languages. Yet, it is difficult to decide whether influence of the contact-languages has prevented a development of [ɣ] > [ğ] *yumuşak g* like in Standard Turkish. A similar difficult constellation is h-prothesis, which is extremely frequent in the Kurdish dialects of the area and may well be connected to language contact influence. Secondary h-prothesis appears with genuine Turkic words such as [hettəlæɹ] < **ettiler* (see 23); it is also to be found with copied stems, such as *helbet* 'certainly' < Arabic *albatta*. On the other hand, there is also an older type of word-initial h-, which combines with Turkic stems such as *hör-* 'to knit' in most Iraq- and Iran-Turkic varieties.[38]

Morphology

With regard to verb morphology, eastern-type forms dominate, such as the eastern copula {+*DE*} (see 9), the present tense morpheme -{*Ir*}, with a personal marker -*E* in the third person singular (see 2, 8) like in most Iran-Turkic dialects, and the non-evidential perfect in {-(*y*)*Ip*} in the 3rd person (see 7, 11) and in {-*mIş*} in the 1st and 2nd persons (which is already attested in the sample of 17th century Mosul-Turkic).

There are also conspicuous features in case morphology; exceptional for the area is the characteristic Iraq-Turkman instrumental in {+(*y*)*dAn*} (see 6). [bʊŋgænɛ] (see 20) is a variant of the typical Iraqi pronominal equative *buncana*/*muncana*. Other wise, the equative has no pronominal /n/, see [ardıdʒæ], in (25).

[38] On the problem of initial h- in Turkic languages see Doerfer (1981, 1982).

Syntax

Copied syntactical structures are the postverbal position of the directive (see 10, 24) and an Iranian strategy to form nominal phrases, the so-called izafet-construction (see 21, the nominal group [ɑlad̥‿ħærbım].

Iraq-Turkic has preserved the Turkic type of forming subordinate clauses by means of infinite verb forms (see 1); in the adjoining Iran-Turkic dialects, the verbal noun in {*-DIK*} is no longer to be found in this function.

Lexicon

Characteristically, the auxiliary 'do, make' is expressed by two different verbs, *ele-* (see 4, 21), which most eastern varieties use, and its western equivalent *et-* (see 5, 10, 12, 16, 17, 23). A third auxiliary appearing in our text is *yap-* in (see 15). In Iran-Turkic, the verb *yap-* has preserved its original meaning 'to bake (bread)'; its usage as an auxiliary in Iraqi Turkman points to an interference of Modern Turkish.

The appearance of different pronominal stems for reflexive and topic reference forms an isogloss separating Anatolian dialects, which use pronominal forms based on *kendi/gendü*, from Iraq- and Iran-Turkic varieties, where *öz* (see 8, 10, 15) takes similar functions.[39]

Fairly widespread in Anatolian and Iran-Turkic dialects is *herkeş* 'everyone' (see 11); the copied conjunctor *maxsadı kı/ke* (see 14, 19), from the Arabic *maqṣad* 'aim' is a typical Iraq-Turkic item. Another characteristic Iraq-Turkic form is tıpʏrɛg for 'spittle'(see 18), which is *tüpürcek* in Iran-Turkic or *tükürük* in the dialects of Turkey.

The eastern isogloss *indi* 'now' (see 22) appears throughout Iran-Turkic dialects, while the contracted form of *getirerem* (see 22) is characteristic for Turkic varieties of West Iran.

[39] Moreover, this usage hints at essential differences between eastern and western pronominal systems, see Bulut (2003).

Further reading and references

al-Bayati, Mehdi 1970. *Die Anfänge der Prosaliteratur bei den Irak-Türkmenen*. Dissertation: Mainz University.

Bayatlı, Hidayet Kemal 1996. *Irak Türkmen Türkçesi*. Ankara: Atatürk Kültür, Dil ve Tarih Yüksek Kurumu Türk Dil Kurumu Yayınları: 664.

Bellér-Hann, Ildikó 1995. *A History of Cathay. A Translation and Linguistic Analysis of a Fifteenth-Century Turkic Manuscript*. Bloomington: Indiana University.

Buluç, Sadettin 1973/74. Tellafer Türkçesi Üzerine, *Türk Dili Araştırmaları Yıllığı Belleten*, 1973-74: 49-57.

- 1975 Mendeli (Irak) Ağzının Özellikleri,. *I. Türk Dili Bilimsel Kurultayına Sunulan Bildirler, 1972*. Ankara:181-183.
- 1979 Hanekin (Irak) Türk Ağzı Üzerine, *I. Milletler Arası Türkoloji Kongresi, İstanbul 1973*: 600-603.
- 1980 Irak Türk Ağızlarının Bazı Ses Özellikleri, *I. Milli Türkoloji Kongresi Tebliğler, İstanbul 1978*. İstanbul: 54/1-54/4.

Bulut, Christiane 1999. Klassifikatorische Merkmale des Iraktürkischen, *Orientalia Suecana* 48: 5-27.

- 2000. Optative constructions in Iraqi-Turkman, in: Aslı Göksel & Celia Kerslake (eds.), *Studies on Turkish and Turkic Languages. Proceedings of the IXth International Conference on Turkish Linguistcs, Lincoln College, Oxford , August 12-14, 1998* (Turcologica 46.). Wiesbaden: 161-9.
- 2003. Pronominal systems in the transitional varieties of eastern Anatolia, Iraq and Western Iran, in Sumry Özsoy (ed.), *Proceedings of the Tenth International Conference on Turkish Linguistics*. Istanbul: 321-335.

Doerfer, Gerhard 1976. Das Vorosmanische (Die Entwicklung der oghusischen Sprachen von den Orchoninschriften bis zu Sultan Veled). *Türk Dili Araştırmaları Yıllığı Belleten* 1975-1976: 81-131.

- 1981. Materialien zu türkisch h- (I), *Ural-Altaische Jahrbücher. Neue Folge* 1: 93-141.
- 1982. Materialien zu türkisch h- (II), *Ural-Altaische Jahrbücher. Neue Folge* 2: 138-168.
- 1990. Die Stellung des Osmanischen im Kreise des Oghusischen und seine Vorgeschichte, in György Hazai (ed.), *Handbuch der türkischen Sprachwissenschaft*. Budapest: 13-34.

Evliya Çelebi. Ms. Bağdat Köşkü 305; Topkapı Sarayı, İstanbul.

Fischer, Reinhard 1993. *Die Türkmenen im Irak*. Freie Universität Berlin: Magisterarbeit.

Hassan, Hussin Shahbaz 1979. *Kerkük Ağzı*. İstanbul Üniversitesi Edebiyat Fakültesi, Türk Dili ve Edebiyat Bölümü. Doktora Tezi.

Haydar, Choban Khıdır 1979. *Irak Türkmen Ağızları. (Metinler - İnceleme - Sözlük)*.İstanbul Üniversitesi Edebiyat Fakültesi Türk Dili ve Edebiyat Bölümü. Doktora Tezi.

Johanson, Lars 1990. Subjektlose Sätze im Türkischen, in: Bernt Brendemoen (ed.), *Altaica Osloensia*. Proceedings from the 32nd Meeting of the Permanent International Altaistic Conference. Oslo: 193-218.

- 1992. *Strukturelle Faktoren in türkischen Sprachkontakten.* Sitzungsberichte der Wissenschaftlichen Gesellschaft an der Johann Wolfgang Goethe-Universität. Bd. 29, Nr. 5. Frankfurt am Main.

MacKenzie, D.N. 1961/2. *Kurdish Dialect Studies I&II.* School of Oriental and African Studies, University of London: 1981.

Marufoğlu, Sinan 1998. *Osmanli Döneminde Kuzey Irak.* Istanbul.

Oberling, Pierre 1985. Afšâr. *Encyclopædia Iranica, I*:582-586.

Pellat, Charles 1969. *The Life and Work of Jâḥiẓ. Translation of selected texts.* (translated from the French by D. M. Hawke). London.

Saatçi, Suphi 1996. *Tarihi Gelişim içinde Irak'ta Türk Varlıği.* İstanbul: Tarihi Araştırmalar ve Dokümantasyon Merkezleri Kurma ve Geliştirme Vakfı.

Spuler, Berthold 1952. *Iran in frühislamischer Zeit.* Wiesbaden.

Sümer, Faruk 1952. Bayatlar, *İstanbul Üniversitesi Edebiyat Fakültesi Türk Dili ve Edebiyatı Dergisi* IV/4: 373-417.

Töllner, Helmut 1971. *Die türkischen Garden am Kalifenhof von Samarra. Ihre Entstehung und Machtergreifung bis zum Kalifat Al-Mu'taḍids.* Beiträge zur Sprach- und Kulturgeschichte des Orients. Bd. 21. Walldorf-Hessen.